W9-CKA-340

THE TRUST-BUILDERS

THE TRUST-BUILDERS
The Remarkable Rise of Canada Trust

Philip Smith

Macmillan of Canada
A Division of Canada Publishing Corporation
Toronto, Ontario, Canada

Canadian Cataloguing in Publication Data

Smith, Philip, date.
The trust-builders
Includes index.
ISBN 0-7715-9535-2
1. Canada Trustco Mortgage Company—History.
I. Title.
HG4360.L6S55 1989   332.2′6′0971326   C89-093301-4

Designer: Don Fernley
Printed in Canada

Macmillan of Canada
A Division of Canada Publishing Corporation
Toronto, Ontario, Canada

Contents

Prologue	vii
1. Boom and Bust on the Old Frontier	1
2. The Meeting at Macfie's Store	10
3. Getting Down to Business	18
4. An Inspector's Notebook Mirrors Hard Times	26
5. A Versatile and Visionary President	35
6. A New Departure	47
7. The Expansion Begins	56
8. The Company Copes with the War	65
9. A Tower Rises into the Gathering Clouds	76
10. The Four Horsemen Battle the Storm	86
11. The Tail Begins to Wag the Dog	96
12. Allyn Taylor Looks to the Future	105
13. The Old Order Changes	117
14. Raising Eyebrows	128
15. Getting the Wagons in a Circle	143
16. Two Mergers Quicken the Pace	154
17. The "Stunts" Begin to Pay Off	165
18. The Challenge of Inflation	175
19. The Struggle to Preserve the "Spread"	187
20. "A Sad Comment on Government Lethargy"	196
21. More Innovations—and the Business Booms	207
22. The "Sitting Duck" is Plucked	217
23. Under New Ownership Once More	234
Epilogue	248
Appendix	253
Index	263

Prologue

THE little cooperative venture that would one day become Canada's largest trust company was founded by a group of storekeepers and other local worthies in London, Canada West, three years before Confederation. It took its name, the Huron & Erie Savings and Loan Society, from the two Great Lakes bordering the peninsula known today as western Ontario.

In those not-so-long-ago days, western Ontario was still largely virgin forest, part of the frontier of what was soon to become Canada, and pioneer settlers were still struggling to topple the tightly packed pines and to plant crops in the clearings they and their teams of horses created. Unless they arrived with a sock stuffed with golden guineas, which few did, the settlers had to borrow the money they needed to begin farming from rapacious money-lenders who charged interest rates as high as sixty per cent a year.

The Huron & Erie was patterned on the cooperative building societies that began to appear in England in the late 18th century. The merchants and businessmen who founded it realized that their best interests would be served by a stable, prosperous citizenry in the farming country of which London was destined to be the centre. Their purpose was to accumulate a pool of capital that could be lent on reasonable terms to settlers striving to buy or improve farms. And since the society undercut the usurers by making its first mortgage loans at an interest rate of six and a half per cent, it was welcomed from the start.

The founding shareholders committed themselves to buy shares at $50 each—no mean sum in 1864, when a hundredweight of beef could be bought for $2.50 and a dress frock-coat for $5. Thirteen years later a local broker was quoting Huron & Erie shares at $130 each. By the turn of the century they were worth

$178; and if some descendant of a founder shareholder were to turn one up in a dusty trunk in the attic today, it would be worth $6,000.

Takeover bids—sometimes friendly, but often most decidedly unfriendly and bitterly resented—have made many headlines in financial pages in recent years. They were not unknown in an earlier age: eight months after the Huron & Erie's formation its directors agreed to take over the affairs of another local building society which seemed to be having financial problems. By 1976 eighteen other companies had been absorbed into what had by then become Canada Trust. And in 1985 Canada Trust itself was unable to fight off a determined takeover bid by an industrial conglomerate which resulted, ironically, in Canada Trust's taking over in turn one of its principal longtime competitors, Canada Permanent.

"The old Huron and Erie," as it came to be called, ended its first year of operations with total assets of $49,566 and 33 cents. Canada Trust's corporate assets at the beginning of 1989 amounted to $29.2 billion dollars, and the assets under its administration exceeded $67.4 billion. This book attempts to tell the story of that tremendous growth and the men and methods that brought it about.

1

Boom and Bust on the Old Frontier

THE first building on the site of what would soon become the city of London was—appropriately enough, in view of the boisterous years that lay ahead—a tavern. A log cabin with a tankard hanging beside the door to advertise its wares, it was built in 1826 by a settler named Peter McGregor.

The enterprising McGregor had been a chain-bearer for the surveyor who had just laid out a plan for a new town in the swampy wilderness around the Forks of the Thames, a river renamed from the French La Tranche by the first lieutenant-governor of Upper Canada, John Graves Simcoe, a little over thirty years earlier. Concerned about the threat of invasion by the newly independent Americans on the other side of Lakes Huron and Erie, Simcoe thought that the Forks, centrally placed on the peninsula between the lakes, would be an excellent strategic location for the capital of his province; and, as a loyal servant of the Crown, he decided it should be named London. However, the officials in the other London overruled him, the capital was established at Toronto, then known as Muddy York, and the Forks remained unoccupied, though the land round about was beginning to fill up with pioneer farmers.

As usual, the first settlements grew up along the shores of the lakes. The administrative capital of the District of London, a million-acre tract extending across the peninsula, was the hamlet of Vittoria on Lake Erie, nearly one hundred kilometres southeast of the Forks. This meant that settlers in the interior with business to transact at the courts or government offices faced long and arduous journeys on rudimentary wagon trails cut through the forest. So it was decided to move the capital to the Forks, the geographical centre of the district.

No sooner had Peter McGregor opened his inn than he received a contract to put up a two-storey log building to serve as courthouse, jail, and school, pending construction of a permanent courthouse designed to house all government services. The building, an imposing brick structure with turrets and battlements reminiscent of an Irish castle, was ready by 1829; it still stands today. All this activity brought in construction workers from as far away as Toronto, and many of them stayed, attracted by the government's offer of free building lots, subject only to an £8[1] fee for the patent granting legal title to the land and the construction upon it of a cabin measuring at least twenty-four feet by eighteen.

Within ten years of the survey that laid out its site, the Village of London was home to more than a thousand people. It had stores and taverns, a stagecoach inn, two churches, a bank, two thriving tanneries, grist mills along the Thames, and a brewery that later became the famous John Labatt Limited. It was also a rip-roaring frontier town, Canada's western outpost. Many of the settlers were Americans imbued with the spirit of the frontiersman, and those citizens bold enough to walk abroad frequently went armed. The handsome courthouse was often the scene of murder trials but the first of the many public hangings outside it was bungled. Cornelius Burley, a pathetic simpleton who some thought had been framed, was found guilty of murdering a constable. The first time the trapdoor opened, the rope broke, and the expectant crowd of three thousand spectators fretted until a second rope was procured and justice was seen to be done.

The flavour of the town, though not its unruliness, was changed by the short-lived Rebellion of 1837. When its defeated leaders fled to the United States, they soon attracted American support for an invasion designed to liberate the Canadian provinces from "the colonial yoke." The invasion never materialized, but the rebels and their allies mounted several raids across the border, and the authorities considered the threat sufficiently serious to warrant the stationing of a garrison of British regular troops in London. At first they were billeted on the local householders, but by 1839 a barracks had been built, at a cost of $200,000. The infusion of all this good British currency, and the pounds and shillings

---

1. In those days, the dollar was only just beginning to supersede sterling. It equalled five Canadian shillings, which were worth somewhat less than their British counterparts: £750 Canadian equalled £650 sterling.

spent by the officers and men who crowded the streets, boosted the fortunes of the burgeoning settlement. Business doubled, buildings sprang up everywhere, and by 1841 when London was incorporated as a town, the population exceeded two thousand.

The arrival of the troops transformed the town. They helped to provide law and order and fought fires as needed. Men convicted of military offences were put to work clearing tree stumps from the emerging road network and piling them up into a fence around the regimental parade ground. During off-duty hours the soldiers naturally mingled with the settlers—not without some notable tavern brawls. Some wooed and won local girls and stayed on as settlers themselves after their military service ended. Their officers were much in demand by the leading ladies of the local society, who fell over themselves arranging balls at which their daughters might catch some young gallant's eye, so that in due course they might marry into the British aristocracy.[2] Within a short time the town lost its frontier aspect and began to take on the air of British respectability for which it became noted in later years.

While all this development was going on in the town, the settlers in the country round about were cutting down the forest and planting wheat in the rich land they cleared. The area was fast becoming the granary of Canada, and as citizens of its major market town Londoners could be forgiven for thinking the boom would go on for ever. But there were some rude shocks ahead.

By 1845 the town's population was fast approaching the four-thousand mark. Then, in a single afternoon, a fire that started in a hotel's stable wiped out three hundred stores, homes, churches, and hotels—in all about three-quarters of the town. Soon afterward the municipal authorities decreed that all new buildings

---

2. One such lady was Mrs. George Jervis Goodhue, whose husband was called London's first millionaire. A Yankee trader, Goodhue hiked into Westminster Township before London was founded. He set up a plank between two barrels and sold his stock for what he later boasted was a five hundred per cent profit. He opened one of the first stores in London, but made most of his fortune by giving unsuspecting settlers loans at usurious rates which in due course enabled him to foreclose on them and sell the now partly cleared property to another innocent. His daughter married a lieutenant in the Imperial garrison during the American Civil War, Hamilton Tovey, and returned with him to England. Their son, Admiral John Cronyn Tovey, commanded the British fleet that sank the German battleship *Bismarck* during World War II.

should be of stone or brick. The town thus lost its ramshackle Wild West appearance, but not its freebooting frontier spirit.

The rebuilding was only slightly interrupted in February 1851 when the south branch of the Thames suddenly overflowed its banks in the first of a series of disastrous floods that took many lives before adequate control structures were built in modern times. Later that same year the town came down with a severe case of land fever when work began on the Great Western Railway, designed to link Hamilton with Windsor. The projected route ran right through London, and well before the rails reached the town in 1853, land for the first time became a medium for speculation. Huge prices were paid, usually on margin, for land along the proposed right of way and even in forested areas that remained undeveloped for many years into the future. The *London Free Press* reported that one lot changed hands several times on one day, with no hard cash being handed over. Within a few years land values increased by three hundred per cent. Some fortunes were made, but mostly on paper. It was a boom that would soon turn into a bust.

In 1853, with the approach of the Crimean War in Europe, the British troops packed their kitbags and left for home. What might have been a devastating blow to the local economy was cushioned by the arrival of the railway and the flurry of activity it brought with it. The thousands of bushels of wheat now being grown by the area's farmers could henceforth be speedily shipped to Windsor and Toronto, whence much of it found its way to the United States or to Europe, where the war expanded the demand for it. As a result, prices skyrocketed. Good fall wheat that could be bought in 1849 for 75 cents a bushel was fetching $2.60 a bushel by 1856.

Unfortunately for the citizenry at large, the price of everything else soared too. Chickens that could have been bought for ten cents apiece in 1849 now cost fifty; their eggs, once five cents a dozen, now cost a quarter. The war, as usual, had brought on the kind of galloping inflation with which the world was to become all too familiar in the century ahead. And, as usual, wage increases did not keep pace with the inflationary spiral.

In 1855, with a population that had now reached twelve thousand, the town of London was accorded city status. One of the first melancholy duties of the new city council was to appoint a committee for the relief of the poor. For a time, prosperity for some marched alongside poverty for others.

Then came the inevitable crash. The end of the war in 1856 brought on a worldwide economic depression. A major British bank went under, ruining thousands of investors, and the repercussions rapidly spread to North America, where British investment was still an important fact of economic life. London was struck a double blow. First, the wheat price collapsed, and then the year 1857 proved a ruinous one for agriculture: there was a wet spring, which delayed planting, a July frost, which wrecked many crops, and a wet fall, which made it difficult to reap whatever harvest remained. London was not alone in its misfortune. All over North America farmers were driven from the land to swell the ranks of the thousands of urban unemployed. Local historians estimate that during the disastrous two-year depression three-quarters of London's businesses went under.

Land prices plummeted—it would be thirty years before they recovered—and many genuine investors as well as speculators were wiped out.[3] In those days the Debtors' Act enabled creditors to engineer the imprisonment of not only men but women for unpaid debts of as little as forty dollars. For some reason, the London courts had a reputation for enforcing this law with unusual harshness. But as the economy collapsed the debtors' cells became so overcrowded that the authorities were compelled to relax their enforcement of the regulations. Between 1855 and 1860 several thousand people left the new city of London; it was believed many of them fled across the border to avoid debtors' jail.

Among those who stayed, the fortunate propertied class practised an unaccustomed economy; the white-collar workers and skilled tradesmen resorted to careful frugality; the unskilled and unemployed and their families went hungry, if they did not actually starve. The city council set up a soup kitchen at the municipal hospital; the demand for its meagre meals was such that the city could not afford to keep it supplied, and the councillors appealed for help to those citizens who still had some resources, through the church congregations, the charitable organizations, and the social clubs. These responded as best they could and at least four more private soup kitchens set about trying to alleviate the suffering.

---

3. In 1905, the *London Free Press* reported the case of an unfortunate investor who bought a lot for cash during the boom, put up a building, and paid taxes on it for fifty years. Finally he sold the property—for a dollar less than he had paid for just the lot.

The economic roller-coaster headed upward again for Londoners in the early 1860s. It was driven by two unconnected events with far-reaching consequences for the whole of North America. One of those events occurred close to home, the other further afield, though it was still considered alarmingly close.

First, oil was discovered in Enniskillen Township, west of London; the first commercial production of crude oil in North America was obtained there in 1858 from a well dug by hand. In the ensuing oil boom, the United States rapidly outstripped Ontario as a producer, but by 1870 the province was exporting some oil to Europe. The first small refineries grew up around Petrolia, about 130 kilometres west of London, but many others soon opened in the larger centre. (A few years later, when a group of sixteen businessmen formed Imperial Oil Ltd. in an ultimately vain bid to counter the powerful competition from the United States, fifteen of them hailed from London.)

The second event that powered the revival of London's economy was the outbreak of the American Civil War in 1861. After the secession of the slave-holding states that led to the war, newspapers in the North began to call for the annexation of Canada to strengthen the Union. Fearful that the war would spread, the British government sent ten thousand troops to Canada to protect its undefended border, and two thousand of them were stationed in London. As before, their presence boosted the takings of those merchants and tavern-keepers who had survived the depression of the previous decade.

The war also restored the fortunes of the area's farmers, upon whose well-being the city had always closely depended. The northern states needed meat as well as wheat to feed their army, and they were prepared to pay good prices for it. Western Ontario's farmers therefore began to raise pigs and cattle and thus freed themselves from the one-crop economy that had been so vulnerable in the past. Mixed farming became the vogue, and it would ensure western Ontario's prosperity well into the future.

By 1864, as the tragic war to the south ground to its close, London was prosperous as never before, and its prosperity was now solidly based on a mixed economy that would make it the metropolis of western Ontario: its thriving agricultural hinterland, its burgeoning oil refineries, and the new factories that had sprung up in response to the Union's wartime need for goods of all kinds.

Yet the Forest City, as it now bills itself in its tourist literature—handsome new trees having been planted to replace the old ones cut down by the settlers—had not yet rid itself of its wild and woolly frontier atmosphere. During the Civil War, the town was crowded with southern whites fleeing the war it was becoming obvious their side could not win, fugitive slaves who had made it to freedom before the Union victory liberated their fellows, and spies for both sides. The latter's presence was occasioned by the "north-west conspiracy," a last-ditch attempt by southerners and some of their sympathizers in the North to harass the Union with raiding parties assembled or even raised within Canada. This proved to be a futile undertaking, but it gave the city something of the ambiance of Lisbon during World War II.

Quite apart from these alien intrigues, London had its own invigorating brand of politics. Its mayor at the time was Francis Evans Cornish, a lawyer born north of the Forks before the city was established. This worthy was once arrested by a constable for drunkenly driving his horse and buggy through an arcade leading to the market square, scattering law-abiding citizens right and left. Next morning, presiding as the town's chief magistrate, Cornish read out his own name in court, delivered a lecture on the evils of drink, and fined the defendant Frank Cornish four dollars, which he took from his right-hand trouser pocket and placed on the desk. In those days, the city's mayor was entitled to keep the fines levied in court, in lieu of salary. So Mayor Cornish picked up the four dollars and popped them into his left pocket. Then, tempering justice with mercy, he remitted half the fine because of the defendant's previous good conduct, and transferred two dollars from his left pocket to his right.

Cornish was first elected in 1861, and he assured himself of re-election for four consecutive terms by his repertoire of strong-arm tactics. Electors at that time did not enjoy the luxury of the secret ballot, and few of them, when faced by a crowd of billy-wielding Cornish hirelings, dared to stand before the returning officer and call out their vote, if it happened to be unfavourable to the incumbent. Just in case any did, Frank Cornish always had reinforcements on hand. The British troops, living in barracks owned by the Imperial government, were not eligible for the local vote. But as British subjects, they could vote if they could prove residence in the city for twenty-four hours. Good old Frank used to put parties of them up at some local hostelry and ply them with the products of the local breweries. Then, before returning to barracks with aching heads, the lads would loyally cast their votes for their genial host.

The soldiers, though, eventually proved to be Frank's undoing. After four terms of his mayoralty the city council had had enough, and it called in the troops to supervise the next election. Cornish lost to his reform opponent and headed out further west to the new frontier. He became the first mayor of Winnipeg and then the first member of the federal parliament for the riding of Poplar Point. This eminence he achieved by having his opponent kidnapped and held on a farm outside the city while he stumped the hustings demanding that the poor fellow show up in public to answer certain grave charges levelled against him—by Frank Cornish, of course.

Other Londoners besides the city councillors were becoming tired of Cornish's high jinks. While the city had not yet completely shed its old frontier disorderliness, the renewed prosperity encouraged those solid citizens who, with the earnestness typical of the Victorian age, were intent on building a stable, orderly community where opportunities for self-improvement would be open to all; where virtue would receive its just reward; where good, sound education would be provided for the young and enjoyable cultural outlets would be available for their elders when the day's work was done.

The first British officers, when they had arrived more than thirty years before, had introduced the city's upper crust to pursuits more genteel than hacking down trees and chivvying oxen from behind a plough. They organized dances where decorum was more in evidence than at some of the indigenous celebrations; they staged amateur theatricals that inspired countless dramatic societies in ensuing years; they formed sleigh clubs and organized winter carnivals; and they introduced the locals to the thrills of steeplechasing, thus sowing the seeds for today's exclusive London Hunt and Country Club. The draughtsmen among them and some of the garrison wives provided most of the first drawings and paintings of the city and the land around it.

There was satisfying evidence in 1864 that the old order was changing, that the rawness of the frontier was being replaced by a sedate respectability. That spring, London society turned out in force to support a three-day Shakespearean festival to honour the three-hundredth anniversary of the birth of the bard. The high point of the program was a performance of *The Merchant of Venice*, with the role of Portia, in accordance with Shakespearean tradition, being played by a young man, Edmund Meredith, a lawyer and scion of one of the most distinguished London families of the day. In the fall of the year a touring Italian opera company in full costume regaled an appreciative audience in the City Hall with two acts from the opera *Norma* and one from *Lucrezia Borgia*.

The leading lights of the local business world may have fretted and grumbled as their womenfolk urged them into their stiff-fronted shirts and frock-coats to attend these performances, but they too were eager for change. The years of boom and bust they had passed through had been just too turbulent. Sure, times were good right now. But to keep them that way there was a need for thrift and caution; good solid investments to replace the crazy speculations of the past; above all, prudence; in short, the financial conservatism for which their city would later become legend.

It was a group of men seized with these sentiments who sat down one March evening around the stove in the room above Daniel Macfie's dry-goods emporium to form the Huron & Erie Savings and Loan Society.

2

The Meeting at Macfie's Store

THE first English building society of which any record seems to exist was formed in Birmingham in 1775. With the other societies that quickly followed, it was a product of the developing Industrial Revolution. The idea was that members of the newly emerging middle class, by pooling their modest savings, would each in turn be able to buy their own little plot of land and build a house on it.

These early cooperative ventures were known as "terminating" societies, because they were designed to be wound up within a specified number of years, perhaps ten or twelve. Each member agreed to buy a share in the society with small monthly instalments, and when all the shares had been paid for, all the society's assets—greatly augmented, it was hoped, by the profits made by lending out the pooled funds through the years—would be distributed to its members.

Each member had the privilege of borrowing an amount equal to the value of the share for which he was subscribing, by increasing his subscription to cover repayment of the loan plus interest. If a society could recruit say a hundred members to pay one pound a month toward shares valued at a hundred pounds, the pool of capital available for lending would amount to a hundred pounds at the end of the first month. This, of course, would satisfy the borrowing needs of only one shareholder, so in the early months of a society's existence the loans were usually auctioned off to the highest bidder. Large sums were often paid for the privilege of taking out a loan, thus increasing the society's assets and the pool of capital it had available to make loans and earn more interest.

The system sounded foolproof, like some of the pyramid schemes that have gulled financial innocents in modern times. But after those shareholders most impatient to build had received their loans, bidding at the auctions began to be less spirited, the bonuses paid for loans fell sharply, and it often became difficult to find borrowers willing to take out loans even at par. Some members, in fact, signed up for shares simply as an investment, with no intention of borrowing; others sometimes had no security to offer when their time came; and still others hesitated to borrow because they did not know how long they would have to continue their payments, which were compulsory until the society was wound up. In addition, those societies that found it difficult to invest their funds profitably likewise found it difficult to gather up enough money to deliver their members' shares and "terminate" their affairs by the agreed date.

Because of the way they were set up, the terminating societies that ran into difficulties could not recruit new shareholders to salvage their fortunes. But in 1849, a British actuary named Arthur Scratchley suggested a new form of "permanent" society in a book that remained the bible of the mortgage lending industry well into the next century. Central to his idea was the admission of new shareholders as societies grew and removal of the requirement that they be wound up at a stated date.

Even before Scratchley proposed his improvements, it was recognized that the idea of building societies was ideally suited to the development of Canada. In the years before Confederation, capital was a scarce commodity in the colonies. There was not much money in circulation, and trade was still largely conducted by barter. A man's land was virtually his only capital, but there was little trade in land: newly arrived settlers seldom had enough money to buy a farm and so they took up the uncleared lands, which cost them little but their back-breaking labour. The few banks then existing were not permitted to lend on the security of land, and in any case had little interest in either small depositors or small borrowers; they occupied themselves with commercial business. A farmer wishing to improve his land or to buy stock had to try to find a storekeeper or richer neighbour willing to advance him money, and these private lenders had a well-stocked armoury of ruses designed to circumvent the Usury Law. Small farmers and those artisans and tradesmen thrifty enough to set a few shillings aside every month from their wages could do little with their savings but stash them under their mattresses, where they garnered no interest.

This was the situation when in 1846 the government of Canada passed "An Act to Encourage the Establishment of certain Societies commonly called Building Societies. . ." All that was required to launch such a society was for twenty or more people to sign a declaration that they would join it, file it with the Clerk of the Peace, and pay a registration fee of two shillings and sixpence.

What must rank as Upper Canada's first, if informal, mortgage loan company had been founded two years earlier, without benefit of the legislation, in Sarnia, west of London. A former military man named Robert Skilbeck, who had been an official of a building society in England, noted the dearth of cash in his new home town and suggested to a group of his neighbours that they should entrust him with any spare funds they might have, which he would lend out to the highest bidder to the benefit of one and all. Skilbeck was evidently well trusted, and an organization known as the Port Sarnia Syndicate was set up, operating from his home. Its members took advantage of the 1846 legislation to turn themselves into the Port Sarnia Building Society. Their infant organization celebrated its centenary in 1944 as the Lambton Loan and Investment Society.[1]

Among those who studied Scratchley with close interest was a young accountant, J. Herbert Mason, who in 1851 was placed in charge of the Farmers and Mechanics Society, which had been formed in Toronto in 1847. Mason turned out to be something of a financial wizard and in 1855 he was able to liquidate the society, with each member receiving his full share, plus a dividend equivalent to fifteen per cent compounded. About the same time, another group, the Toronto Building Society, was wound up successfully.

By this time Mason had worked out a plan for a new permanent society and he put it to the directors of both groups. They thought it a good idea, with one reservation. Part of Mason's plan was to augment the capital raised by the members' purchase of shares by opening an office to accept from the public the kind of small deposits scorned by the banks. The directors, well versed in the ways of building societies, wondered whether this would be permitted under the 1846 Act, and so a committee was appointed to

---

1. The locally well-regarded Lambton Loan was bought by the larger Victoria and Grey Trust in 1969, as the wave of consolidation of smaller trust and loan companies gathered momentum, but it retained its own name until 1979.

make inquiries. In due course the committee reported that "[Its members] have examined the Building Society Act and find nothing therein provided which in any manner prohibits such societies from receiving money on deposit, allowing interest, and loaning such funds on real property or other securities in the same manner as the other funds of the Society. . ." Thus was born the Canada Permanent Building and Savings Society.

Another new feature of Mason's plan was that it made a distinction between two classes of shareholders: investors and borrowers. The difference between them was that investors shared in the society's profits but the borrowers did not. This apparent inequity arose from the fact that a borrower did not actually have to buy any shares. He would sign up for shares equivalent to the amount he wanted to borrow, thus becoming a nominal shareholder; but instead of paying for them, he would execute a mortgage on his property for the amount and receive his loan. The advantage of this arrangement was that a borrower did not have to pay instalments on both his shares and his loan.

Both new aspects of Mason's plan proved popular with the public, but as time went on the directors still wondered whether they were strictly legal. The problem was put to the government and in 1859 the 1846 Act was amended to confirm that they were. The amendment also authorized permanent building societies to treat "accumulating shares"—those subscribed for but not yet paid up in full—as fixed capital, upon which dividends could be paid.

This legislation began the evolution of the early self-help building societies into the mortgage loan companies that succeeded them. Five years later, when the founders of the Huron & Erie Savings and Loan Society gathered around Daniel Macfie's stove, they were to all intents and purposes planning to invest in a normal business corporation, a fact given formal recognition in 1875 by legislation changing the society's name to the Huron & Erie Loan and Savings Company. As investors, they naturally planned to make a profit. But they did not intend to be grasping landlords grinding the faces of the poor—the terms and conditions of their loans demonstrated that. If they had any vested interest at all, it was in the stability and prosperity of the surrounding farming communities upon which their city and businesses so much depended. Certainly they did not found the society with the intention of taking out loans themselves, for they were men of substance and local prominence, some of whom would later make their mark on the national scene.

Their host on this evening of 15 March 1864 was a forty-five-year-old Scot who, like so many in the group, had succeeded in his adopted country by his own industriousness. One of ten children born to a barrel-maker on the Isle of Bute, Daniel Macfie began work in a cotton mill as a boy and came to Canada at the age of twenty-one as a salesman for a Glasgow company. After working in Toronto and St. Thomas, he settled in London in 1844 and opened a dry-goods store, which flourished to the extent that when he became one of the founders of the august London Club years later his occupation was listed as "gentleman."

Macfie had been elected to the city council in 1860 and was chairman of its finance committee. At the time of the founding meeting he was already a director of another local loan and savings society, the president of which, Adam Hope, was elected first president of the Huron & Erie. Thus the new society, unlike so many of those that had foundered in both Britain and Canada, was blessed with experienced direction from the start.

Like most of the men at the meeting, Adam Hope[2] was also a dry-goods merchant. But there were other businesses represented. E. A. Taylor was a bookseller, and to judge from his advertising that year he was doing a brisk trade in the novel *Our Mutual Friend* by Charles Dickens. Ellis W. Hyman owned a tannery and had a wide range of other business interests: during his career he was a founding director of the London Life Insurance Co., two railroads, a bank, and an oil refinery. Luxuriantly bearded Simeon Morrill was another tannery owner, who had served three terms as a more seemly mayor of the city than Frank Cornish. William Robinson was an Irish-born builder and surveyor who later became city engineer.

The Anglican church, too, was represented at the meeting, in the person of the Reverend Isaac Hellmuth, a Polish Jew who had

---

2. Adam Hope was in partnership with his brother Charles, who also attended the founding meeting, as a wholesaler of dry goods, groceries, and hardware. After four years as president, he moved to Hamilton and went into business there with another Huron & Erie founder, John McKenzie. Adam, who in later life became a senator, also founded and became president of the Hamilton Provident & Loan Corporation, which was bought by the Huron & Erie in 1926, at which time its president was George Hope, Adam's nephew.

converted to Christianity and had first visited London as General Secretary for North America of the Colonial Church and School Society. Hellmuth, who went on to become the second bishop of the Anglican diocese of Huron, founded several schools and colleges in London, one of which, Huron College, evolved into today's University of Western Ontario. In later years, the Anglican diocese would have substantial investments in the Huron & Erie, and its representatives were frequently invited to address the company's annual shareholders' meeting.

Two powerful men who did not attend the meeting, but who ranked high among the founders and were both elected to the first board of directors, were the Honourable Elijah Leonard and Frank Smith. Elijah Leonard was an American, born into a family of Welsh origin whose members had been ironmongers for more than two centuries. He came to Canada in 1830 to work at one of the first successful ironworks in Ontario, at Normandale, on Lake Erie. Four years later he set up in business on his own at St. Thomas, and in 1838 moved his operation to London, where he built a foundry that was for many years one of the city's leading industries. Leonard was elected to the Upper Canada legislature in 1862 as a Liberal and remained there until Confederation, when he was named a senator. His family's connection with the Huron & Erie survived through three generations, until 1958, when his grandson, Col. Ibbotson Leonard, D.S.O., retired from his post as chairman of the board of directors.

Frank Smith was among the richest of London's merchants. Born in Ireland, he came to Canada with his parents at the age of ten, and set up in business in London in 1849 as an importer and wholesaler of groceries, wines, and spirits. A contemporary advertisement announced to the city's storekeepers and tavern-owners that he had a large consignment of Hennessy's brandy, deKuyper's gin, Booth's Old Tom, Bass's Ale, and Blood's Porter, all available for sale "in wood and bottle." He had been a city alderman, and would soon be elected mayor. Shortly thereafter he moved his business to Toronto, where he became the chief owner of the Toronto Street Railway, president of half a dozen companies, including the Dominion Bank, and a director of many others. It is some indication of the varied make-up of the founding group that Smith was a Tory, and a prominent figure in the Roman Catholic church, one of the originators of the Ontario Catholic League. He was summoned to Ottawa as a senator in 1871 and held office in five successive Tory governments. His career was capped with a knighthood in 1894.

Some idea of the financial standing of these men can be gathered from the assessment of Frank Smith in the register of a contemporary credit-rating agency. It was "undoubted"—the second highest category, denoting a personal capital of from $300,000 to $500,000. Elijah Leonard's rating was "very high to very good," denoting personal capital of from $50,000 to $75,000. The brewer John Labatt, who was not one of the Huron & Erie's founders but joined the board later, was rated as "good," which signified that he had capital between $6,000 and $10,000.

If any written record was made of the proceedings at that founding meeting it no longer survives. But presumably the twenty-five men present discussed their plans for the society and agreed that the shares would cost $50 each and could be bought outright or by monthly instalments. It was also agreed that deposits from $4 to $500 would be accepted from the public. The founding members then signed the declaration required to constitute themselves a permanent building society, which was filed with the Clerk of the Peace for Middlesex County three days later by Benjamin Cronyn, a twenty-four-year-old "student at Law."

There was another meeting on 8 April, at which twelve members were elected to the board of directors. The board met a few days later and elected Adam Hope as their president and Ellis Hyman as vice-president. At that same meeting, William Boyer, an English immigrant who filled the same position in the other society headed by Hope, was appointed secretary and treasurer—in effect, general manager. It was resolved that "he be paid for the first year a salary not less than one per cent on the invested capital of the Society during that period." Boyer was required to "give as security himself in $4,000 and two sureties in $2,000 each for the faithful fulfilment of his duties in the office."

The meeting also set the fees that could be charged by the society's solicitor for drawing up mortgages: $4 for loans up to $400; $5 for loans between $400 and $1,000; and $6 for loans over $1,000. The solicitor was enjoined that no extra charges were to be made "unless for the drawing of necessary documents to complete the title." He was also to make no extra charges for letters. And the board instructed the secretary that if any extra charges were levied he must "lay the account of costs on the table at the next meeting."

The lawyer appointed to the post of solicitor was Benjamin Cronyn's brother Verschoyle, his senior by seven years. Thus began a family association with the Huron & Erie that has continued unbroken to the present day: John B. Cronyn, one of Canada Trust's directors at the time of writing, is Verschoyle's great-grandson.

3

Getting Down to Business

VERSCHOYLE Cronyn was the driving force behind the Huron & Erie during its formative years and for long afterwards. He inherited his financial acumen and his nose for a real estate deal from his father, the Reverend Benjamin Cronyn, a young Irish curate who had arrived in London in 1832, and who, in recognition of his energetic furtherance of the interests of his church and its parishioners, was in due course elected the first bishop of the Anglican diocese of Huron.

Born in Kilkenny in 1802, Benjamin earned a B.A. and an M.A. at Trinity College, Dublin, along with the distinction of being Divinity Prizeman. He sailed for Canada with his wife and two children in the summer of 1832, bound for the recently established settlement of Adelaide, about thirty-two kilometres west of London. The family trundled into London, in a wagon carrying all their worldly goods, on a Saturday evening. The local Anglican congregation, whose minister had fled the village with many other inhabitants because of a disastrous epidemic of cholera, asked the young curate to conduct a service for them the next day. Impressed with his style, they invited him to stay on in the village. Since Mrs. Cronyn was expecting their third child, Verschoyle, this seemed like a good idea, and after assuring the Adelaide Anglicans he would look after their interests too, Benjamin accepted the invitation.

Under the Canada Act of 1791 one-seventh of the land granted to settlers in each new township was set aside "for the support of a Protestant clergy." Benjamin's predecessor had acquired some land from the government and had begun to build a church on it, but the congregation had run out of funds and only the frame of the building had been completed. Finishing it became Benjamin's first priority, and he soon showed his astuteness in matters of property: he journeyed to the provincial capital of York, received permission to sell the land on which the partly built church stood, and extracted a grant of four acres in what is now the centre of the city upon which to build a new one.

Back in London the young curate divided the church site into lots and sold them, buying one for himself. The proceeds amounted to £877, more than enough to cover the cost of moving the frame of the church to the new site and completing it.

This was the first of a long series of canny land deals by which Benjamin enhanced his church's fortunes and laid the basis for his family's. His first church, St. Paul's, burned down in 1844, and despite his enthusiastic fund-raising the building of its replacement saddled his congregation with a £4,000 debt. Benjamin therefore sought and received his bishop's permission to sell part of the church's original land grant, use the proceeds to buy cheaper acreage elsewhere, and apply the profit he confidently expected from the deal to paying off the church's debt. As his son would do in later years, Benjamin had gauged the state of the real estate market with remarkable accuracy. He was soon able to report to his bishop that "the sale of lot 13 took place and after deducting expenses it produced £6,650. Of this, one-fifth—the first instalment—has been paid and applied to the liquidation of the debt. And as the annual payments come in, the debt on the church, amounting to £3,100, will be paid, and the price of the lands purchased in exchange will also be paid."

While more orthodox churchmen might have frowned at the ease with which he combined the service of God and Mammon, the rector of St. Paul's was not an avaricious man. He once bought sixteen acres of land from a settler who had moved away. Three years later it was worth six times what he had paid for it, but since his church at the time needed a cemetery, he sold it the land at the price he had paid for it, to the church's considerable benefit many years later when part of the acreage was sold off as building lots.

The young minister was also a man of action. In the great fire of 1845, as chaplain of the Imperial garrison, he recruited a squad of gunners and spent the day supervising their removal of furniture and personal belongings from doomed buildings into the middle of the street, where they were protected from potential looters by another squad he had summoned from the 2nd Regiment of Foot. Fourteen years later, in 1859, when he had been bishop for two years and was no longer young, he spent the year travelling 3,946 kilometres around his diocese, visiting 84 congregations, preaching 130 sermons, consecrating 5 new churches, and admitting 1,453 communicants to his faith.

Benjamin's son Verschoyle thus brought a formidable inheritance to the newly formed Huron & Erie. In 1864 he was in the prime of life, thirty-one years old, four years out of the University of Toronto, and comfortably married to Sophy Blake, daughter of the Honourable William Hume Blake, solicitor general for Canada West and a pioneer law reformer.[1] He also brought experience to the new society; like his friend Daniel Macfie, he was a member of the board of directors of the City of London Building Society under Adam Hope's presidency.

Though there seems never to have been any formal connection between these two societies there was certainly a close link between them. They employed the same secretary-treasurer, William Boyer, who must have been a busy man, since he was employed in the same capacity by another society, the London Permanent. And when the Huron & Erie took its first office space, in a building known as the Crystal Block, the City of London Society moved in and shared the rent.

The discussion on the question of premises at an early board meeting demonstrates the caution and frugality that characterized the society from its formation. According to the minutes, "The Secretary reported that Mr. Gunn had offered to build a vault and let the shop west of Murray Anderson's store for $168 a year, the Society to pay the taxes, provided the Society will lease for five years." Another potential landlord, Mr. Lawrason, offered "the store on Talbot Street north of his office for $150 per annum," but a note in the margin of the minute book said, "No vault." Verschoyle Cronyn then offered "that in the event of the Society

---

1. Among Benjamin Cronyn's fellow passengers on his voyage across the Atlantic were two close friends who, like him, were members of the Anglo-Irish gentry, the Reverend Dominick Blake and his younger brother William Hume Blake. Dominick's wife was Anne Margaret Hume, and that surname recurs as a Christian name through both the Cronyn and Blake families, whose destinies became inextricably intertwined. Sophy Blake's brother was Edward Blake, the Toronto lawyer who became the second premier of Ontario and later a federal cabinet minister and leader of the federal Liberal party. Edward married one of his brother-in-law Verschoyle's sisters, Margaret; his brother, Samuel Blake, married another, Rebecca.

taking the store occupied by Messrs. Noble and Lewis in the Crystal Block, with the cellar and rooms above, at a rent of £65 per annum, [he would] pay half the rent for the second storey [for his own office], leaving the ground floor for the office and the third flat for the Board Room. Should the City of London Building Society move into the same office, they will pay £10 per annum, which would reduce the rent [to the society] to £22 and two shillings."

The matter of the vault was resolved by the offer of a local lawyer, John Scatcherd, to sell the society "a large iron safe" for two hundred dollars, which sum he was prepared to take in shares. But the deal with Messrs. Noble and Lewis apparently broke down when they too wanted the society to lease the premises for five years. The board decided instead to take "the store in the Crystal Block lately occupied by Mr. McCabe as a temporary office at $15 per month, provided the City of London Building Society pays at the rate of $40 per annum for their share."

Much of the business at those early board meetings was devoted to the appointment of valuators in the outlying areas; these were men of some position and trust whose job it was to assist prospective borrowers in filling out the application forms required by the society, and to report to the directors on the value of the property being mortgaged and the credit-worthiness of the aspiring borrower. That the chosen valuators were men of some substance is shown by two appointments made at an early meeting: John P. Harding, solicitor, of St. Mary's, and James Hart, county clerk, of Chatham. The valuators' pay scale was set out in the following terms: "On an advance not exceeding $500, $1; on an advance from $500 to $750, $1.50; on an advance from $750 to $1,000, $2; and fifty cents additional for every $1,000 or fraction of $1,000." For their valuation and report to the directors, the valuators earned "$2, and mileage ten cents per mile, one way only."

Before opening for business, the society decided to adopt the loan table used by the Canada Permanent society in Toronto, "with interest calculated at 6½ per cent per annum. . ."[2] This was

---

2. Since the society paid depositors six per cent interest this seems surprisingly low. Then, as now, mortgage loan companies made their profit from the "spread"—the difference between the interest paid on money deposited with them and that charged to borrowers. For many years companies aimed at a spread of two per cent; one half of one per cent would seem hardly enough to cover the society's expenses. Indeed, a couple of years later, the directors voted to raise the rate to ten per cent.

a much more favourable rate than those available to borrowers from private lenders, and the terms were also much easier. Previously, a borrower's loan extended over a period of years without his being able to reduce the principal by regular payments. If he were unable to repay the loan in full when it fell due, he had either to take out a new loan at exorbitant rates or lose his property. The Huron & Erie's terms called for amortized payments covering principal and interest, payable monthly, quarterly, half-yearly, or yearly, for periods of five years and upwards, at the option of the borrower.

With the preliminaries satisfactorily attended to, the directors of the society approved its first mortgage loan on 29 April, a little over a month after its formation. It went to Edward Talbott, a farmer at Bayfield, on the east shore of Lake Huron south of Goderich, who, to quote the minutes, "offers as security for $400 for five years, the south half of Lot No. 19, Lake road east, in the Township of Stanley, containing 70 acres, 40 cleared, log buildings. Valued by A. Campbell at $1,250."

Right from the start, the directors of the Huron & Erie set limits on what they would lend that were far more stringent than the seventy-five per cent of assessed value permitted by legislation today. The second loan they approved that day went to James Whitely, who wanted $300 over eight years and offered as security a property assessed by the society's valuator as worth $1,500. Robert Porteous was not so fortunate: he wanted $3,000 on a property valued at $4,965; the directors would give him only $1,600. In all, that day, the directors considered valuators' reports on six applications for mortgages. They rejected one and approved five, which together amounted to an investment of $3,500 of the society's funds.[3]

At that same meeting the directors set the conditions upon which the Huron & Erie's savings bank would operate. It was resolved to accept deposits from $4 to $500 and pay interest on them at the rate of six per cent a year. Sums up to $50 could be withdrawn on demand, but depositors wishing to withdraw more than $50 would have to give the society fourteen days' notice. If

3. The requirement that each individual mortgage application be reviewed and approved by the board of directors persisted into the 1930s. That practice would obviously be impossible today, when in an average month the company approves new mortgages and renewals amounting to approximately a billion dollars.

anyone wanted to deposit more than $500 the board would have to give its approval "subject to special agreement as to rate of interest and time of withdrawal."[4]

Among the first customers of the savings bank was Edward de la Hooke, for many years London passenger manager for the Great Western Railway. But a few weeks after it opened, when one William H. Ash wanted to deposit "about $3,000," the board turned him down and agreed to take only $500 of his money.

For some reason, perhaps because the Crystal Block premises were becoming too small for the growing volume of business, the society moved its office in October to "the Brick Building on Talbot-st. in the rear of Mr. Macfie's store." In an advertisement carried by the local newspapers the directors took the opportunity to address local "capitalists." (Karl Marx had not yet published his *Das Kapital* and brought down upon that appellation the opprobrium that would later attach to it in some quarters.) "Capitalists," the advertisement said, "will be convinced, on investigating the principles upon which this Society is established, that it offers a most desirable medium for investing either large or small sums of money."

It seems there were plenty of local capitalists who shared the anonymous copy-writer's sentiment. In January 1865, at the society's first annual general meeting of shareholders, Adam Hope was able to report that during the first eight months of the society's existence subscriptions had been received for shares totalling in value $77,600. Of this amount the society had actually taken in $34,769.53. Its receipts also included $10,812.33 deposited by the public in its savings bank. Of its total assets of $49,566.33, the cash value of the mortgages it had given out amounted to $41,445.05. It had $7,921.28 in the Gore Bank, a bank founded in Hamilton in 1835 and later (in 1870) merged with the Canadian Bank of Commerce. The only other asset deemed worthy of men-

---

4. This condition may have been imposed because the legislation at that time limited the total deposits a society could accept to "three-fourths of the amount of capital actually paid in on unadvanced shares . . ." This deposit limit, which eventually became known as the "multiple," was raised several times through the years. In 1914, for instance, it was raised to four times a company's paid-up capital and reserve. The present multiple is twenty-five times a company's capital.

tion was Mr. Scatcherd's large iron safe, which was still carried on the books at its cost price of $200.[5]

Addressing the shareholders, President Hope said that ever since the society's formation the cash paid in for shares had been "promptly invested in unexceptionable securities," which enabled the directors to declare a ten-per-cent dividend to stockholders for the year and place the sum of $279.83 in the contingent reserve fund. This profit, he observed, had been declared after all the initial expenses of founding the society had been met. "Many serious items of expenditure," he said, "will not again occur, such as for the publication of a large number of the Prospectuses and Rules of the Society, and in the purchase of the Books of Account, etc."

President Hope also stressed the basic principle of caution and financial conservatism underlying the society's mortgage loans: "The amount advanced has been in nearly every case less than one-third of the cash value of the property given in security, and has in no case amounted to one-half the cash value of the bare land."

The phrase "the bare land" was significant. At first the society would lend only on farm property, and loans to farmers remained its dominant business for many years into the future. Even twenty years later the annual meeting was told that only seven per cent of the company's loans were on city property. The rest were on farms in the "prosperous counties" around London, "counties unsurpassed in the fertility of their soil, and occupied by a class of thrifty farmers, where farms offered for sale can readily be sold at good prices."

Though it was not mentioned in the president's report at that first annual meeting, the directors had already agreed in principle to a request for a merger from the London Permanent Building Society. Founded four years earlier, with Adam Hope as its first president, the London Permanent had already been outstripped by its new rival, the Huron & Erie. Its total assets were only a little over $14,000, and it was beleaguered by an unexplained claim

5. The safe proved its worth a month later when thieves broke into the office, blew open the City of London's safe, and stole $114. A news report at the time said an attempt had also been made to drill the Huron & Erie's safe but "the villains may have been startled by their own fears for the safe was not injured further."

against it by yet another society, the County of Middlesex Building Society. The merger was approved by legislation in March 1865, whereupon the Huron & Erie assumed all the London Permanent's assets and liabilities and the London Permanent's shareholders became "shareholders of a like degree" in the Huron & Erie. Among the Huron & Erie's shareholders who voted for the merger was Edward Blake.

In August of the following year another Act of the Legislative Council sanctioned a merger on similar terms with the Western Counties Permanent Building and Savings Society. The Huron & Erie was growing fast, and when Adam Hope delivered his annual report for the year 1866 he was proud to announce that the society's invested capital now amounted to $215,764.04 and that another ten-per-cent dividend was in order.

By 1867, the year in which Hope resigned to move to Hamilton, the society's total assets had grown to $318,849 and its paid-up capital to $210,482. There was $89,222 on deposit in the savings bank and, cautious as ever, management had increased the reserve fund to $16,000.

That year was, of course, the year of Confederation, but the board minutes around 1 July make no mention of that event. It must be presumed, though, that the directors discussed among themselves from time to time an issue with which the local press had been much preoccupied: the question of what the new nation should be called. As Canadians today, we must be thankful that some of the names proposed in the London newspapers were passed over. They included Niagarentia, Canotia, Laconia, and West Britain.

4

An Inspector's Notebook Mirrors Hard Times

IN 1868 the society's directors decided to appoint a travelling inspector to check up on its many valuators and their assessments of mortgaged properties. The importance they attached to this position is indicated by the salary set: $800 a year plus travelling expenses, at a time when the secretary-treasurer's annual salary was $1,100. Hugh Forbes McDonald, the first man appointed to the post, quit after a few months and was succeeded by a rising young financial man, Joseph Jeffery. Jeffery, too, resigned after three months—amicably enough, it would seem, since soon afterward he was named to the board of directors. Four years later he founded the London Life Insurance Company.

The high turnover rate among travelling inspectors is perhaps explained in the work book kept by his successor, H.D. Cameron, which survives in the company's archives. This reveals that between 19 July and 11 October 1870 Cameron made 179 inspections in the townships around London in something less than comfortable travelling conditions. On 27 July, for instance, he visited a property of fifty acres, "none of them cleared," in Egremont Township, a "very backward" area. "The roads are almost impassable," he writes. "A sledge or an ox team might get along but horses and wheeled vehicles are out of place in this terrible place. At one time I was nearly mired; at other times my horse was in danger of breaking his legs walking over old, rotten and ill-laid cross lays."

A couple of weeks later he encountered similar conditions in Keppel Township. "The township is one of the roughest I have been in," his notes read. "It is quite recently settled and I had very great difficulty getting around on horseback. It is utterly impossible to drive a buggy."

Cameron's notes also mirror the hardships faced by the pioneer settlers even as late as 1870. Of one farm he writes: "There is a good well with a pump on it, which enhances its value very much as water is very scarce. I met a woman carrying water one and a half miles." On a farm owned by Samuel Slack, of which 50 acres had been cleared and 115 were still wild, Cameron set a value of $1,000. "It's a good farm," he wrote. "The soil is very good clay soil. There are no buildings worth anything on it. There is a small shanty but of no value."

The inspector obviously had considerable sympathy for the inhabitant of this poor shanty. "He seems an industrious man," he wrote, "but I very much fear his ability to pay the instalments. He is very poor. God help the poor fellow. The wheat crop at Keppel was a total failure last year. Mr. Slack told me that all he made out of his whole crop was enough to pay his taxes and buy himself a pair of boots, which he pointed to on his feet. It will be a hard struggle for him to meet his payments. I believe if it could be arranged that he would pay simply interest the first few years, until he gets a little better off. It would be better for him, and us too."

In Bruce County, Cameron came across a settler in an even more pathetic plight: John Ebert, a Dutchman living on a hundred acres, with thirty cleared, his only companion his dog. "I very much fear Ebert will never be able to pay off this loan," he wrote. "At present, he is lame, and has been all spring and summer, quite unable to work. A week ago he lost his wife with a paralytic stroke. The farm is very much out of the way, and not being fenced or cleared at all in a square form, would not bring much. I have placed it, all things considered, at all it is worth." Ebert told Cameron he would not take less than $1,000 for his farm, but the inspector, though a kindly man, took his duties seriously; he valued it at $750. His compassion comes through in the final note on that page: "It was pitiable to see the poor man in his hovel, and in such misery and poverty. God help him."

Cameron did not always agree with the valuations of properties made by the men on the spot. "Doyle's valuations," he writes in one place, "are much higher than mine. Land is not worth as much as the people here seem to think." One valuator, a Mr. Philips, seems to have incurred his special displeasure. On his fifth inspection in the book, Cameron looked over a hundred-acre farm owned by a Mr. Hunt. He found eighty acres cleared, five partly cleared, and about fifteen wild. But the soil was "excellent, a clay soil but not stiff." He described the fences as "pretty good," the log house, about twenty feet by twenty-six, as "not very good," and the small stable as "of not much account." But there was "a small young orchard of about forty to fifty trees, last spring's planting," and there was expected to be a railroad station a few miles away soon.

All in all, Cameron figured it was a pretty good property. "Before Mr. Hunt knew who I was," he writes, "I inquired what he asked for the lot, in cash. After some consideration, he said, 'I think if I had all that piece cleared up, the fences a little better, and some other small improvements, I would not take less than $3,000.'" Cameron had come to the conclusion that it was worth $2,500. But in an "extraordinary valuation," Philips had placed it at $4,500.

On another inspection Cameron asked a farmer named Cowan how much he would take for his hundred-acre farm, only forty-five acres of which had been cleared. The farmer replied, "I would not like to part with it for less than $1,200 or $1,300." Somewhat acidly, Cameron notes: "And yet Philips values it at $2,275. It is not worth half of that."

These may have been examples merely of lack of judgment on Philips's part, or perhaps of excessive optimism about the prospects ahead for his district. But then Cameron came across a more serious lapse. Examining a "capital lot" in Luther Township owned by William Nelson, who kept his farm "in excellent condition," he was pleased to find that his valuation of $1,000 was exactly what Nelson had paid for it two years earlier. But he also reported to the Huron & Erie's directors: "Mr. Nelson thinks that our valuator, Mr. Philips, has cheated him. Attached I place Philips' account to Mr. Nelson. [This survives in his notebook as a faded piece of blue paper, practically illegible today.] It is to be remembered that Philips never inspected this lot at all and never corresponded to any extent with Mr. Nelson and still he makes a charge of $15. Methinks the Society should make Philips pay him back any overcharge." It is doubtless significant that Philips's name as a valuator promptly disappears from the Huron & Erie's records.

Despite his conservative valuations Cameron believed in playing fair with the customer, a quality the society tried to instil in its staff from the beginning. On one occasion he reported to the directors, a farmer named William Cooke and his son complained that it had cost them $25 to take out their $250 mortgage. As soon as he arrived back at the office, he dug out the Cookes' account and found that $10.42 of that amount had gone to pay off outstanding taxes on the lot. The Cookes had not realized this, and when Cameron told them "they were quite pleased—their opinion of the Society rose 100 degrees at once."

When Cameron resigned in 1871 to accept a better job as secretary-treasurer of the Hamilton Provident society, the directors obviously regretted losing such a conscientious employee. It seems they were also a bit miffed, because they resolved "that the travelling inspector be required to covenant not to enter into the service or direction of any similar society for a period of two years after he ceases to be in the employment of this Society, and that such be the rule in future in regard to all officers of the Society." Notwithstanding this caveat, the advertisement seeking a successor to Cameron drew sixty applications, with supporting references.

By 1870 the society's assets had grown to $680,233, and it made a profit that year of $51,929 after fattening its reserve fund to $43,000. But in the business boom that followed Confederation there was what the minutes of one directors' meeting referred to as "an abundance of money" in the hands of the populace at large, and the society noticed a steep drop in applications for loans. Consequently, besides declaring a dividend of only nine per cent that year, the directors considered lowering the ten-per-cent interest charge on its mortgages.

Ellis Hyman, who had taken over as president after Adam Hope left for Hamilton, told a board meeting in June that the Canada Permanent was about to lower its rate to eight per cent, and that in view of the fact "that the interest on money all over the Province is lower than the rates of this Society," the Huron & Erie should reduce its rate to nine per cent.

As cautious as ever, the directors took the matter under consideration. At their next meeting they decided against the rate reduction but agreed that henceforth the society would pay the solicitors' fees on mortgages, and offer valuators a one-per-cent commission to inspire them to greater efforts on the society's behalf.

Even though business was slow, the directors retained enough confidence in the society's future to circularize the city's architects inviting them to submit plans for "a building three storeys in height and a basement, estimated to cost $6,000." Cost overruns on construction projects were apparently not unknown even in those days, because the eventual cost of the building the society moved into during the summer of 1871 seems to have been $12,000. However, with their customary thrift and foresight, the directors had rounded up tenants to help offset the expense, including the local Masons, who rented the top storey for $125 a year. The new building, on Richmond Street near Dundas, still the heart of London's downtown, remained the Huron & Erie's headquarters for the next sixty years.

Even in the new building business remained disappointingly slow, and at a board meeting in 1872 there was an interesting anticipation of a sales tactic by which the company would steal a march on the banks a century later: "It was suggested that in view of our bank account being now heavily overdrawn and the present being an unfavourable time for selling new stock, it is desirable to increase the savings bank as much as possible, and that for this purpose and to afford facilities to mechanics and others who cannot attend during business hours, it would be well to keep the savings bank open for a couple of hours on Saturday evenings."

At that time the normal work day everywhere lasted from 8 a.m. to 6 p.m. six days a week, though at the Huron & Erie the employees were permitted the privilege of leaving an hour early on Saturdays. The board minutes do not disclose whether they lost that privilege as a result of the "suggestion" made to the board, but during 1873 deposits in the savings bank increased by $58,000, to a total of $636,000.

The society's assets passed the million-dollar mark for the first time in 1872, a satisfying advance on the $49,000 with which it had finished its first year of operation only eight years earlier. In the annual report for 1873 the president, John Birrell, another Scots-born dry-goods wholesaler who had succeeded Ellis Hyman in the post, said: "In inviting the attention of the shareholders to the accompanying financial statement, your directors feel bound to add that the time has now come when this society, both as regards wealth and popularity, ranks as one of the foremost institutions of its class in the country."

In 1874 the Dominion parliament passed legislation that proved to be an enormous benefit not only to the Huron & Erie and the other building societies but to the country as a whole. Its most important feature was that it permitted the societies to issue debentures, that is, bonds paying fixed interest over a set period of years. This gave the societies what became a popular new instrument to offer to Canadian savers. Even more important, since the debentures could be sold overseas, it gave them access to the rich British capital markets. In the years that followed, a steady stream of capital flowed in from Britain to fuel Canada's development, so that by the turn of the century it was estimated that British investment in Canada totalled more than $1 billion. (U.S. investment in Canada at the same time was estimated at $168 million.)

When the possibility of issuing debentures came before the Huron & Erie board for the first time in the fall of 1874, the directors, deliberating with their customary conservatism, seemed to feel that their little society, growing though it certainly was, could hardly compete with the mighty financial moguls in that other London over the sea. They were "of the opinion that in order to dispose of the debentures successfully a considerable amount, say £200,000 or £300,000 sterling, should be placed upon the market at one time, and as no one society would be able to issue such an amount, it was suggested that two or three societies might unite for this purpose."

Nothing came of this suggestion, but the directors continued to ponder the matter from time to time and to receive approaches from various apparent brokers offering to place debentures for them. It was not until 1877, however, that they appointed the firm of Messrs. Alison and Dickson, of 21 St. Andrew's Square, Edinburgh, sharebrokers, "as the agents of the Company in Scotland for the purpose of contracting for the sale at par of £50,000 sterling debentures."

Presumably after consultation with their Scottish agents, the directors had decided the issue should consist of debentures priced at either £500 or £100, with an interest rate of five per cent on those redeemable after three or five years, and five and a half per cent on those extending over seven years. Some graying heads may have been shaken ruefully and there may have been mutters of "I told you so" around the board table that December, when "a letter was read from Messrs. Alison and Dickson in reference to the very limited applications for our debentures at present, which they attribute to the business being overdone."

The Huron & Erie was clearly not the only Canadian company lining up to tap the funds of Scotland's landed lairds and canny industrialists, and by the end of 1878 it had sold only $16,452 of its debentures. This was a tiny item on its balance sheet: the company's total assets now exceeded $2 million and its paid-up capital was fast approaching the million-dollar mark. These statistics, and the company's reputation for cautious dealing—its reserve fund now amounted to the substantial total of $220,000—must have been pushed energetically by Messrs. Alison and Dickson, because ten years later the Huron & Erie listed $855,073 in sterling debentures on its balance sheet, against only $322,500 invested in its certificates by Canadians. And the inflow of capital, mostly from Scotland, continued: by 1914 British investors held more than $5 million in Huron & Erie debentures.

Back in 1878, whatever concern the Huron & Erie directors felt over the discouraging start to their debenture marketing in Britain was overshadowed by a scandalous discovery right in their own closet. That spring, a man named DeLatre, who appears to have been a company employee, voiced his suspicion that all was not well with the company's accounts.

The company's president at the time was Charles Stead,[1] one of the founder-directors who had succeeded to the post when John Birrell died in 1875. Stead was born in Leeds, Yorkshire, in 1806 and came to Canada as a boy with his family. His father founded a stage-coach line in Toronto; Charles pushed on west as a "carpenter-builder" and settled in London in time to be one of the contractors who built the original British barracks in the city.

To this solid Yorkshireman, whose obituary in the *London Free Press* a few years later described him as "a clear-headed, thoughtful municipal officer whose opinion carried great weight with his associates," fell the unpleasant duty of investigating DeLatre's suspicions. And what his inquiry disclosed horrified his colleagues: their secretary-treasurer, Lawrence Gibson, an agent of the Merchants' Bank at Prescott who had been chosen from dozens of applicants for the post back in 1870, had been systematically fiddling the books ever since.

A thorough investigation of the company's accounts by the

---

1. Family legend has it that Charles Stead was a relative—perhaps an uncle—of the English journalist W. T. Stead, editor of the *Pall Mall Gazette*, whose many crusading articles included an exposé of white-slave traffic which brought him a three-month jail sentence but also resulted in legislation to correct the abuses he complained of. W. T. Stead embarked on the *Titanic* in 1912—perhaps on a visit to his North American relatives—and was drowned in that famous disaster.

well-known local auditor George F. Jewell[2] revealed that by "erasures, alterations, the addition of figures in one account and the omission of them in another," Gibson had managed to defraud the company of $14,651.50—a considerable sum when the company's profit for the year was $18,780. Gibson was promptly fired but the company does not seem to have prosecuted him. It did, however, seize and sell his house and some stock he held in the company and insist on payment of his "sureties" by his reluctant bondsmen.

There were eighty-six applications in response to the advertisement seeking Gibson's successor. The man chosen for the job was Robert W. Smylie, manager of the local branch of the Bank of Commerce, who had assisted Jewell in his investigation and recommended some changes in the company's bookkeeping methods to the board.

In the years 1871 and 1872 there was a worldwide financial crisis, and the period from 1873 to the mid-1890s became known as "the long depression." There was a brief recovery in Canada after the introduction of Sir John A. Macdonald's National Policy in 1879, which spurred the development of Canadian industry by increasing tariffs on most manufactured goods and reducing import duties on raw materials, and it continued during the early 1880s, when spending on the construction of the Canadian Pacific Railway gave business in general a boost. But the Huron & Erie's minute books throughout this period make frequent reference to the slow state of the economy. At the annual meeting in 1877, for instance, Charles Stead "congratulated the shareholders upon the continued prosperity of the company, notwithstanding the general depression which had prevailed last year and the constantly increasing competition with which we have to contend."

That competition, as well as the economic climate, led to reduced interest rates. By 1880 the company was paying only four and a half per cent on its sterling debentures and four per cent on savings deposits. Those rates were reduced again the following year, and Manager Smylie recommended to the directors that "in view of the present state of the bank balance" the minimum interest charged on mortgage loans be raised to six and a half per cent—

---

2. George F. Jewell was the Huron & Erie's auditor for many years. In keeping with the continuity upon which the company has always prided itself, that post later fell to his son, and then his grandson.

a far cry from the ten per cent of a few years before. The directors agreed.

In 1880 the Dominion parliament enacted a bill whose provisions have governed the mortgage business ever since. This was the Mortgage Regulation Act, known also as the Orton Act after its crusading sponsor, a Dr. Orton. There had been growing public resentment against the system of long-term "sinking fund" mortgages, in which the interest charged was not spelled out in the loan tables, enabling unscrupulous companies or agents to misrepresent the rate in order to drum up business. Dr. Orton fanned the discontent in Commons debates by citing examples of extortionate rates levied on unsuspecting borrowers.

The Act he succeeded in having passed stipulated that mortgages with blended principal and interest should spell out both the principal amount and the interest being charged on it. And it provided that borrowers with mortgages for terms longer than five years could pay them off at the end of that period, with a penalty of three months' interest. The effect of this, of course, was that five years became the customary mortgage term down to modern times.

The Orton Act undoubtedly benefited the consumer, and it probably put some of the shadier loan companies out of business. But it had little effect on the Huron & Erie. The first booklet ever issued by the company said: "It has been urged against some loan companies that the borrower can never tell how much he will have to pay, nor when his payments will cease. The Huron & Erie, however, has found it to its advantage to make the mode of repayment so plain that any man can understand what he has to pay for his loan and when he will be entitled to a discharge." And at a meeting six months after the company was formed "the Board considered the terms upon which parties should be allowed to pay their mortgages in full in advance, and the Secretary was instructed until further ordered by the Board to give a discharge of any mortgage upon payment of a sum approximating as near as possible to the unpaid principal, with interest, up to the first of the month subsequent to the said payment."

5

A Versatile and Visionary President

BY 1882 all the Huron & Erie's authorized capital of $1 million had been paid in, and its total assets, which had amounted to only $319,000 at the time of Confederation fifteen years earlier, now stood at more than $2.5 million. Charles Stead had retired from the presidency four years earlier and had been succeeded by William Saunders, the most remarkably versatile man ever to hold the position. Saunders's predecessors had all been entrepreneurs, *money* men—men who understood money, how to make it, how to make it work for them, and above all how to conserve it. Saunders shared all these abilities: he was president for nine years and had been a valued director before that. But he was also a scholar, a self-taught scientist.

William Saunders was born in Devon in 1836, the ninth child of a shoemaker and Methodist lay preacher who emigrated to London, Ontario, when young William was twelve. Such formal education as the boy acquired was imparted to him during his apprenticeship to Dr. Salter, a pioneer London druggist. At the age of nineteen William opened his own drug store on Dundas Street, and by 1857 he was well enough established to be able to marry Sarah, the daughter of the Reverend Joseph Hiram Robinson, London-based superintendent of the Methodist New Connexion Church in Canada.

Joseph Robinson had edited church magazines in England and had one of the finest libraries in Canada, in which William, and his sons too as they grew up, were encouraged to browse. In 1864, the year the Huron & Erie opened for business, William moved to a new store nearby, where he offered for sale "botanical medicines, eclectic preparations and Swedish leeches." His competitors at the time were advertising such products as "Bristol's sugar-coated vegetable pills," said to be efficacious in all cases of "Dyspepsia, Indigestion, Lung Complaints, Constipation, Headache, Dropsy and Piles," and "Dr. Radway's Pills," of which one to six boxes would allegedly cure any of a list of forty-four complaints, ranging from diseases of the liver to bad dreams.

Pharmacy, like medicine itself, was not exactly a precise science in those days, but William's practice of it obviously stimulated his inquiring mind, and since plants were the basis of most of the pharmaceuticals he sold, and was beginning to manufacture, his interest turned to the natural world around him. Sarah bore her first two children in rooms above the store, but as William's business prospered he bought a seventy-acre farm about three kilometres east of town. There he planted 2,500 apple trees, together with plums, peaches, cherries, and hundreds of grape vines. As many a hobby farmer since has found, this concentrated his mind wonderfully on bugs, and in 1863 he became a co-founder of the Entomological Society of Canada, which earned government financial support for its research on insect pests.

A man of inexhaustible energy, Saunders helped to found the Fruit Growers' Association of Ontario and at its first meeting in 1868 gave a paper on "The Apple Worm." That same year he was admitted to the American Association for the Advancement of Science, of which he was soon elected a Fellow, and later general secretary for the customary one-year term. In 1871 he helped to found the Ontario College of Pharmacy, and in 1877 he was elected president of the American Pharmaceutical Association. When the Royal Society of Canada was formed in 1881, Saunders, by now recognized as Canada's foremost authority on agriculture and horticulture, was one of its first Fellows. Back in London he encouraged Isaac Hellmuth in his school-founding endeavours, and when the University of Western Ontario's medical faculty opened in 1882 he embarked on a two-year stint there as a teacher of *Materia Medica*. In that same year, he was appointed public analyst for western Ontario, in which capacity he supervised the hygiene and wholesomeness of the milk, butter, cheese, and canned goods produced in the area.

In 1884, at a time when half the Canadian electorate still made its living off the land, the government decided the country needed a network of experimental farms to introduce new varieties of plants, test fertilizers and seeds, and investigate methods of controlling plant and animal pests and diseases. With his wide-ranging knowledge and demonstrated administrative talents, William Saunders was the obvious candidate to take charge of this important new venture. In 1885 he toured experimental farms already established in the United States and Europe and submitted a voluminous report on their activities to Ottawa. And in 1886, a year during which he exhibited a selection of his pharmaceutical manufactures at the World's Fair in Paris, he was appointed the first director of the federal experimental farm system. The day after his appointment he left on a tour of potential farm sites which took him to the Maritimes, Manitoba, what was then the Northwest Territories, and British Columbia; and within two years he had five farms in operation, at Ottawa; Nappan, Nova Scotia; Brandon, Manitoba; Indian Head, Saskatchewan; and Agassiz, British Columbia.

One of the objectives the government had set for the experimental farm system was the development of a strain of wheat suited to the short growing season on the prairies, where a new generation of pioneers was beginning to occupy the land opened up by the transcontinental railroad. Saunders had experimented with the cross-breeding of plants on his farm at London, and he had developed many successful new varieties of raspberries, blackberries, gooseberries, and currants. Now he began to import wheat seed from all over the world, and within ten years of his appointment the Dominion experimental farms had developed fifteen new varieties of hybrid wheat.

Saunders had always tried to interest his five sons in his activities and his nature studies. He appointed one of them, Charles,[1] whose previous career had included a professorship at Central University, Kentucky, and a couple of years teaching music in Toronto, to the post of Dominion Cerealist. Charles continued his father's experiments and was in due course knighted for his development of the Marquis strain of early-ripening wheat, which both expanded far to the north the area in which wheat could be grown

---

1. William and Sarah raised a remarkable family. Fred, their youngest son, became a professor of physics at Harvard. Percy taught at Hamilton College, Clinton, N.Y., and was a well-known horticulturist. Henry, a musician in Toronto, accumulated one of the most important collections of the works of Walt Whitman. Only Will, the eldest, stayed on in London, where he became one of the city's business and civic leaders and a naturalist whose work attracted notice in the United States as well as in Canada.

and established Canada's reputation as an exporter of the highest-quality hard wheat for making bread.

With a man of William Saunders's vision and breadth of accomplishments at the helm, it is not surprising that the Huron & Erie became one of the first companies in London to introduce a "high-tech" aid to its operations: in 1883, only a few years after its invention, Manager Smylie was authorized to install a telephone in the office.

At that time, and indeed for many years thereafter, the work of the company was carried out laboriously by hand. Clerks spent their ten-hour days bent over heavy ledgers bound with thick cardboard, recording transactions with customers in meticulous copperplate handwriting, dipping their steel-nibbed pens frequently into their inkwells. Letters, when they were considered necessary, were also painstakingly written by hand and copied in a letter-book by hand press. Practicable typewriters were still some years away, and it is not known when the company first acquired one.

Coffee breaks and cafeterias were not yet in vogue and fifteen minutes was considered ample time for the men to eat their box lunches at the board-room table. The obligatory working garb was a thick serge or worsted three-piece suit, with a high-collared, stiff white shirt and a tie. One clerk was dismissed as "lacking in decorum" for having the effrontery to take off his coat on a particularly hot summer's day. In those Victorian days, of course, the employees were all male; the first woman to join the staff, as a typist, was not taken on until 1895, and even then the appointment raised many eyebrows around town.

Notwithstanding all this stringency, a job at the Huron & Erie was considered a plum, and applicants lined up eagerly for any vacancy that arose, even at a time when the lowliest junior clerk was required to have someone post a substantial bond as a guarantee of his trustworthiness. Young Malcolm Kent, for example, was engaged for a trial period of two months in 1873 for a job that paid $200 a year. He was required to "furnish security to the amount of $1,000," even though it seems likely that his father or an uncle was a member of the company's board of directors.

The evidence for this relationship, while not conclusive, comes in the board minutes for February 1875. At the annual meeting that year, one of the directors, Benjamin Cronyn—the "student-at-law" who had filed the society's charter and was now not only a full-fledged lawyer in partnership with his brother Verschoyle but mayor of the city—"made some remarks as to the small amount which appeared in the financial statement for expenses of management, and advocated liberality in the payment of officials." A couple of weeks later, when Benjamin put a motion approving salary increases for the staff to a meeting of the directors, it was seconded by Charles W. Kent. The motion was approved, and the manager's salary was raised to $2,400. Young Malcolm Kent was included, too: he got a raise to $400 a year. A couple of years later, when Malcolm resigned, presumably to move on to better things, and a Mr. Gillean was promoted to take his place, the minutes noted: "In return for his new salary of $400, Mr. Gillean was required to give additional security to the amount of $1,000, making $2,000 in all."

After the discovery of Manager Gibson's defalcations in 1878, and presumably because of the reluctance of his sureties to pay up, the company decided that in future it would pay to have all its senior employees bonded by a company specializing in that form of insurance, the Canadian Guaranty Company. But the minute books for 1882 show that Manager Smylie had to match the Canadian Guaranty's $10,000 bond on him by a further $10,000 of his own. The company's accountant at the time, William E. Turner, was bonded for $4,000—a circumstance that was to prove fortunate for the company after he left their employ.

In October 1884 President Saunders and Manager Smylie reported to the board that they had discovered that Turner had misappropriated $150 from two mortgages before leaving the company. "The Manager further reported," the minutes record, "that Mr. Turner had called at his house last evening and acknowledged further misappropriations, bringing up the total to about $300, and had offered to make immediate restitution." The directors authorized Smylie to receive from Turner any sums he acknowledged having taken, "while reserving full liberty of action to the company in regard to further proceedings." And they instructed him to send the borrowers whose funds the accountant had pilfered "corrected statements of their accounts crediting the sums taken by Mr. Turner."

This kind of conduct did not sit at all well with Verschoyle Cronyn, the company's solicitor, and in his prompt investigation of the situation he apparently found that $300 was only the half of it. He made a report to a special board meeting a couple of days later and the directors resolved to refer the matter to the Canadian Guaranty Company unless Smylie reported that the sum of $600 had been repaid "before the closing of the Montreal mail." Turner paid up, and it seems he persuaded a friend to provide the company with a letter of guarantee for a further $1,000, just in case.

That seems to have been a wise precaution, because on 25 November Smylie reported to the board that he had billed Turner for another misappropriation he had traced, amounting to $15.04, and on 9 December he discovered that Turner owed the company a further $65. In both cases, the accountant settled up. But Smylie, or the company's auditor, kept after him, and in January he came up with what seems to have been his last repayment: $288.12.

Earlier in 1884 the company had received permission from the legislative authorities to increase its authorized capital from $1 million to $1.5 million by an issue of 10,000 new shares. President Saunders explained one reason for the new issue to the shareholders at the annual meeting: "Our borrowing power in the savings bank is limited to one million of dollars, and this limit we have nearly reached." The legislation then in force also empowered the company to issue $1 million worth of debentures, but up to that time it had managed to sell only $160,500 worth of debentures in Canada and $86,870 worth in Britain. There was therefore an opportunity, as the president explained, to raise a further $752,630 in capital, thus increasing the company's earning power. This was another reason for the new stock issue.

"We find it difficult to obtain Canadian debentures to the extent we require," Saunders said, "as there is not much money here seeking permanent investment at low rates, and hence all loan companies look to Great Britain for the bulk of their debenture money. There is a prejudice existing there amongst investors in favour of those companies which have uncalled stock. The Directors believe our not having stock of this character [all the company's authorized capital having been paid in two years earlier] militates against the sale of our debentures and, with the view of providing for the natural growth of the company, accompanied with the advantages of increased profits, have asked for the power to make this new issue in order to place the Huron & Erie on the same vantage ground as other companies competing with us in the debenture market of Great Britain."

The proposal for the new issue was that shareholders would be permitted to buy one share for each two they already held. But there was to be no free ride. Huron & Erie shares were being traded on the market at considerably more than their $50 par value, and so those who bought the new ones would have to pay a forty-five-per-cent premium, amounting to an extra $22.50. But they would not have to put up all the money right away. Since it was proposed to "call" only $10 of the share purchase price initially, the buyers faced an extra payment of only $4.50 at the outset.

When this plan was put to the annual meeting, a couple of shareholders, scenting the opportunity to make a nice killing, proposed an amendment suggesting that the premium be only thirty-three and a half per cent. That would have enabled those who did not want to hold on to the new shares to "flip" them on the open market at an assured profit.

It would also, of course, have reduced the amount raised by the issue for the company's treasury, and the proposed amendment outraged Saunders's sense of morality. "The stock of the Huron & Erie," he responded, "is held by about 450 individual holders, many of whom are widows or people advanced in years, who depend mainly on their dividends from this stock for their support. Many of these have not the means of taking their stock, no matter what price it might be issued at. Some live in England, and others in various distant parts of the Dominion and elsewhere, and would not be able to participate in the temporary advantage which would result to shareholders were the stock issued below its value. . . . Why should the shareholders, who get good interest for their money at the rate proposed, ask the Directors to sacrifice a principle which they believe to be based on true justice, and tax the poorer shareholders even to this extent, for the sake of obtaining their stock at fifty cents less per share? I think you will hold with us that those who have money to invest should be satisfied with reasonably good interest and not seek to place a tax on those who are least able to bear it, in order to save themselves so small a sum."

When the amendment was put to the vote, principle triumphed over avarice: it was defeated by 13,558 votes to 844. The whole issue was duly taken up by the shareholders. The company's authorized capital now became $1.5 million, of which $1.1 million was fully paid up, and the directors prudently added the $45,000 paid in premiums to the reserve fund.

Amid the hectic whirl of all his many and varied activities

William Saunders had continued to preside at the frequent meetings of the Huron & Erie board, but with his appointment to head the Dominion experimental farm system, he clearly could not continue as the company's president, and a well-established local lawyer, William P. R. Street, Q.C., was elected to succeed him. In his last report to the shareholders, in February 1887, the retiring president reviewed the progress of the company during his nine-year stewardship. Its total assets had grown from $2.1 million to $3.4 million. When he took over, the company had issued only $16,452 worth of debentures; that figure had now grown to $754,000. And the reserve fund had been nearly doubled, from $220,000 to $417,000.

William Street's tenure of the presidency was a short one. In the fall of 1887 he was gazetted as a justice of the Queen's Bench division of the High Court of Ontario.[2] It therefore fell to Saunders, who had remained on the board as vice-president, to present the company's financial statement for 1887 at the annual meeting early in 1888. At the outset of his remarks, he said: "Notwithstanding the financial disturbances which have occurred during the past year, attended by revelations which might have been expected to lessen public confidence in all monetary institutions, the Huron & Erie has grown stronger amid the storm and has transacted a total volume of business never before equalled in its history."

He did not need to be more specific. His audience was well aware that not all Canadian financial institutions were as dedicated as the Huron & Erie to the eradication from their operations of any form of roguery or what was, to the Huron & Erie's directors, the only slightly less reprehensible sin of laxity. By the end of 1887 thirteen of the chartered banks that had been operating in Canada at the time of Confederation, twenty years earlier, had failed owing to one or other of those human frailties. And the "storm" to which Saunders referred had raged distressingly close to home. It revolved around the activities of a spectacularly successful con man named Henry Taylor.

---

2. Street's successor was a militia colonel named John W. Little. A prosperous dry-goods merchant and prominent civic leader, Little presided over the company's activities for the next twenty years. A bequest in his widow's will provided the University of Western Ontario with its football stadium, which still bears his name.

Taylor had been born in England in 1841, and had arrived in London with the Commissariat department of the Imperial garrison in 1862. He soon retired from the service and set himself up as a private banker. It was alleged years later that he provided himself with the capital for his new career by swindling the Commissariat. If that was so, he covered his tracks skilfully, for his climb into the upper reaches of the London business community was swift.

He became an agent for a British shipping company, the Great Western Railway, the Merchants' Bank of New York, and Molson's Bank. He organized an oil company and was in on the foundation of the Carling Brewing and Malting Company. He was also a director of the British-American Assurance Company of Toronto and several local companies. In 1880 he formed a mortgage company, the Ontario Investment Association, whose first board of directors included the president of Imperial Oil, the manager of the Federal Bank, the brewer John Labatt, and William Meredith, leader of the Conservative opposition in the Ontario legislature until 1894 when he became chief justice of Ontario. And that was not the end of Taylor's rise to prominence. In 1883 he became the first president of the Bank of London, which soon opened branches in five other western Ontario centres.

His house of cards began to collapse when "irregularities" were discovered in the accounts of the Ontario Investment Association in the summer of 1887; in fact, as an investigation by the auditor George Jewell soon found, the association was completely insolvent. Its collapse brought down the Bank of London, whose funds its president had apparently used in a vain attempt to prop up the association. The bank closed its doors for ever on 19 August 1887. By that time Taylor had fled with his family to the New York resort of Alexandria Bay, across the St. Lawrence River east of Kingston. The association's manager and its solicitor had also found it expedient to take refuge across the border.

Jewell's investigation of the association's affairs revealed, in the words of the *Monetary Times*, that "the entire 'reserve fund,' so-called, stated to amount at one time to $500,000, has been entirely swept away." In all, something over $700,000 had been lost in disastrous speculations or stolen. Jewell estimated Taylor's take at around $389,000. The association's manager, Charles Murray, by now safe in Nebraska, had got away with $126,000. And what the *London Free Press* described in an irreverent sub-heading as "the solicitor's whack" amounted to $131,000.

Respectable Londoners were appalled by the scandal, none more so than Verschoyle Cronyn, for the Ontario Investment Association's solicitor was his brother Benjamin. The bishop had harboured a black sheep in his fold, though mercifully he had not lived to see his name disgraced. Verschoyle paid off the substantial debts his brother had left behind him in London and refused to speak to him again as long as he lived. Not that he had much opportunity to do so: Benjamin never returned to London. He took his family first to Marion, Alabama, and then to Burlington, Vermont, from where he decamped to England in 1896, having misappropriated $15,000 worth of insurance premiums and other funds entrusted to him.

By that time Benjamin's wife Mary, daughter of the wealthy George Goodhue, had had enough. In addition to all the large sums of other people's money, Benjamin had frittered away her inheritance of $130,000. She returned to London in straitened circumstances and struggled to bring up her children alone, to such good effect that one of her sons in due course became secretary of the Bank of Montreal.

By the time the scandal erupted into torrents of newsprint, Verschoyle Cronyn was no longer in business with his brother: he had formed a partnership with his son-in-law, Frederick Pimlott Betts. Nor did Benjamin have any official connection with the Huron & Erie, having resigned his directorship twelve years earlier. But the magnitude of the disaster, which according to a contemporary account ruined several of London's wealthiest citizens, reinforced the determination of Verschoyle Cronyn and his fellow directors not to countenance even the slightest taint of dishonesty in the dealings of their company. Retribution was accordingly rapid when Manager Smylie was caught fiddling his expense accounts a year later.

In 1964, when the company was about to mark its hundredth anniversary, its secretary, Bob Knighton, explored the archives for anything that might be useful in the coming celebrations. He decided it was time to open a locked cash box that had been in the company's records vault as long as he had been around. He had the lock broken open. Inside he found a stoutly bound old ledger fitted with a solid brass lock. When that lock too was forced, he discovered a record of the proceedings at an investigation conducted by Colonel Little and several other directors on 1 November 1888.

The committee assembled in the board room at 10:15 that morning and President Little began to grill Smylie, pointing out several contradictions in his explanation for various inspection visits he claimed to have made. The president himself had visited several of the places named in the manager's expense accounts and had talked to farmers who said they had never even seen Smylie. The sums involved seem small a century later, ranging from $3.00 to $14.75, and they were mostly for such things as "hire of horse and buggy."

The committee met again that afternoon, recalled Smylie, and questioned him about two telegrams he had sent, at a cost to the company of 76 cents and $4.63. Smylie admitted that the telegrams dealt with his private affairs but said he had called at the telegraph office to settle them. The record goes on: "The President pointed out the fact that neither of these credits were made until after inquiries had been made by him regarding telegrams which he thought were not on the company's business."

Junior members of the staff gave evidence against their boss, stating that on several occasions they had been ordered by him to take parcels from the office to his wife at his home. They contained such things as cakes of soap, toilet paper, stationery, and pencils. One employee, John S. Moore, said that not long ago he had heard Mr. Smylie telephone a Mrs. Winslow at the Tecumseh Hotel and arrange to take her out for a drive. Next day he submitted an expense account for three dollars for the buggy rental.

The committee was determined to get to the bottom of the matter and it met again that evening in Verschoyle Cronyn's office, when a witness named Holmes said he had "a suspicion that the Manager gets a premium on insurances effected with Mr. Hammond." The record continues: "He thinks this for the reason that the Manager is always so anxious to have the business go to Mr. Hammond and from the frequent private conferences they have together in the office."

Next day President Little reported to the board that the committee was satisfied that there had been "transactions where the Manager has profited at the expense of the company" and his explanations had been "contradictory and untruthful."

In the circumstances, the directors were surprisingly lenient with Smylie. He was permitted to resign when he promised to deposit one thousand dollars cash in the company's savings bank to cover any deficiencies in his accounts discovered later, and within a week he had hung out his shingle as a free-lance accountant and auditor.

There were said to be eighty applications to succeed him. The man chosen for the job, George Anderson Somerville, would soon re-establish the scrupulous standards of employee conduct desired by the directors, and a few years later he would lead the company into an important new venture.

6

A New Departure

GEO. A. Somerville, as he invariably signed his name, was a man of formidable intellect but modest bearing; a contemporary account speaks of his "cordial smile and his kindly and sympathetic greetings." He was born in 1855 at St. Mary's, Ontario, and went to school there and at the University of Toronto. His first job was as a mathematics teacher at Guelph High School, and at the age of twenty-three he was appointed an inspector of schools. But the business world beckoned and Somerville soon abandoned the schoolroom to put his mathematical talents to good use as manager of the Guelph and Ontario Investment and Savings Society. When he left for London nine years later to become the Huron & Erie's new manager, a writer in the *Guelph Mercury*, while regretting his departure, consoled himself with the observation that he was going to take over "the oldest and best institution of the kind in the western part of Ontario."

Somerville went on to build from there. At the end of his first year as manager, 1889, President Little saluted his achievement by telling the annual meeting: "The increase of the business has been greater by far than in any former year, and at the same time a saving has been effected in the expense of management equal to about one-twelfth of the entire cost." The company's total assets were now more than $4.3 million and the cash value of its mortgages, which had increased by more than $500,000 during the year, was $4.1 million, on properties valued by the company's own inspectors at $8.9 million.

Because of the continued growth in the volume of business, the directors had considered it necessary that year to increase the company's capital again, and 20,000 new shares had been issued, with shareholders entitled to buy two new shares for every three they already held. As in the earlier issue in 1884, subscribers were charged a premium of forty-five per cent. At the same time, the company's authorized capital was increased from $1.5 million to $2.5 million, of which more than $1.2 million had been paid in by the end of the year.

At the time Somerville joined the company, agriculture, like every other form of economic activity, was suffering through the long depression, and the value of farmland was declining. But in his remarks accompanying the annual report for 1890 President Little told the shareholders that the arrears on mortgages held by the company—$80,903—were less than at any time since 1881, although the business had almost doubled since that date. "In every respect," the president said, "the business of the company is in a most healthy and prosperous condition. There has been an increase of $312,007 in the cash value of the securities without any corresponding addition to the expense account; in fact in the controllable portion of that account a slight saving has been effected."

Seconding the motion to adopt the annual report, the vice-president, John Beattie, said: "This gratifying result is due very largely to the scrupulous care which has always been taken in the selection of investments. We have always avoided loaning on unproductive property, and the more hazardous investments, such as mills, factories, machinery, village property etc.; when loaning in cities or towns, which we have only done where the margins were very large, we have always insisted upon having central productive property. In fact, I might here say, our motto is 'a fair rate of interest and undoubted security'." And, a later observer might add, "prudence and caution," the qualities that had characterized the company since its beginning.

During the year under review the company had placed about £100,000 worth of sterling debentures in Britain, almost as much as the total issued in any previous two years. It was left to Verschoyle Cronyn to point out to the shareholders that this satisfying result was largely due to President Little's own efforts on a trip to the Old Country. The president himself merely said, as a result of his visits to the various British agents, "I feel quite justified in saying that the standing of the Company among British investors is such that we shall have no difficulty in securing what funds we require at the lowest current rates of interest."

President Little had more good news for the shareholders the following year: the company's total assets now exceeded $5 million, more than double what they had been ten years before. Even more remarkable, since the whole population of the city was only a little more than 30,000, the number of customers with accounts in the savings bank stood at 3,206, and their average balance was $404.55, making a total contribution to the funds available for investment of almost $1.3 million.[1]

And so the company's growth continued, although at the annual meeting in January 1893 President Little felt bound to "warn the shareholders against expecting for the current year an increase of business such as is reported today, the Company having nearly reached the legal limit of its borrowing powers."

This restraint on the company's ability to expand was eased later that year by yet another new issue of 10,000 shares. This time shareholders were allotted one new share for every five they held and, as a reflection of the company's flourishing state, the premium was raised to fifty per cent. The authorized capital was now up to $3 million, and since the reserve fund was approaching $700,000, George Somerville and the directors were given new leeway to continue taking in money and lending it out in profitable investments.

The directors were so successful in their efforts that in January 1896 Little told the shareholders: "As you are aware, the legal borrowing powers of the Company were about exhausted at the end of last year, so that we cannot show much increase in the business done; but the net profits have been well maintained." In

---

1. At the end of this annual meeting in January 1892, the Huron & Erie's oldest director, Philip Mackenzie, rose to pay tribute to his fellow founder, Elijah Leonard, who had died during the previous year. In passing, Mackenzie reflected that this was the company's twenty-eighth annual meeting, and he was proud to have attended them all. A year later he was elected vice-president and he went on attending the meetings until after the fortieth, in 1904, when he retired owing to ill-health. He died in 1923, the last survivor of the company's founders.

an attempt to remove this recurring impediment to its operations the company applied to the Dominion parliament for a special Private Act to increase its multiple—such Acts governing the activities of individual companies were common in those days. The application was approved, and in April 1896 legislation was passed enabling the Huron & Erie to borrow from the public twice the amount of its authorized (not just paid-up) capital.

George Somerville's role in the company's continuing progress had earned him considerable admiration elsewhere in the financial community, and in 1896 he accepted an invitation to become a director of the Mutual Life insurance company in Waterloo. His talents in that office became so apparent to his fellow directors that two years later he was invited to take over active direction of the Mutual Life as its general manager, a position that would today be styled "president and chief executive officer."[2] He declined the post, perhaps because he was already formulating new plans for the Huron & Erie.

In 1899, the Dominion parliament enacted a General Act that considerably enlarged the borrowing powers of mortgage loan companies and broadened the range of investments they were permitted to make to include, among other things, the shares of trust companies. These institutions were the last to appear on the Canadian scene of what later became known as the four pillars of the financial world—the others being the banks, the insurance companies, and the investment dealers. The first one to be given a charter, the Toronto General Trusts Company, was incorporated in 1872. Edward Blake, doubtless benefiting from his experience with the Huron & Erie, became its first president. By the turn of the century fourteen charters had been issued to various trust companies, some by the federal authorities and some by the provinces.

The distinguishing feature of the trust companies was that they, alone among the four pillars, were empowered to conduct fidu-

2. Somerville's head for figures was inherited by Walter H. Somerville, one of his three sons. Walter joined Mutual Life as a junior in 1900 and rose through the ranks to become its general manager from 1926 to 1943, after which he remained in harness as vice-president until his death in 1959.

ciary[3] business, that is, to act as trustees, executors, and administrators of wills and trusts, and to perform a variety of functions as agents, such as managing property, collecting rents, and supervising stock issues and the payment of dividends for other companies. This latter corporate trust function is an important part of the business today, but at the turn of the century trust companies were largely concerned with the management of estates, and they were permitted to invest the funds entrusted to them in mortgages and provincial and municipal debentures.

These activities, of course, directly impinged upon the business of the mortgage loan companies, which had hitherto had this field to themselves. (Banks were not permitted to make mortgages until 1967.) George Somerville appears to have been an early believer in the adage "If you can't lick 'em, join 'em," and he realized that the operations of the Huron & Erie and those of an allied trust company would make an ideal "fit." By now the long depression had ended and the whole country was basking in unprecedented prosperity. Agricultural products were once again fetching good prices, and some of the farmers who had taken out mortgages with the company years before had long since paid them off and were now men of substance with estates to leave to their dependents. London's manufacturing industries, too, had flourished and substantial fortunes were being accumulated by the city's emerging tycoons.

The Huron & Erie had now been in operation for more than thirty years and had earned the confidence and trust of thousands of customers. Somerville clearly felt that, given the opportunity, those of his customers who had estates to be cared for would entrust them to the company they had dealt with while they were alive. There was already one trust company operating in the city,

3. This rather intimidating term stems from the Latin *fiducia*, which in Roman law meant the transfer of some right to a person who thereupon assumed the obligation to pass it on again at some time in the future. In modern trust companies, there is still a legal distinction between the fiduciary or trust side of the business and the intermediary or banking side. A trust company issuing a savings certificate to a customer is deemed to hold his money in trust; a mortgage loan company issuing a savings certificate assumes the same debtor-creditor relationship as a bank. In practice this legal nicety makes no difference to the customer.

the London and Western Trusts Ltd., formed by a group of local businessmen in 1896 to safeguard their own interests and estates. Among the group was the second John Labatt, and it doubtless distressed Somerville that one of the Huron & Erie's most stalwart directors was unable to keep his fortune in the family, so to speak.

Even before it was permitted to do so by law—though probably the 1899 legislation was already foreshadowed at the time—Somerville had persuaded the Huron & Erie's directors that the company should plan for the acquisition of a trust company charter. The record does not show how his choice fell on a company in far-away Calgary. The General Trust Corporation of Canada had received its charter from the Dominion authorities in 1894. Its president was Senator James A. Lougheed, a prominent lawyer whose grandson would years later become premier of Alberta, and its board of directors included wealthy ranchers and land-owners such as William Hull. But, having procured their charter, those early westerners do not seem to have done much with it, since references to it through the years in the Huron & Erie's records describe it as "largely inactive."

At any rate, in December 1898 Somerville and a group of the Huron & Erie's top brass, acting as individuals, bought control of the General Trust Corporation. Seven of them put up $15,000 each to buy 150 shares at $100 per share. In addition to Somerville, they were President Little, Vice-President Philip Mackenzie, Frank E. Leonard, who had inherited his father Elijah's seat on the board, Verschoyle Cronyn, his son-in-law and partner Frederick Betts, and Verschoyle's son Hume, who had followed his father into the practice of law. The former Huron & Erie president William Saunders chipped in $10,000 for 100 shares, making an apparent total purchase price of $115,000.

That they were acting as agents of the Huron & Erie rather than as independent entrepreneurs is indicated by later developments. Senator Lougheed remained president of General Trust Corporation only long enough for permission to be obtained from Ottawa to transfer its head office to London and change its name to the Canada Trust Company. Then, as soon as the legislation of 1899 permitted, the purchasers transferred most of their shares to the Huron & Erie at cost, retaining only the twenty-five shares each required to qualify as a director of the new company. The Canada Trust Company thus opened for business early in 1901 with a capitalization of $200,000, of which the Huron & Erie had paid in

$177,500, giving it almost ninety per cent ownership of its new subsidiary. Verschoyle Cronyn was elected president of the new company, George Somerville became its managing director, and all its work was carried out by the well-versed staff of the Huron & Erie [4]—an economy frequently mentioned in subsequent annual reports.

The experience and professionalism of the Huron & Erie's management was emphasized in Canada Trust's early advertising. A booklet issued soon after the company opened its doors, with the title *Why a Corporate Executor?* began: "A generation ago men named friends or relatives as their executors. Seldom, therefore, did the same man act in that capacity twice. Hence it took him longer to learn what to do than to do it. By the same reasoning (or want of it) you would select a tailor to shingle your house or a plumber to make your shoes—because he is your friend or relative."

Another booklet issued about the same time posed a set of six questions calculated to sow doubt in the minds of men of property about the wisdom of entrusting their estates to friends:

> THE result of a generation of patient toil should not be lightly left at the command of inexperienced individuals. The executors you have in mind for your estate may be **perfectly honest, but—**
> *ARE YOU SURE* they will live to fully carry out your commands?
> *ARE YOU SURE* they will take from their own occupations sufficient time to carefully fulfil your desires?

---

4. Initially, both federal and provincial legislators tried to prevent the trust companies from encroaching on the territory of the banks and mortgage loan companies by excluding them from the intermediary, or banking, function, and prohibiting them from issuing debentures. But these walls were soon breached. In 1922 a Special Act of the Dominion parliament permitted Canada Trust "to receive money on deposit in trust and allow interest thereon at such rate as may be agreed upon between the Company and the depositor." This wording was soon afterward incorporated in the general legislation governing all trust companies. By that time the trust companies had long been taking money in trust from savers in the form of guaranteed investment receipts, or certificates, which to all intents and purposes were debentures. Henceforth, the business activities of the Huron & Erie and its subsidiary became virtually indistinguishable, and the Huron & Erie's staff continued to do Canada Trust's work for many years.

ARE YOU SURE they will resist the temptation to speculate with the money belonging to your dependents?
ARE YOU SURE they have the necessary experience with "the ways of the world" to cope with difficult situations that may arise?
ARE YOU SURE they will impartially and without showing favour divide your estate as you have directed?
ARE YOU SURE they will never move away—take sick—or become incapable of transacting business?

A line from a Canada Trust advertisement in 1911 made that last point more succintly. A company acting as an executor, it said, "cannot die, abscond, or become insane." It can, of course, as several unhappy experiences in recent years have shown, go broke, but the men who ran the Huron & Erie had no intention of allowing that sad fate to befall their creation. "The Canada Trust," another early booklet proclaimed, "aspires to be a Trust Company in fact as well as in name. It eschews those seductive and dangerous methods which make promise of sudden wealth, and is content with a natural growth which fits an institution to withstand the shocks of time."

The "natural growth" of Canada Trust, if slower than the Huron & Erie's had been, was no less sure. The first estate entrusted to its care, in February 1901, was $100,000 left by Martha L. Wood Eccles. It was handed over to the company by her executors, President Little and Dr. F. R. Eccles; the latter, perhaps her son, would later become a director of both the Huron & Erie and Canada Trust. The terms of the trust agreement stipulated that the company guarantee that the income from the estate, which was to be paid to Mrs. Augusta W. Aikins "during the term of her natural life," would be not less than four per cent. Since the rate being charged on mortgage loans at that time was five per cent, Mrs. Aikins presumably received more than her guaranteed income. The one-per-cent "spread" did not go to the company; then, as now, trust companies administered estates for a fee, agreed in advance or set by the Surrogate Court. This same guarantee of four per cent was given by the company in 1904 when it undertook "to receive and invest the endowment fund" of the University of Western Ontario.

In that same year, 1904, the assets in the hands of Canada Trust passed the million-dollar mark and the company's net earnings amounted to almost $17,000. Of this amount, $15,000 was salted away in the reserve fund. For the first five years of its existence the company continued to apply its profits to the reserve, until by the beginning of 1906 it amounted to $50,000, or a quarter of the paid-up capital. Only then did the directors pay a dividend—$10,000—to the parent company. From then on Canada Trust's growing volume of business continued to bolster the growing prosperity of the Huron & Erie.

7

The Expansion Begins

EARLY in 1903 the North American stock markets shuddered through what is euphemistically referred to these days as a "correction," though the uglier word "slump" serves just as well. Among its most prominent victims was Alfred Ernest Ames, a Methodist minister's son from Lambeth, Ontario, now a suburb of London. Ames began his meteoric career in banking as a lad of fifteen, and by the time he was twenty-one, he was a bank manager at Mount Forest. Two years later he founded a private bank and brokerage business in Toronto.

Within a few years A.E. Ames & Co. was one of the leading institutions on Bay Street. Its founder was president of the Toronto Stock Exchange in 1897 and 1898 and president of the Toronto Board of Trade in 1902. He was married to the daughter of one of the leading tycoons of that day, George Albertus Cox, a former telegraph operator who became president of the Bank of Commerce and the Canada Life Assurance Company and founder, president, or director of more than forty other companies. Like his fellow-Methodist father-in-law, who was a generous contributor to such institutions as the Toronto General Hospital and the University of Toronto, Ames was widely known as a philanthropist and supporter of his church.

The Toronto financial community was accordingly horror-stricken when, on 2 June 1903, the firm of A.E. Ames & Co. suspended payments. In the words of a contemporary account: "The notice hung out says that owing to the continued declines in stocks held by them they wish to examine their standing." The examination was less than reassuring: one report said the company had large holdings of Dominion Steel shares bought at more than $70 which were now worth only $15.

Ames himself was reported at the time to have lost more than a million dollars, but the company ultimately survived. Its convulsions, though, had a ripple effect that engulfed the prosperous little railroad centre of St. Thomas, about thirty kilometres south of London. One of Ames's partners, A.E. Wallace, was also president of the Atlas Loan Company, the leading institution of its kind in St. Thomas. The Atlas closed its doors for ever the day after A.E. Ames & Co. suspended payments.

Before 1898 the Atlas had done a modest business borrowing from local savers at around four per cent interest and issuing mortgages at around six per cent—a comfortable two-per-cent spread. But in that year a Special Act of the Dominion parliament gave the company much wider investment powers than those granted to other mortgage companies, and Wallace began to invest his customers' funds in speculative securities, many of which were held by the Ames company. Wallace told reporters at the time that he had personally lost more than $300,000, and when the dust settled his customers recouped less than fifty cents on the dollar.

That was not the end of St. Thomas's travail. Two weeks after the Atlas collapsed another city institution, the Elgin Loan & Savings Company, also closed its doors for ever. The Elgin's manager since its formation twenty-four years earlier had been George Rowley, a much-respected man of fifty-eight, prominent in civic affairs and treasurer of his church. Rowley disappeared from the city the day the Elgin went out of business, and it was soon discovered that he too had been speculating with the depositors' funds and had been ruined by the market crash. He returned to the city ten days later to face the music, to the tune of a twelve-year penitentiary sentence for theft and forgery.

The three other loan companies in St. Thomas, weakened by investors who lined up in droves during the panic to withdraw their money while they could, were forced to merge.[1] This reduction in the number of local loan companies from five to one created a vacuum which the Huron & Erie decided to fill. Before the end of 1903 the managers of two of the merged companies, displaced through no fault of their own and untainted by the scandalous goings-on at the Atlas and Elgin, were appointed to open the company's first branch office.

---

1. The merged company, named the Southern Loan and Savings Company, was bought by the Huron & Erie a quarter of a century later.

The Huron & Erie's deliberate policy, of course, was to refrain from any investments in stock, apart from its holding in Canada Trust. As President Little told the shareholders and customers, the company restricted its investments to mortgages and government and municipal debentures. This conservative policy appealed to those investors who had been able to salvage anything from the speculative binge, and the new St. Thomas branch was soon contributing handsomely to the company's steady growth.

An even larger contribution to that growth was made in January 1906, when the Huron & Erie absorbed a smaller London company, the Canadian Savings & Loan Company. The Canadian Savings had total assets of only $2.4 million, compared to the Huron & Erie's $8.7 million, but it was solidly based. In 1905 its shareholders had received a dividend of six per cent, and since the Huron & Erie had for years been paying nine per cent they were glad to vote in favour of the merger. They received two shares in the amalgamated company for every three Canadian Savings shares they held; Huron & Erie shareholders received the new shares on a one-for-one basis.

From the Huron & Erie's point of view, the amalgamation removed a competitor and increased business at one stroke. Also, as President Little told the shareholders early in 1907: "It was scarcely to be expected that any material reduction in the expenses could be made during the first year, but the report shows that already a large saving has been effected." Furthermore, the Canadian Savings' building had been sold for $12,000 more than its book value, a welcome addition to the amalgamated company's profit.

Credit for the smoothness of the transition and for the reduction in the amalgamated company's expenses undoubtedly went to George Somerville. But that summer the company lost his services when he went to Toronto as general manager of the Manufacturers Life Insurance Company. During his eighteen years at the helm the Huron & Erie's total assets had risen from a little over $3.7 million to $11.2 million, and its reserve fund from just over $400,000 to $1.6 million.

There was some criticism of the Manufacturers Life in Toronto insurance circles for appointing an outsider from a loan company to its top position. But as one editorialist pointed out at the time, the critics were evidently unaware that Somerville had for seven years been one of the most active directors of the Mutual Life company. Somerville did not need the editorialist's support; in his first five years in his new post he increased the Manufacturers' business volume by fifty per cent, from less than $50 million a year to more than $75 million. And his counsel remained available to the Huron & Erie, since he continued to be a director of Canada Trust until his death in 1914.

Somerville's successor as manager of the Huron & Erie was Major Hume Blake Cronyn, Verschoyle's second son. Though he was born into one of London's richest dynastic families—in 1864, the year the company was founded—Hume Cronyn, as befitted a grandson of the activist Bishop of Huron, was no effete spoilt brat. When he was nine years old, his father founded the London Street Railway, which operated with horse-drawn trams, and it was not long before young Hume found that on Sundays, when the stablemen were off duty, he was expected to water and feed the horses at the car barns and muck out their stables.

Later, while taking his B.A. at the University of Toronto, Hume played in the scrum as captain of its rugby team and was an enthusiastic member of the officers' training corps. He was twenty-one when the North-West Rebellion erupted on Canada's distant frontier, and he suspended his studies long enough to ship out with the Queen's Own Rifles and fight at the battle of Cut Knife Hill. Back in Toronto, he graduated from Osgoode Hall and joined his father's law firm, Cronyn and Betts.

When he abandoned his law career to join the Huron & Erie, Hume Cronyn was forty-three, married to a daughter of John Labatt, and father to three children, all of whom in due course would carry on the family connection with what was now popularly referred to as "the old Huron & Erie."[2]

2. Hume's elder son, Richard, joined the company after service in the Royal Flying Corps during World War I and spent his life climbing the ladder to an eventual position as vice-president. Richard's brother, Verschoyle Philip, joined the company as an office boy in 1912, went away to the war as an infantry officer, and returned as a Royal Flying Corps fighter pilot with seven "kills" to his credit. He spent the rest of his life in the insurance business, apart from a stint as an officer in the Royal Canadian Air Force during World War II. He was made a director of the Huron & Erie in 1929 and was its chairman from 1957 until his retirement ten years later. Hume's third child, Katherine, after driving ambulances for the Red Cross in France during World War I, married John Harley, a Nova Scotian war veteran who worked as an investment broker in New York before joining Canada Trust in 1939. Only Hume's third son, born four years after his father joined the company, had no interest in the business. Instead, the second Hume Cronyn went on to become a star of the international stage.

Hume Cronyn took over the company at a time when the prosperity of the first half of the decade had been superseded by a worldwide financial panic, which contemporary commentators usually referred to more delicately as "financial stringency." But during 1907 there was a general suspension of cash payments in New York for two months, and prospective borrowers found it virtually impossible to get bank loans. And as usual, when the United States sneezed, Canada caught the cold: three Canadian chartered banks failed in the first half of 1908.

The hard times gave President Little yet another opportunity to expatiate on the fundamental soundness of "the old Huron & Erie." He told the company's annual meeting in January 1908: "In view of all that has recently been said about monetary stringency and the criticism of financial institutions who accept deposits from the public, especially in the United States, our shareholders will be pleased to find the Company in the exceptionally strong position shown by the report which has just been submitted. At the end of the year, besides a large amount invested in what are called quick assets, we had in cash over $440,000, or about 22½ per cent of our total deposits." That ratio, as he pointed out, compared very favourably with the average twelve-per-cent deposits-to-cash ratio maintained in the country's thirty-five chartered banks.

The "criticism of financial institutions" to which Little referred had apparently been at least partly directed at some shady self-dealing, because he reminded the shareholders that under the company's Special Acts, passed at its own behest, "we are prohibited from making loans on our own stock, and no Director or Officer can borrow from the Company on any security whatever."

As to the "exceptionally strong position" of which he spoke, the company's net profit for the year was $237,872, only a modest advance of $2,000 on the previous year, but enough to add a further $55,000 to the precious reserve fund and still pay the usual nine-per-cent dividend. In fact, despite the generally prevailing "financial stringency," the company's position was considered so sound that voices were now being raised suggesting that the dividend be increased.

This view had first been put forward at the annual meeting a year earlier by the Venerable Archdeacon Young, representing the Anglican diocese of Huron. His view was countered by a former Canadian Savings director, Adam McMahen, who had joined the amalgamated company's board. McMahen said it was more important to have a strong reserve than to pay a large dividend, since this enabled the company to borrow money cheaply. The Very Reverend Dean Davis supported his fellow churchman, saying that "a company with such a magnificent showing" could safely increase its dividend. It was his judgment that "such a course would be very preferable to heaping up a large Reserve Fund for posterity."

The board's position was put by a recently elected director, Thomas Graves Meredith, K.C. "Everybody feels," he said, "that it would be a nice thing to have something extra coming into his pocket." But there were good reasons for not increasing the dividend at that stage. Meredith, it seems, had already absorbed the principle of caution behind the Huron & Erie—or perhaps he had been chosen for the board because he himself embodied that principle—for he went on to say: "To over-estimate the value of the Company's assets would be a great mistake and entirely contrary to the principles underlying the whole institution and governing all its actions. The utmost conservatism is desirable." It would be better, he said, to defer an increased dividend until there was every reasonable assurance that it could be maintained.

When the matter was raised again at the next annual meeting early in 1908, Meredith returned to this theme. The directors, he said, "will be glad, just so soon as the position of the Company justifies an increase which may be steadily maintained, to authorize the same." President Little spoke in his support. "The Huron & Erie," he said, "has made a larger return to its shareholders than any other loan corporation in Canada, and to be over-cautious is at least to err on the safe side."

Thus was tradition maintained. But in other ways the old order was changing. At the end of his remarks President Little saluted Verschoyle Cronyn, who had retired from the board after more than forty years' service. The founding father, now seventy-four years old, had suffered a stroke that left his face partially paralyzed for the rest of his long life: he died in 1921 at the age of eighty-eight. The old stalwart William Saunders returned to the board to replace him, and continuity was assured by the election of Verschoyle's son Hume as a director at the end of the meeting. At the next annual meeting, in 1909, President Little also retired, to be replaced by lawyer Meredith.

Thomas Graves Meredith was one of the eight remarkable sons

of John Meredith who, though of Welsh extraction, was born in Ireland. After studying at Trinity College, Dublin, John came to Canada in 1834, became clerk of the division court in London, and married Sarah Pegler, the schoolteacher daughter of a local gardener. Four of their sons distinguished themselves as lawyers and four as businessmen.[3] "T.G.", as he was universally known, was born in 1853, articled with his brother Edmund, and became London's city solicitor, a post he held for fifty-one years. A pompous little man, not much over five feet tall, he was addicted to punctuality. Retired members of the staff who joined the company in the early 1930s recall that he would strut into the Huron & Erie building at precisely 10 a.m.—and woe betide the janitor if the elevator was not stationary and empty awaiting his arrival. Borne aloft to his office, he would deal swiftly with whatever business awaited him—the presidency of a company was not a full-time job in those days—and then stride over to his city office, which he would enter at precisely 11 a.m. Unfortunately, he had an imperious manner that alienated many of those with whom he had dealings, including some of the Huron & Erie's staff. But if he lacked popularity, he was an effective president, and under his conservative stewardship the company continued to prosper.

In the absence of the retiring president, it fell to Meredith at that 1909 meeting to announce an important departure from the company's longstanding policy of investing only in its own rich bailiwick of southwestern Ontario: the decision to begin lending some of its funds on farm mortgages in Manitoba and Saskatchewan.

As early as 1879 a man named Girdlestone had written to the board from Winnipeg, suggesting that the company extend its business to Manitoba and offering his services as its agent. The offer was declined, even though there was an extraordinary boom in Manitoba land at that time. That the directors' caution was

---

3. William Ralph Meredith led the opposition in the provincial legislature for sixteen years before becoming Chief Justice of Ontario and earning a knighthood. Richard Martin Meredith became Chief Justice of Common Pleas in Ontario. Edmund became London's pre-eminent criminal lawyer. Henry Vincent was successively general manager, president, and chairman of the Bank of Montreal. Charles became a wealthy and influential stockbroker in that same city. John Stanley became manager of the head office of the Merchants' Bank and a financier who left an estate of almost half a million dollars. Llewellyn became a successful real estate agent in London.

justified is suggested by an article that appeared in the *Monetary Times* in 1882. "Every day brings its new city, three feet square or more on paper," it said. And describing one land auction, it went on: "The name of every new 'city' existing in ink and paper was spelt out by a wondering crowd; a crowd which jostled for elbow room [and] which, if just let loose from Bedlam, could not have acted more irrationally; which bought all the parcels offered, knowing no more about them or the city they were presumably in, than if they had been in Timbuctoo. It was quite clear that so long as the fools, the dupes and the money lasted, the supply of new 'cities' would not fall short." The bubble eventually burst, of course, and many of the speculators were ruined. Indeed, it was speculation in Manitoba lands that was blamed by some for the demise of Henry Taylor's Ontario Investment Association and the collapse of the Bank of London.

But by the early years of this century the arrival of the Canadian Pacific Railway and the tide of immigration to the west had created another boom; and this time it was genuine. The 1901 census counted 42,340 people in Winnipeg, about the same number as there were in London. In 1911 Winnipeg's population had grown to 136,035, almost three times London's size. Regina's population grew even more spectacularly during the same period, from 2,249 to 30,213. And as the new arrivals broke the prairies to the plough, Canada's wheat production, and hence its prosperity, soared. In 1897 total wheat production was 39.6 million bushels. Ten years later it had reached 135.6 million bushels, and by 1912 it was 231.2 million bushels.

So the Huron & Erie directors decided to take the plunge, but only after Hume Cronyn had made a careful fact-finding tour of the west. In 1908 they appointed W.J. Christie, son of a Canadian Savings director who had joined the amalgamated company's board, as their agent for loans in Manitoba and Saskatchewan. And by 1911, with more than $2 million invested in those provinces, they decided it was time to open the company's second branch office, in Regina.

The man entrusted with the responsibility of running the new branch was Harold W. Givins, who had been with the company twenty-two years and had risen to the post of assistant manager. A retiree who joined the company in Winnipeg in 1935, by which time Givins had long been superintendent of all western branches, recalls him as a tall, very formal but kindly old gentleman who invariably wore a grey stovepipe hat and an old-fashioned high stiff collar. But Harry Givins in his youth had been both athletic and gregarious. He managed his church's baseball team and among the players he coached was George (Mooney) Gibson, who went on to be catcher for the Pittsburgh Pirates when they won the World Series in 1909.

The move from the now sedate and settled London to the raw new city of Regina must have been something of a culture shock for Mr. and Mrs. Givins and their family. But life in Regina would not be without it amenities. No doubt a man in Givins's comfortable position would have had one of Edison's phonographs, and among the best-selling records he might have played in the evenings were "The Lost Chord," sung by Enrico Caruso, and "Silver Threads Among The Gold," in the stentorian tones of Count John McCormack. And during their first summer in their new home the Givins family would have had the opportunity to attend the performances of a touring English theatrical company which included a young actor named Pratt, who later became known to a wider world under his Hollywood stage name of Boris Karloff.

Karloff and his companions were fortunately out of the city on a picnic on 30 June 1912 when in three minutes a tornado destroyed much of the downtown area, killed at least thirty-one people, and injured hundreds more. A paragraph in the *London Free Press* a couple of days later reported that the Givins family and the Huron & Erie's small staff in Regina had also survived the storm unharmed, and Givins went on to build a flourishing business for the company in the west. He lived an active life for many years after his retirement, and owed his death to an entirely uncharacteristic lack of the caution he had practised throughout his business life: in his eighties, he was helping a daughter to repair a roof on a farm building when he fell and broke his neck.

8

The Company Copes with the War

THE years leading up to World War I, notwithstanding the 1907–08 financial panic, were years of unprecedented development for Canada. The boom in wheat production in the wide-open west was matched by a rapid acceleration of industrialization in the older, more settled parts of the country. Southwestern Ontario, in particular, benefited from the harnessing of Niagara Falls and the building of transmission lines to distribute the cheap electricity generated there to its embryo manufacturing centres. Aided by American capital, now flowing in to supplement the continuing investment from the still potent Old Country, existing factories were expanded and new ones built to turn out hitherto unheard-of products such as automobiles.

The Huron & Erie shared in the general prosperity. In 1910 it reported a record net profit and the restive churchmen finally received a little extra money for their church's pockets: the dividend was raised to ten per cent. The "balance available for distribution," to use the time-honoured wording of annual reports, was $314,620.55, and of this sum $100,000 was transferred to the reserve fund, bringing it up to $1.9 million—exactly the same as the company's paid-up capital. As President Meredith told the annual meeting: "We are, I believe, the first of the Canadian Loan Companies to arrive at this much desired goal." (The reserve fund of the much larger Canada Permanent at that time amounted to not much more than half its capital.)

The profits increased again in 1911 and the ten-per-cent dividend was supplemented by a one-per-cent bonus. It was the same story in 1912, and at the beginning of the fateful year 1914 Meredith told the shareholders at the company's fiftieth annual meeting: "Although it may be monotonous to hear that the past year was the most prosperous in the Company's history, unless we disregard the figures in the statement just presented, no other conclusion can be reached." The company's assets had increased during 1913 by more than $600,000 and now exceeded $15 million, and the net profits were $36,000 larger than the year before. In response to this, the dividend had now risen to eleven per cent, once again supplemented by a one-per-cent bonus. The company's business in Manitoba and Saskatchewan now surpassed $3.3 million, and "contrary to our expectations, the farms which during 1913 came into our hands in the West were, by our Regina branch, all disposed of without loss, so that for the sixth consecutive year the Company has no real estate on hand other than office premises."

By now those office premises had been extended to take in two more new branches. One was opened in 1912 on Market Square in London, a few blocks from head office, to serve farmers who sold their produce at the popular Covent Garden; the other, opened in Winnipeg in 1913 under the management of William Whyte, Jr., was designed to handle the expanding business in Manitoba. Hume Cronyn had met the socially prominent Whyte on one of his trips to the west. When he asked him to open a branch of the Huron & Erie in that city, the young man displayed the streak of caution considered essential in Huron & Erie employees: he took counsel of his father, Sir William Whyte, a powerful vice-president of the Canadian Pacific Railway. Sir William assured him it was a capital idea: there was no finer company in the country; why, he himself had opened his first savings account with "the old Huron & Erie" years before, when he was living in London.

All this heady growth by the parent company was paralleled by the slower but nevertheless steady progress of its smaller subsidiary, Canada Trust. Being under the same management, the two companies naturally conducted their business along the same prudent lines. As early as 1907 the former Canadian Savings director Adam McMahen had said at the annual meeting that "he had noticed with pleasure that the Company had confined its business to Executorships, Administrations, and similar conservative operations, and had shunned the more hazardous, though perhaps more remunerative, work of underwriting commercial enterprises."

Taking advantage of the good times, the Huron & Erie directors invested more money in their subsidiary in 1911 and 1912, so that by 1913 Canada Trust's capitalization had increased from the original $200,000 to $1 million. Its assets were now nearing $5 million, and its net earnings for the year amounted to almost $67,000. With typical restraint, its board of directors[1] declared a dividend of only five per cent, contributing a little over $33,000 to the parent company's net profits of $371,970, and stashed the rest of the money in the reserve fund.

The Huron & Erie's growth during those years would probably have been even more rapid had it not been for the limitation on its borrowing powers imposed by the crucial "multiple." The only way to increase this, of course, was to increase the company's capital and reserves. So in 1911 it issued 10,000 new shares, its shareholders being permitted to buy one new share for every seven they already held. But since this was "twenty-per-cent stock"—in other words, the shareholders initially had to put up only $10 of the $50 par value (together with a $9 premium)—this increased the company's fully-paid capital by only $100,000. At the annual meeting early in 1912 President Meredith reported that "the additional borrowing power gained from this issue is nearly exhausted." Consequently, that same year there was another issue of 2,000 shares, this time fully paid, with a premium of one hundred per cent, which went straight into the reserve fund. And in 1914 a further 8,000 fully-paid shares were issued, again at a premium of one hundred per cent.

This brought the company's fully-paid capital at the outbreak of World War I to $2.4 million, and its reserve fund, standing at $2.7 million, now exceeded that amount. The company gained new elbow room to grow that year when the first comprehensive Act governing loan companies passed by the Dominion parliament raised the multiple to four times the combined total of their paid-up capital and reserve funds.[2] But the top priority for the management and board of the Huron & Erie, and for many other companies as well, now became not growth but survival.

---

1. Then, and for many years thereafter, the Canada Trust board consisted of a nucleus of Huron & Erie directors, supplemented by approximately the same number of outsiders, usually lawyers and insurance men.

2. After this legislation was passed, the company applied for permission to change its name to the Huron & Erie Mortgage Corporation, presumably to reflect the nature of its business more accurately. The permission was granted and the change was made in 1915.

For the Canadian business world, the outbreak of war in August 1914 brought about a state of chaos and confusion bordering on paralysis. The whole country was seized by fear and uncertainty. The stock exchanges closed for almost two months and reopened only when new restrictions had been imposed by the federal authorities. Those same authorities, fearing a run on the banks, announced new federal guarantees to soothe the nerves of both depositors and bankers.

Things had calmed down somewhat, and the country was gearing for the grim years ahead, when President Meredith told the Huron & Erie shareholders in February 1915: "So much depends upon the duration and outcome of the great war in which we are engaged it is impossible to forecast the future, but your Directors have since its outbreak spared no effort to render the Company's position safe beyond any contingency. To do this calls for a large increase in available cash and cash resources and entails of necessity a curtailment of normal profits; while, therefore, the present dividend may be reasonably considered assured, Shareholders must not expect a continuance in the growth of the net profits, which for years past has been a striking feature of the Company's history."

When Meredith uttered this warning, one of the first of the many problems the company would face during the war had already arisen: in January 1915 the British Treasury imposed an embargo on the export of capital. This not only dried up new injections of funds from the Old Country; it meant that as the sterling debentures issued by the company in past years matured, their owners were unable to renew them and they had to be repaid. The Huron & Erie had to send $1.6 million back to British investors between 1914 and 1918.

Also, as Canada's economy switched over to war production, all sorts of material shortages developed, domestic building virtually ceased, and with so many young men joining the services the demand for mortgages fell off drastically. Faced with the need to keep its money at work, the company took up the slack by directing more of its investments into government and municipal bonds and the Victory loans floated by the federal government to finance its heavy wartime expenditures. The high interest rates these paid were not an unmixed blessing, since the Huron & Erie had to raise the interest rates it paid to its own depositors. Some old and valued customers, either from patriotic motives or from a desire to benefit from better interest rates, cashed in debentures to buy the government's Victory bonds, even though, as company legend has it, one manager, asked by a customer about their security, replied, "Well, they're all right, I suppose, but of course they're not guaranteed by the Huron & Erie."

The company's activities were further complicated when several of the provinces enacted various forms of moratorium legislation. These were no doubt well intentioned, since they were designed to protect borrowers from any panic that might have led to a general calling of loans, but their effect was unfortunate. The tremendous increase in wartime production and the departure of so many men for the services had created an acute shortage of labour; unemployment had virtually disappeared and women had entered the work force in unprecedented numbers. Yet despite the general prosperity, some borrowers took advantage of the legislation to postpone paying their debts at a time when they could well have afforded to do so, thus tying up some of the funds lenders would otherwise have had available for investment.

Faced with all these disruptions of their normal business, the Huron & Erie directors had good cause to congratulate themselves on the wisdom of their policy of lending mostly to farmers, for the demand for food at home and abroad mounted steadily, and the prices paid for agricultural products rose with it. Though farmers, too, suffered from the labour shortage, they were able to sell everything they could grow at good prices and had no difficulty paying their debts; the 1917 annual report said the repayment of farm mortgages in both Ontario and the west had been "extraordinarily good."

In fact, as the war dragged on, the production of food came to be considered a patriotic duty, and as early as 1915 the company put up five hundred dollars in cash prizes for the cultivation of the best fields of wheat, oats, corn, potatoes, and mangels in Middlesex County. The contest was evidently deemed a success, because later in the war the company organized a "patriotic vegetable garden competition" to encourage city gardeners in London. Home-owners with green thumbs were assured that their crops would not only save them money; they would "help to enlarge the urgently needed surplus of produce for export" and "save the labour of others whose effort is needed for other vital war work." The competition was judged by members of the London Horticultural Society, but this time the prizes were not in cash. It seems that someone on the company's staff with well-honed promotional instincts had scented an opportunity to attract more customers: the winners were awarded Huron & Erie passbooks with the prize money entered to their credit.

Even with five branches now operating, the staff from which these initiatives sprang still numbered only a few dozens, in contrast with today's thousands. They formed a close-knit, hard-working group with a notable *esprit de corps* no doubt bolstered by the directors' decision in 1913 to set aside ten thousand dollars to establish a pension fund, a fringe benefit enjoyed by few Canadian workers at that time. And their loyalty to the company was matched by the company's trust in them. In 1964 a publication issued to celebrate the company's centenary contained this reminiscence by George E. Metcalfe, who had joined the staff in 1911:

"When the first pay day came along I expected to get my pay ($5 a week) in an envelope. However, one of the boys on the staff said to me: 'You had better get your pay. See that money piled on the desk in that office. Just fill in and sign a receipt form for the amount of your salary, walk in, lay it face down on the desk, and count off your salary from those piles of money.' I thought my leg was being pulled, but sure enough I watched other members of the staff get their pay, so I did the same. You were absolutely trusted or you would not be on the staff."

By the end of 1915 forty per cent of the male employees had volunteered for the services; the company granted them leave of absence and continued to pay them half their salary. Their absence imposed an extra burden on the older men left behind, and also on the women employees, who still wore ankle-length skirts and buttoned boots but whose presence in the tellers' cages was no longer considered a curiosity. The absence of so many men also led to an increase in the responsibility entrusted to women staff members.[3] In all, twenty-two Huron & Erie men served in the war, and four of them never returned.

---

3. According to the directors' minutes for 14 April 1919, it was resolved "that during the absence of the accountant of the Market Branch from the office, Miss Nellie Fletcher be appointed accountant pro tem, and that for the purpose of signing cheques and other documents Miss Fletcher be substituted for the accountant in accordance with the by-law to that effect." It was Miss Fletcher who originated a slogan that appeared on the company's stationery for many years: "Older Than the Dominion of Canada."

The company's popular general manager, Major Cronyn,[4] was now too old for military service, but in 1917 his patriotism induced him to enter his country's service in another way. With the country riven by the contentious issue of conscription, the Conservative prime minister, Sir Robert Borden, decided to form a coalition government. Cronyn, who was a Liberal, though more by philosophy than from any strong political partisanship, was asked to stand for the Union Party in the resulting election. He accepted, but only on condition that the Huron & Erie directors approve his decision. At a special meeting summoned to consider the matter on 9 November 1917, "the Board unanimously consented to the general manager becoming a candidate as it was felt that it was a sacrifice that the Company was called upon to make."

Cronyn won election without difficulty, and press reports at the time touted him as cabinet material. In fact, family tradition has it that he turned down the post of minister of finance in the Union government, pleading pressure of other obligations. He served only one term in Parliament, refusing to accept nomination again, but before he returned to private life he gained respect on both sides of the House for his chairmanship of the parliamentary committee that strongly recommended establishment of the National Research Council.

With the departure of the general manager for Ottawa, responsibility for the day-to-day operations of the company passed to Morley Aylsworth, who was both its superintendent of branches and its secretary. Aylsworth was born on a farm in Dorchester Township, but he was not without connections: he was advised to

---

4. Notwithstanding his patrician background and appearance, Hume Cronyn was entirely without Meredith's hauteur, and his kindnesses were legendary. A keen golfer, he took a lead in the establishment of London's first municipal golf course, believing that the sport should not be restricted to those, like himself, rich enough to join an exclusive club.

Once, when he heard that his tailor's young son was in hospital, he visited the lad on a Saturday afternoon and presented him with a Tom Swift book. The boy was of a serious bent and thought Tom Swift corny. Cronyn detected his disappointment and asked him what *did* interest him. "History," the boy replied. So Cronyn returned the following Saturday with a book called *Ancient Cities in the New World*. Reading about the achievements of the Maya, Incas, and Aztecs, the lad was enthralled. He grew up to graduate through journalism into the church and is today the Reverend Orlo Miller, a London historian with a more than purely local reputation.

look for a job in the financial field by one of his father's cousins, Sir Allen Aylsworth, minister of justice in Sir Wilfrid Laurier's cabinet. Young Morley joined the Huron & Erie from high school in 1902 with the proud title of junior clerk, but since the company had only fourteen employees at that time and he was the rawest recruit, his first duties ran to such lowly tasks as sharpening pencils and replenishing inkwells. He soon graduated to successively more imposing positions such as ledger-keeper, teller, mortgage clerk, and accountant, and in 1912, when the new post of secretary was created, he was considered the best candidate to fill it. In all, he served the company for fifty-six years, retiring in 1958 as its president.

When the Armistice finally came in 1918, the company had not only survived but had kept on growing. Its profits had gone on rising each year though, as Meredith had warned at the beginning of the war, at a slower pace: from $409,844 in 1914 to $474,069 in 1918. Its assets, too, even though they actually shrank by $124,000 in 1917, had grown from $16.4 million when the war broke out to $18.2 million when it ended. And thanks to its careful management, it continued to pay a twelve-per-cent dividend every year.

Canada Trust's performance was even more impressive. Its assets almost doubled during the war, from $5.5 million to just under $10 million, and in 1917 it was able to increase its six-per-cent dividend to seven per cent.

The two companies also grew physically during the war years. Aylsworth had prepared a report for the board in the summer of 1915 supporting his recommendation that the company extend its operations to the province of Alberta, and a new branch was opened in Edmonton in 1916. The next year land was purchased and "a compact office building" was erected to serve "the thriving City of Windsor and the neighbouring border towns." The expansion continued in 1919 when the company opened its third branch on its home turf, London-East.

Back in 1915 Meredith had told the annual meeting that the company proposed to apply to Parliament for "certain additions to its existing powers. . . in view of our future expansion." The main clauses of the legislation sought, he said, would "empower the Directors by by-law duly sanctioned to increase the capital stock and provide for converting the same into shares of $100 each." These plans had had to be shelved in favour of weightier matters, but as soon as the war was over they were revived.

A special meeting of shareholders was held in February 1919 to approve a recapitalization which seems to have been merely a change in the company's accounting methods, for reasons that are obscure at this remove. At any rate, the Huron & Erie's paid-up capital was increased to $5 million by the conversion of $2.5 million from the reserve fund into capital stock. That left $800,000 in the reserve, so that the combined total of paid-up capital and reserve—crucial to the multiple—remained at $5.8 million. At the same time, the par value of the shares was increased from $50 to $100. Again, the reason for this is unclear now, but it may have been to bring the company into line with other similar institutions, the 1914 legislation having stipulated that any new loan company formed after the passage of the Act must have capital stock "not less than $250,000. . . divided into shares of $100 each." Alternatively, the directors may have thought that hundred-dollar shares would have a more substantial ring to British investors, who still held $3.8 million in Huron & Erie debentures and whose money was still desired, even though they had now been overtaken by Canadian investors, with $5.2 million.

Whatever the reasons for this recapitalization, for the shareholders it was a mere technicality. Since the new shares were issued on a one-for-one basis, the company's dividend rate was halved, from twelve to six per cent. In practice, this made no difference: the shareholders now received $6 a year for each $100 share they held, instead of, as before, $6 on each $50 share.

A few days after this meeting, Hume Cronyn received the directors' approval for a shuffle of his senior staff. Morley Aylsworth stepped up to the post of assistant manager and Danbert McEachern replaced him as secretary. Charles J. Clarke was appointed to the newly created post of treasurer, and Robert P. Baker was named investment manager for a branch the company had been planning for some time to open in Toronto.

Dan McEachern, another country boy, had joined the firm as a lad of fourteen just two weeks after Aylsworth (thus, presumably, relieving young Morley of some of his inkwell duties). He too showed the talent for learning on the job that was essential in those days. Ten years later he was made accountant at the main branch in London, and in 1914 he became its manager for a brief spell before becoming assistant secretary.

Charlie Clarke, who had grown up in London as the son of a shoe manufacturer's salesman, conformed to the pattern of that day: he joined the company as a junior straight from high school in 1900 and worked his way up so successfully that when McEachern was promoted assistant secretary he took over as manager of London-Main.

Bob Baker was a comparative newcomer. He had joined the company, again fresh from high school, in 1908, and a mere eight years later he was sent out to open the company's new branch in Edmonton.

These four men, dubbed by a long-retired employee with retrospective affection "the Four Horsemen," remained the nucleus of the Huron & Erie's management until long after World War II. As befitted their time and place, they were a conservative, sedate, even austere group, and for the most part their work was their life. In the summer months Morley Aylsworth and Charlie Clarke would enjoy a round of golf on Saturday after the office closed, their plus-fours topped by the obligatory collars and ties. In the winter there would be occasional bridge games in the evenings, and on special occasions a glass of sherry might be served.

Dan McEachern's passion was his garden, and in the spring he delighted to invite visitors to admire his riotous display of peonies, but without serving sherry. (Dan was a pillar of his Presbyterian church, superintendent of its Sunday school for many years, and a rigorous teetotaller.) Stern moralist though he was, he was well liked and trusted by the staff, and he practised his Christian faith sincerely. Younger staff members who hesitated to drink where any of their bosses might see them would occasionally repair to Detroit, in post-Prohibition days, for a Saturday night on the town. One young clerk who clearly did not share McEachern's abhorrence of alcohol was once arrested for impaired driving and spent the night in a police cell. On Monday morning he confessed his transgression, and the Horsemen met to consider his fate. Most were for firing him on the spot, but McEachern demurred. "Judging by the example that is set around here by some of the head office officials," he said, "I think we have to stand behind this boy."

His gaze at the time might have been directed toward Bob Baker. Though no roisterer, Baker was a big, bluff, gregarious man, much more outgoing than his colleagues. Perhaps his years in Edmonton and Toronto had stripped him of some of the parochialism to be found in London. At any rate, when he returned from Toronto to become investment manager at head office, he seemed to find the pace of life in London a little slow, and he sometimes offended the locals by letting it show.

By the standards of today's young upwardly mobile executives, the Four Horsemen might be judged impossibly formal and conventional, overly cautious, fuddy-duddies even. But they were solid, responsible citizens, and they would need all their dedication and capacity for hard work to shepherd their company safely through the apocalyptic years ahead.

9

A Tower Rises into the Gathering Clouds

THE end of the war that was to have ended all wars brought Canada a period of bitter disillusionment. Factories that had worked night and day to turn out armaments closed or suspended operations for retooling to meet peacetime needs. The wartime labour shortage was replaced by unemployment, which became worse as the troops were demobilized and returned to the labour force. The world price of wheat slumped and Canadian farmers received disastrously low prices for their products. Prices of other goods rose as inflation took over, and efforts to stem the inflation by raising interest rates brought on a recession in the early 1920s which some commentators preferred to term a depression.

The Huron & Erie sailed serenely on through the storm, if not immune to all the commotion, at least insulated from its worst effects by its vigilant management. It was even able in 1920 to increase its dividend to seven per cent, which would have been an unprecedented fourteen per cent on the old fifty-dollar par shares.

But the depression took its toll of other financial institutions. At the beginning of 1924 Hume Cronyn, now the company's first vice-president, told the shareholders at their annual meeting: "As those present know, 1923 has passed into Canadian history as a year of financial crisis. To almost every Canadian the question of the safety of deposits became of moment during that year, and the stability of all financial institutions formed the topic of conversation in home, factory, and office. Throughout, I am happy to report, the old Huron & Erie stood firm as a rock, and its impregnable position as a safe depository for savings was undoubtedly recognized by the public."

The financial crisis to which he referred, still fresh in his listeners' minds, was occasioned by the collapse of the Home Bank, the last bank failure in Canada until modern times (though there had been twenty-five before it, beginning just a year after Confederation). Originally a building and loan society, the Home Bank received its bank charter in 1907. It grew rapidly, and when it closed its doors it had seventy-one branches, forty-seven of them in Ontario, three in Quebec, and the rest in the western provinces. Its assets were listed at $27.4 million, but it had been badly managed and had made a series of bad loans, some of them to its directors and to companies they had interests in. The scandal led to an inquiry by a Royal Commission and fraud charges against several directors and executives. The bank's depositors lost half their savings, a sum amounting to millions of dollars, and its shareholders lost everything.

In contrast, as Cronyn told the annual meeting with obvious satisfaction, 858 new customers had opened savings accounts with the Huron & Erie during the year, bringing the total number of its depositors to more than 19,000. The money entrusted to the company's care in savings deposits and debentures had increased by almost $1.5 million during the year, and the combined assets of the Huron & Erie and Canada Trust now exceeded $42 million. The Huron & Erie's net profit for the year was a record $571,914, and to celebrate that fact, and the fact that 1924 was the company's diamond jubilee year, the directors declared a bonus payment of one half of one per cent, making the total dividend seven and a half per cent.

For the rest of the decade the company's earnings kept on growing, as the country emerged from the postwar slump. The automobile age had arrived with Henry Ford's Model-T. New technology spurred the development of new manufacturing industries and the demand for their products. The pulp and paper and mining industries boomed. Jobs became more plentiful and wages rose. It was the Roaring Twenties, the Jazz Age; and the Huron & Erie shared in the good times.

The long-planned new Toronto branch had opened early in 1920, in a building purchased for $200,000 at King and Yonge—not quite Bay Street but close enough to it. It was followed the same year by a new branch at Chatham, closer to home, and in 1921 by a fourth branch in London, London-South. In the meantime Harry Givins was expanding the western business, and in 1924 the directors took the plunge and opened a new branch in far-away Victoria, B.C.

The company grew through acquisitions during those years, too. In 1921 the Ontario government passed legislation providing for the regular inspection of all loan and trust companies' books by the registrar of loan companies. The registrar was not pleased when he examined the records of the Dominion Savings and Investment Society, a company founded in London eight years after the Huron & Erie. In fact, he found "a serious condition which convinced the department and the minister that the society could not be allowed, with safety to the public, to receive moneys on deposit or by the sale of its debentures." One of the Dominion Savings shareholders went further: he alleged that the society was insolvent and filed suit to have it wound up.

At that stage the Huron & Erie came to the rescue. Having a financial institution collapse right in its own backyard would not be good for business; and so it took over the society's affairs in the summer of 1922, guaranteeing its depositors' claims of $500,000 and debenture-holders' claims of $200,000. The president of Dominion Savings was T.H. Purdom, a well-known Liberal lawyer and proprietor of the *London Advertiser*, longtime rival of the *London Free Press*. Purdom and members of his family owned more than half the shares of Dominion Savings, whose assets included the *Advertiser* and its commercial printing press, a local weaving mill, and a dyeing plant. The takeover agreement provided that "when the public liabilities have been satisfied, [the shareholders] will be entitled to any surplus remaining from the assets after the payment of the costs and expenses of the Huron & Erie Mortgage Corporation in connection therewith." Since those assets were transferred a year later to the Trustee Guaranty Company, the Huron & Erie records do not show what happened to them. But the *Advertiser*, after being operated for a time by the *Toronto Star*, disappeared from the local scene in 1936.

The next stage in the expansion came in 1926 with the purchase of a company that was by no means ailing. The Hamilton Provident & Loan Corporation had something of the same substantial standing in that growing steel city that the Huron & Erie had in London. Founded by Adam Hope in 1871 soon after he left London, it was housed in its own imposing four-storey building constructed in the heart of the downtown area a few years later with stone imported from Vermont, and surmounted by a revolving clock that was a local landmark. It had one branch office, in Brandon, Manitoba. Its assets amounted to $5.4 million, and it had paid a ten-per-cent dividend in 1925. Its shares, with a par value of $100, were sufficiently valuable that the Huron & Erie shareholders voted to buy them for $227 each—$100 in cash and $117 in Huron & Erie debentures. (The remaining $10 was set aside in a reserve fund to cover any losses on Hamilton Provident investments—not that any were expected at that time.)

The purchase contributed to a record increase of $8 million in the Huron & Erie's assets that year. Explaining it to the shareholders at the beginning of 1927, Hume Cronyn[1] said it increased the company's mortgage portfolio by $5 million. The Hamilton Provident's Brandon branch was closed, and the $1.9 million it held in mortgages in Saskatchewan and Manitoba was henceforth administered by the Huron & Erie's Regina and Winnipeg offices. The sign-painters moved in to the Hamilton Provident's head office and it became a branch of the Huron & Erie, under the continuing management of D.M. Cameron, who was transferred to the Huron & Erie's staff. The deal brought the Huron & Erie's savings bank almost two thousand new customers in Hamilton, with accounts totalling $900,000, and mortgage investments in the city of $2.1 million. The company already had $3 million invested in Hamilton properties, its policy of confining its loans largely to farm properties having changed through the years.

The growth continued a year later, when the company bought the Southern Loan & Savings Company in St. Thomas. The Southern Loan had been founded in 1870, and in 1903 it absorbed two of the companies undermined by the Atlas scandal. It had a paid-up capital of $900,000, a reserve fund of more than $400,000, and total assets of more than $3 million. Its manager, J.W. Stewart, who had worked for it for forty-five years, continued to run it as a Huron & Erie employee.

Canada Trust, too, was growing through these years. Since 1922, when Dominion legislation had been passed permitting it to take deposits, the operations of the two companies had been more than ever indistinguishable, except, of course, that the Huron & Erie was not empowered to undertake trust functions. By 1927 Canada Trust's assets amounted to $20.5 million; it registered a net profit for the year of more than $135,000 and paid a dividend of ten per cent—$100,000—to its parent company.

---

1. Cronyn was by now president of the company. At the beginning of 1926, T.G. Meredith had been elevated to the newly created post of chairman of the board, and Morley Aylsworth moved up to general manager, replacing Cronyn.

At the beginning of 1929 Chairman Meredith invited the shareholders at the annual meeting to contemplate the company's continuing upward progress. Net profits for 1928 were up, assets were up again, and the dividend was up by a further one half of one per cent, to eight per cent. All this, the chairman said, was "evidence of the growth and expansion of the Dominion of Canada during recent years." While expressing his confidence that the company would "continue to share in the bright future of our country," he permitted himself a slight digression. Though not noticeably bucolic himself, Meredith naturally had a keen interest in the success of farming operations, which, he said, had not been as remunerative as they should have been.

As the decade of the 1920s had roared on, more and more farm workers had left the land for the cities, drawn by the increasing number of industrial jobs available there and the higher wages they paid. As a result, farmers were once again suffering from a shortage of labour. But this was not the burden of Meredith's complaint. "A serious problem for farmers in parts of the province of Ontario and in some of the other provinces," he said, "is the spread of noxious weeds, not only on the farms but also upon the highways, and it seems to me that something should be done to overcome this menace if farmers in these districts are to prosper."

General Manager Aylsworth, with his keen eye for the bottom line, was more to the point. "What we own," he told the shareholders, "totals $42,013,578; the amount we owe is only $34,437,871. We can repay Depositors and Debenture owners every dollar of their money and still have the splendid surplus of $7,575,707."

His pride was pardonable, but in the words of the familiar misquotation from the book of *Proverbs*, pride often goeth before a fall. The nation's farmers, and the nation itself, would soon face much graver problems than noxious weeds.

The stock-market crash of October 1929 was still haunting the shareholders when they gathered for the annual meeting early in 1930, but they could not have envisaged the horrors of the depression that would soon follow it. Some may have had forebodings, and no doubt Meredith was attempting to allay their fears when he pointed out that the company had been able to show an increase in its profits for twenty-five consecutive years and that an eight-per-cent dividend was once again in order.

Meredith avoided the unpalatable topic of the stock-market

crash, and it was left to the company's vice-president, Maj. Gen. the Honourable S.C. Mewburn, K.C., C.M.G.,[2] to draw the predictable moral from it. "It has been apparent to all," he said, "that a large volume of private funds was employed in speculative ventures during the past year. Unfortunately, many who can ill afford to lose have seen the savings of a lifetime swiftly disappear in the stock markets. On the other hand, many thousands of savers and investors who are numbered among the customers of the Huron & Erie have steadfastly adhered to principles of soundness and safety, and have refused to be attracted by the glitter of unreasonably high interest rates or the deceitful promise of quickly made 'profits.' In these days of high pressure salesmanship of questionable securities, it is a tribute to the standing of the old Huron & Erie to find that investments in the corporation's debentures increased substantially during 1929."

Certainly, the old conservatism seemed to be justified, for the depression was slow to affect the Huron & Erie. At the beginning of 1931 Morley Aylsworth was able to report another record net profit for the year 1930: $593,495. "Following the turmoil in the stock market," he said in a circular letter to shareholders, "savers in general have been thinking seriously in terms of safety, with a reasonable interest return. As a result, an unusually large number of new investors in Huron & Erie debentures was secured during the past year." Savings deposits and debenture investments had increased by more than $3 million during the year, giving the company the second greatest year in its history.

By now the company had absorbed yet another local loan company—but this time reluctantly. The People's Loan & Savings Corporation had been founded in 1887, and though much smaller than the Huron & Erie it seemed solid enough. But in the fall of 1930 the auditors dropped in while the corporation's accountant

---

2. Born in Hamilton in 1863, a year before the Huron & Erie was founded, Sydney Chilton Mewburn was called to the Ontario bar in 1885. Twenty-five years later, at the age of forty-seven, he joined the militia as a private and rose through the ranks until in 1917 he was director-general of the Canadian defence force. He was elected as a Unionist member of Parliament in the same election as Hume Cronyn and entered the cabinet as minister of militia and defence. He had married into the Labatt family in 1888, and in 1920 he resigned his portfolio to devote his time to his extensive business interests. In addition to his ten-year term on the Huron & Erie's board, he was for many years vice-president of the Bank of Montreal.

happened to be on holiday. He returned to find the police waiting for him and he was charged with the theft of $1,345 from the company in October 1929. Before the case came to court, the auditors' continuing investigation revealed that he had been systematically embezzling funds ever since he joined the company twenty years earlier. He was eventually jailed for eight years for the theft of more than $150,000.

This was enough to threaten the People's Loan with collapse, and the superintendent of insurance for Ontario and a group of Toronto financial leaders headed by the rich and influential Sir Joseph Flavelle, chairman of the National Trust Company, urged the Huron & Erie to step in and guarantee the corporation's customers their money and liquidate its assets. It was clear by now that the country was heading into a depression, and they feared that if even one small financial institution closed its doors with losses to the public there might well be a run on the banks all over the country.

The situation was urgent, and with no time for a thorough investigation of the People's Loan's assets the Huron & Erie directors hesitated to commit themselves to possibly enormous losses. Only when six major trust companies got together and gave them a $100,000 guarantee against losses did they agree to the proposition and assume all the public liabilities of the People's Loan. These totalled $1.5 million, which it was agreed would be repaid to the Huron & Erie out of the People's Loan's assets, which had a book value of $1.9 million. The assets were transferred to Canada Trust for liquidation, and any surplus after the Huron & Erie had been repaid was to go to the People's Loan's shareholders.

The People's Loan's customers were thus protected against any losses. But much of the corporation's mortgage portfolio consisted of loans on modest workers' houses in Hamilton and other cities hard hit by the depression. These were difficult if not impossible to sell, even at distress prices, and it was 1948 before the last of the assets had been sold. The Huron & Erie eventually lost more than $30,000 on the deal, but it did not invoke the trust companies' guarantee. There was no money left over for the People's Loan's shareholders, who lost everything.

When it took on this "thankless task," as it was described in a company memorandum detailing it in 1948, the Huron & Erie was in the throes of preparing to move into a spanking new head office building. A year earlier it had bought the London Loan & Savings Company, which had been founded in 1877 and whose chief attraction seems to have been that its head-office building stood on a piece of choice real estate at Dundas and Clarence streets, in what is still the heart of London's downtown area.

The old Huron & Erie incurred some unwelcome publicity early in 1930 when it became known that it had hired the Toronto wrecking contractor Teperman and Sons to dismantle the old London Loan building to make way for its new headquarters. That April, when a Teperman crew arrived from Toronto to begin work, a crowd of a hundred unemployed local workers marched on City Hall in an angry protest. News reports at the time described the demonstration as a near-riot, but the men dispersed after the mayor had explained that skilled demolition workers were essential in the early stages of the project and that the Teperman company had promised local labour would be employed as soon as possible.

A few weeks later the Huron & Erie directors met to consider bids for construction of their new nine-storey building. The lowest—$685,000—came from a Detroit company, but after some deliberation, and no doubt with the demonstration by the unemployed in mind, the directors resolved that "it would be very unwise for the corporation to give the contract to an American firm." So at the beginning of July they accepted the second lowest bid—$725,000—from the Hamilton firm of Pigott & Sons.

Construction began in September, and in June 1931 the company moved in to the "tower," as it was called in the many columns of newsprint that celebrated the occasion. A handsome building that still houses the London-Main branch, it was for many years the dominant landmark in London and the surrounding countryside, since it was floodlit at night and topped by a revolving 11.5-million-candlepower beacon whose searchlight beam could be seen from eighty kilometres away.

A writer in the *London Free Press* who was given a guided tour of the building before it opened for business waxed lyrical about its wonders. "From the comparatively low level of the city," he wrote, "the squat towers on the roof thrust forth their eminences above the smoke pall and welcome the stranger, approaching by rail or by highway to the commercial keystone of Western Ontario. . . . Down, down, twenty-three feet below the level of the streets, is the vault, an island of steel and reinforced concrete defying any possible attempt at forcible entry, short of such a catastrophe as would move the whole structure."

The visitor was mightily impressed by the vault's seventeen-ton steel door. "A dozen sweating horses," he wrote, "might strain at the load of this door on a trolley, yet so nicely does it set on its hinges that it will yield to the push of an ordinary man to shut or to open. . . . Steel, steel, steel. This is the song of the vault. Smooth, adamant, polished, colorless, grim as a fortress, efficient as the universe, this vault rests deep down in the bedrock of London, guarding the treasures and securities of the corporation and its customers."

The enraptured reporter was similarly awed by the building's main entrance, "a masterpiece in bronze, a tremendous double door set . . . accepted today as the finest single piece of commercial bronze in Canada." The doors, he said, were designed by "Ulysses Ricci, of New York, one of those Italian geniuses who have followed so surely in the footsteps of Michaelangelo and the long line of Italian designers and modelers in stone and metal, who have made the Mediterranean kingdom synonymous with the art of sculpture."

More prosaically, a modest accompanying advertisement disclosed that the new building's boilers had been built at old Elijah Leonard's foundry. "Made in London," this said, simply. "LEONARD BOILERS, again the choice of discriminating clients." Elijah's grandson, Col. Ibbotson Leonard, D.S.O., who had joined the Huron & Erie's board of directors in 1923, was similarly succinct many years later when, on his retirement as chairman in 1958, he told a reporter: "The price for our building was fantastically low. There were so many people out of work we could get all the men we wanted."

In spite of this retrospective silver lining, the storm clouds of the advancing depression must have cast something of a pall over the staff banquet held in the Crystal Ball Room of the old Hotel London to mark the move to the new headquarters. There were more than two hundred guests, representing all the company's fifteen branches in five provinces, new offices having been opened in Vancouver in 1929 and in Montreal earlier in 1931. There were the customary presentations and speeches, including one by Harry Givins, the oldest serving member of the staff, who had started out forty-two years earlier under George Somerville's tutelage and had travelled east with the managers of his western branches to attend the festivities. Then the guests adjourned for dancing in the large convention room on the eighth floor of the new tower.

That room was crowded with anxious shareholders a few months later, when the annual meeting in February 1932 heard disturbing news. For the first time that anyone could remember, the Huron & Erie's net profit for the year was down—by more than $60,000. Chairman Meredith hastened to assure his audience that nevertheless the company would once again pay a dividend of eight per cent. In passing, he permitted himself to grumble a little about the perennial topic of taxes. Faced with mounting expenditures to finance what turned out to be an unavailing effort to alleviate the worst hardships of the depression, the Dominion government in 1931 increased the corporation tax by two per cent, raising it to ten per cent. "This added levy," said Meredith, "was made not only upon the earnings of the year 1931, but was made retroactive, and applied to the profits of the year 1930, and accounts for much of the increase in the taxes shown in the report. The ever-increasing taxation by Dominion, provincial, and municipal governments creates a heavy burden[3] upon the corporation."

Clearly trying to reassure his nervous shareholders, the chairman ended his remarks with a sentence that was, for him, uncharacteristically florid: "The clouds of financial depression are still hanging low over the world, but the clouds will break, and the sun of returning prosperity will appear."

Notwithstanding the illumination provided to London's night skies by the Huron & Erie's floodlights and beacon, Chairman Meredith—and one imagines he suspected it—was whistling in the dark. Many nightmarish years would elapse before the sun again broke through the clouds.

---

3. By later standards, the added levy might not be considered unduly burdensome. In 1929, with a net profit of $590,910, the company paid a little over $60,000 in federal and provincial taxes. In 1931, with a net profit of $533,459, it was able to maintain its usual dividend, amounting to $400,000, and pay federal, provincial, and municipal taxes of $82,969.

10

The Four Horsemen Battle the Storm

HUME Cronyn, who suffered from hardening of the arteries and had been in failing health for some years, died in June 1933. It might have been expected that his successor as president would be the seasoned Morley Aylsworth; but Aylsworth was too valuable, and too busy piloting the company through the gravest crisis in its history, to be kicked upstairs into what was still essentially only a part-time job. So Meredith assumed the dual title of chairman and president.

In his remarks at the annual meeting early in 1932, Meredith had not mentioned an ominous new item that appeared on the 1931 balance sheet. For many years the directors had been accustomed to reporting to the shareholders, with considerable satisfaction, that the company had no real estate on hand;[1] in other words, any property that had been repossessed or had fallen into its hands by default had been successfully disposed of before the end of the financial year.

Now, at the end of 1931, the properties that had fallen into the company's hands and which it had been unable to sell were valued on the books at almost $243,000. A breakdown of that figure suggests that city-dwellers were hit by the depression before it began to take its toll of farmers: more than $235,000 of the total was accounted for by city properties and only $7,700 by farm properties.

That dread balance sheet item, "real estate held for sale," a

1. This category, of course, excluded the office premises of the company. It now owned four buildings in London and one each in Toronto, Winnipeg, Windsor, Chatham, St. Thomas, and Hamilton. Altogether, they were carried on the books at a valuation of $2.1 million.

barometer of the suffering of Canadians during the depression, mounted steadily during succeeding years until it reached a peak of $1.25 million in 1937. By that time farm properties accounted for more than $532,000 of the total, and city properties more than $722,000.

Through all these desperate years Aylsworth travelled constantly, visiting all the company's branches, trying to keep up the spirits of the staff, most of whom he knew by name, and personally examining every loan on the company's books. It was a sad time for everyone, and doubly so for Aylsworth: early in the 1930s he was driving to Toronto when he was involved in a traffic accident in which his wife was killed. Perhaps the travelling eased his loneliness. At any rate, he was given credit for holding the company together at a time when it could easily have foundered.

The Huron & Erie went into the depression with a least $18 million invested in mortgages in the west, most of it in Saskatchewan, the province hardest hit by the depression and the searing drought that struck western farmers at the same time. "Mr. Aylsworth believed strongly in the top five inches of Saskatchewan," the author was told by Burd McNiece, a retired company veteran who was still driving his own car when he was well into his nineties. When the company made its western farm loans, that top five inches of soil sustained waving fields of golden wheat that made Saskatchewan farmers the most prosperous in the country. The drought of the Dirty Thirties turned much of it into clouds of blowing dust so thick that motorists had to drive with their headlights on in the daytime.

In 1930 no marketable crop was harvested from almost a third of Saskatchewan's farm land, and fodder had to be shipped in for livestock. Even those farmers who had crops to sell were faced with disastrously low prices on the world market: by December 1932 the price of wheat on the Winnipeg Grain Exchange had fallen to 38 cents a bushel, its lowest point in history. The average cash income generated by Saskatchewan farms in 1928 was $1,164; by 1933 it had slumped to $66, and eighty-five per cent of the province's farmers were receiving some form of relief. City-dwellers were no better off: the province's per capita income fell during the depression years by seventy-two per cent. There was no unemployment insurance then, of course, and relief payments were not exactly munificent: ten dollars and a ninety-eight-pound bag of flour for a family of five, once a month.

In a privately printed book of memoirs, Verschoyle Cronyn, Hume's son, wrote: "Large sections of the west became nothing but a dust bowl. In 1931, crops there were virtually wiped out by a plague of grasshoppers. That summer I went west with other Huron & Erie directors to view the conditions at first hand. What we found was very disheartening. Even in the normally most productive area of the Regina Plain farms had been abandoned. There was desolation everywhere. On approaching one farm we were met by the wife who, throwing her apron up over her head and crying, called to her husband that we had come to take their farm. We were able to convince them that nothing was further from our thoughts, because we already had too many deserted properties on our books. Before we left, the man of the house showed us what food they were living on. In a barrel of brine were skinned gophers and prairie dogs."

The image of the greedy landlord, cruelly profiting from others' misfortunes, was a staple of Victorian melodrama. As the foregoing excerpt from Verschoyle Cronyn's memoirs indicates, the Huron & Erie directors had no disposition to assume that dastardly role. Indeed, they could not have done so had they wished. Conditions were so desperate during those years that city property was difficult to sell even at distress prices; there was no market at all for western land at a time when farmers fortunate enough to have seed to plant often saw it blow away with their topsoil.

Faced with that troubling and constantly mounting balance sheet item "real estate on hand," it was clearly in the company's own interest to keep its farm borrowers working their land. To that end, it often supplied destitute farmers with livestock or machinery to keep them in business. And when the rains at last returned to the west, it provided seed to farmers who were too poor to buy their own, to enable them to revive their operations. Sometimes these supplies were provided free; sometimes, according to circumstances, their cost was added to the mortgage, but at a reduced rate of interest.

The board minutes for the depression years record dozens of these transactions. On 1 September 1931, to cite one example, the directors approved "the expenditure of $275.00 for the purchase of livestock, to be supplied to Mr. Ledat." On 12 July 1932 "it was decided to advance to farm borrowers in Saskatchewan small amounts so as to enable these farmers to continue and complete their summer-fallowing, provided Regina branch, before any such advance is made, investigate each case carefully, and that advances be made only where farm operations would cease if such advances were not made."

On 20 January 1936 it was reported to the board that "the requirements for seed grain advances in Saskatchewan during 1936 will amount to $150,000 to $185,000." Subsequent meetings were informed that the Winnipeg branch would need about $10,000 for seed and Edmonton from $25,000 to $30,000.

Perhaps because of this need for seed, the company sometimes contracted to accept harvested crops as payments on its mortgages. Early in 1934, for instance, the Edmonton branch sold a farmer a repossessed property for $5,120. The farmer agreed to pay $200 down and "the balance in half-crop payments at seven per cent interest." The entry in the minute book does not disclose the size of the property, but it seems that it had not been fully used by the farmer who had walked away from it, because the new mortgagor accepted as part of the agreement a condition that he "break twenty additional acres each year."

Negotiating deals such as this—and there were many of them—called for more flexibility and practical judgment than might in normal times have been required of a bookkeeper who was merely expected to record monthly mortgage payments in a ledger. And the directors back home in London supported the men in the field when, as often happened, they had to resort to unconventional solutions to the many problems they faced. In September 1935, for instance, they approved the Regina branch's decision to accept a thousand bushels of wheat in settlement of a company claim against a property, with "four hundred bushels to be turned over this year and the balance during 1936 to 1937."

The company's problems, and the general misery, were not, of course, confined to the west or to farmers. With well over half a million workers unemployed out of a total Canadian population at that time of only slightly over ten million, the nation's cities suffered tragically, too. Hamilton was a particular problem for the Huron & Erie. Many of its mortgage loans there, including a lot of those inherited from the Hamilton Provident, were on modest working-class houses in the east end, which had grown up as the city's heavy industries expanded during the boom of the 1920s.

When the depression hit, thousands of those east-end workers lost their jobs. Some factories closed entirely, others operated only spasmodically. The huge blast-furnaces stood cold for weeks at a time, and when they were fired up again they operated at only a fraction of their capacity. In January 1930 there were 1,380 people on relief in Hamilton; by January 1932 that figure had risen to 19,763, almost thirteen per cent of the city's population.

Here again, and for the same reasons as elsewhere, the company repossessed properties only as a last resort, but inevitably many borrowers fell so far behind with their mortgage payments that they lost their homes. Jim Brown, a retired company veteran who began work as a junior in Hamilton in 1931, recalled: "We had 'real estate on hand' coming out of our ears. We were selling properties without down payments just to get them occupied, because neighbours were breaking down the back fences and verandahs, the back steps and so on, to get firewood." When, as often happened, it was impossible to sell repossessed houses, the company would try to lease them at nominal rents, sometimes to families on relief, again just to keep them occupied and in the hope of at least covering the municipal taxes due on them.

At their weekly meetings during those terrible years, the directors listened anxiously to crop forecasts from the men in the field, wrote down loans or wrote them off altogether, and waived or postponed payments of interest and even, on occasion, of principal. On 8 January 1934 the directors totted up the figures for 1933 and wrote off a total of more than $329,000 in overdue interest payments, $153,500 of it in Saskatchewan. The directors' minutes for those years are full of entries recording the forgiveness of overdue principal payments. On 24 April 1933, for instance, the board approved the Hamilton branch's waiver of overdue principal payments on 107 loans, ranging from $25 to $750. Again, on 1 April 1935 they forgave a long list of principal payments in Hamilton, most of them less than $100 but one amounting to $1,000. These may seem small sums today, but they bulked large in those hard times to both borrowers and lenders.

There was a limit, of course, to how far the company could go to assist its borrowers. It was not, after all, a philanthropic institution but the custodian and investor of other people's savings, funds entrusted to it by its depositors and debenture holders, by no means all of whom were, to use a term that acquired wide currency in those days, bloated capitalists. In 1934, for example, the average balance in the company's 35,000 savings accounts was $256.

This situation, which boiled down to the question of how to help Peter without hurting Paul, was addressed by one of the Four

Horsemen, Bob Baker, in a long and thoughtful speech to the Canadian Political Science Association in Montreal in May 1934. "Perhaps the most difficult and discouraging situation confronting the mortgage lending institutions in this country today," he said, "is the persistence with which some governments seek to ameliorate the suffering of certain classes of debtors, apparently oblivious to the fact that they are merely transferring the distress to other and larger groups of our citizens. The utter futility of attempts to wipe out debts by legislation has been demonstrated so often that it should be unnecessary to argue the point. Nevertheless, it is evident that many people—some holding positions of responsibility—still believe that various forms of moratoria legislation are not only desirable but necessary in an emergency such as we have been facing in common with the peoples of other countries for the past two or three years. . . ."

To try to cope with the undeniable emergency, several provinces contemplated, and some implemented, plans for government agencies to give farmers credit at cheaper than commercial rates. Baker produced figures to justify the commercial rates. Over a ten-year period, he said, the Huron & Erie had found that the cost of borrowed capital, in the form of savings deposits and debentures, averaged five and a half per cent. The average rate being charged on farm loans in the prairie provinces by thirteen representative loaning corporations at the time was just over seven per cent. The gap, Baker said, was necessary to cover overhead costs, provide reserve funds to cover losses, and return a reasonable profit to the lenders.

"The ratio of delinquency with western farm loans," he said, "has always been considerably in excess of that in eastern loaning fields and this is a further fact militating against lower interest rates for the western farmer. . . . I am fully convinced that the Province of Ontario cannot provide loans to farmers at a five and a half per cent rate on an economic basis, nor can the Province of Saskatchewan, for instance, furnish loans at a six and a half per cent rate, and charge all proper expenses to the farm loan organization, including rates paid by the province for the money, together with the cost of securing the money, all legitimate administrative expenses, and reasonable provision for losses."

In fact, Baker went on, the Saskatchewan Farm Loan Board—he was speaking five months into 1934—had already lost roughly $4 million on business capitalized at $17 million at the end of 1933.

"We are faced with two alternatives," he said. "Either the governments must recognize that they must continue this 'sop' to the farmer, and deliberately set forth to bonus our basic industry of agriculture—a dangerous path to follow—or they must conclude that economics must ultimately determine the country's policy, in which event it will be admitted that the great institutions that have provided mortgage credit in the past—after serving the country splendidly for almost a century—have been treated shamefully by some of our governments."

One piece of depression-era legislation that the Huron & Erie people considered particularly shameful was the Dominion government's Farmers' Creditors Arrangement Act, under which borrowers could appear before "Boards of Review" which often arbitrarily reduced their mortgages, sometimes by substantial amounts, or cut the interest rates on them. Jack Wilson joined the Huron & Erie as a teenager in 1928 and rose through the ranks to be its vice-president in charge of western branches and one of its directors. In his retirement in Vancouver he recalled a board hearing he attended when still a young man: "I went down to Leamington and had to go into court. There were four mortgages on this farm. We had the first—we were always first—then there were the Bank of Montreal and two others. And the judge ruled that we'd all take a cut in capital, and he went right across the board, all four mortgages, and we all took a capital loss in the same proportion. I drove back that night to London, and as I say I was then very young, but boy, I was upset. I said, 'What's the use of being in a preferred position?'"

Bob Baker did not mention this Act specifically in his speech, but on the topic of moratorium legislation in general he said: "If mortgagors are left free and unhampered in dealing with their borrowers it should be possible to work out mutually satisfactory solutions in a vast majority of cases. If, however, governments must interfere it is not unreasonable to suggest that they should be prepared to reimburse creditors for any losses that are attributable to such interference. Our governments should give due consideration to the rights and needs of the creditor lest we destroy the commercial morality of the country. It has been pointed out time and again that a very large proportion of all mortgage loans in this country have been made by our loan, trust and insurance companies and it has also been shown that the money so invested represents the savings of countless thousands of small investors in every walk of life. These are facts that should be kept clearly in mind whenever a new Moses appears to offer a panacea for our financial ills. . . .

"The heavy blows that have been struck at the principle of sanctity of contracts during recent years would indicate that many people forget that credit is nothing more, nor less, than confidence. . . . It should be patent to all that iniquitous legislation such as we have witnessed only tends to aggravate an already difficult situation and retard recovery."

Obviously, forces other than just "iniquitous legislation" were at work during the depression, but confidence was indeed slow to return, and as the economic stagnation dragged on and on the financial position of the Huron & Erie worsened with each passing year. Its record net profit of $593,495 in 1930 dwindled until by 1942 it was less than half that sum—$292,554—and still the eroding effects of the depression persisted. The 1930 level of profit was not achieved again until the early 1950s. The continuing write-downs and write-offs of loans and interest also took their toll of the company's assets, which had until then been constantly rising; they fell from just over $47 million in 1930 to a little over $42 million in 1942.

The healthy eight-per-cent dividend that had been paid through the good years was cut to six and a half per cent in 1933, and thereafter it fell year by year until it was down to four per cent in 1938, and it did not begin to rise again until the directors were able to declare a bonus of one half of one per cent in 1947. The worsening financial performance was naturally reflected in the price of the company's shares on the stock market. Before the depression they sold for $170; by 1942 they had tumbled all the way down to a $55 high for the year. Interest rates, too, followed the downward trend. One-year debentures, which paid five per cent at the start of the depression, were paying only three per cent by 1936, by which time the interest paid on savings deposits had sunk to two per cent.

There was little management could do to stem the tide, except to practise even more rigorously the company's traditional close attention to operating expenses. A note in the board minutes in 1934 said that "budget methods" introduced during 1933 had reduced expenses by thirteen and a half per cent during the year. Those methods were not detailed, but the directors several times voted to accept ten-per-cent reductions in their fees, which were

$500 a year at the start of the depression, and the Four Horsemen and other top managers took pay cuts which were not restored until World War II.

Only one of the many retired employees interviewed by the author could remember any lay-offs; there had been a tearful scene in which the accountant and a couple of tellers at one of the branches were informed that they had to go. Some staff salaries were reduced, and for a long time there were no annual raises. But morale among the staff remained high, partly because anyone who held on to a job during those lean years was considered fortunate, but also because of the management-fostered sense of company kinship.

There were company hockey and baseball teams which played in what was known as the "financial league," and the whole staff used to turn out to watch their games, particularly when their opponents were the London Life team, their particular rivals. One Huron & Erie junior who played on the hockey team, Ray Getliffe, quit his job to turn pro and made it to the Montreal Canadiens. Bowling was another popular sport and some of the executives would join the staff in the alleys after work. Charles O'Hara, a particularly athletic junior in those days, recalled that he was captain of a bowling team whose members included Bob Baker.

While the Four Horsemen, with the possible exception of Baker, were rather formal people, they did not confine their relationships with the staff to the office. Morley Aylsworth, for instance, was a keen curler and would invite the junior O'Hara and other staff members to his home for a nightcap after an evening at the rink. Dick Cronyn, Verschoyle's brother, who eventually became the company's chief trust executive, was a keen tennis player and often invited O'Hara, who won the company tournament a couple of times, to play on his family's court on Sundays.

The new building opened in 1931 contained a club room, and Baker and Charlie Clarke would sometimes join junior members of the staff there for a rubber of bridge during their lunch break. There were two company clubs, one for the men and the other for "the girls," as they were still called. The girls were all single in those days; until the staff shortages of World War II a woman had to leave her job if she married. Nevertheless, some inter-company marriages did occur, even though the directors put aside their other preoccupations one day in 1933 to decree that "no male member of the staff should marry without the consent of the

Board, unless receiving a salary of not less than $1,200 per annum and a yearly income from other sources of at least $300."

"It was like a family, really," O'Hara recalled. And nowhere was that spirit more evident than at the annual summer picnic, when staff members from all the Ontario branches would flock with their families to Port Stanley, on Lake Erie, which used to be known as "London's Coney Island." The company's directors continued throughout the depression to vote several hundred dollars every year to provide prizes for the sports events and refreshments at this morale-boosting event.

All this socializing, of course, was not permitted to detract from the strict attention paid to the company's business during the working day—and often long into the night. A teller who was even a couple of cents short at the end of the day had to stay on until the books were properly balanced, no matter how long that took. During the depression, there were frequent weekend sessions when the senior executives and any staff members involved would go on examining "close loans"—loans whose borrowers seemed to be having difficulty in meeting their payments—until late on Sunday evening. And none of the staff counted on arriving early at a New Year's Eve party; all the year-end figures from all the branches had to be gathered together at head office on the evening of 31 December and properly balanced so that the directors could go over them at their traditional meeting on the morning of New Year's Day.

This was all, of course, long before the day of the computer and the pocket calculator, and it became second nature for members of the staff to tot up any column of figures they encountered. There survives in the company archives a copy of the annual report for Canada Trust for the year 1903. One entry in the assets column was "Balance in banks – $1,224.17." That seventeen cents is neatly circled and transposed to seventy-one in the margin. Underneath, in handwriting that could have been treasurer Charlie Clarke's, is a note: "Error caught in Nov/42."

11

The Tail Begins to Wag the Dog

CANADA began to emerge from the misery of the depression in the second half of the Dirty Thirties, and the outbreak of World War II in 1939, tragic though it was, set the seal on the recovery. During the next five years, years that changed the face of the nation for ever, Canadian industry was galvanized into an explosive expansion to turn out munitions, ships, planes, military trucks, armoured vehicles—anything needed by the Allies to wage the war against Hitler's tyranny.

Recovery for the Huron & Erie was a slower process. In retrospect, perhaps it had too large a proportion of its assets concentrated in mortgages. Certainly it suffered from an imbalance in the deployment of its resources, with such huge sums invested in the west, where the depression both bit deeper and persisted longer than in the industrializing east. In 1942, by which time the factories and shipyards were working three shifts a day and business in general was booming, the Huron & Erie's net profit was lower than it had been during the years before World War I, even though its assets were now well over twice the size they had been a quarter of a century earlier. For a variety of reasons, there was not much Morley Aylsworth and his colleagues could do about it as long as the war lasted. Circumstances compelled them to mark time; in effect, they were reduced to simply holding the fort.

Resolved to harness all the country's energies for the war effort, the federal government discouraged expansion by financial institutions and even exhorted them to retrench, urging them to practise whatever economies they could by combining their operations wherever possible.[1] Since production was concentrated on wartime needs, all sorts of domestic shortages developed and the building of residential housing once again virtually ceased; that, and the departure of so many young men for the services, dried up the demand for mortgages. As in the earlier war, large amounts of savings were funnelled into the Victory bonds floated by the government to finance the war effort, and the Huron & Erie people considered it their patriotic duty to sell the government's bonds when they might otherwise have been pushing their own debentures.

Like many other businesses, the company was also plagued during the war years by a lack of trained staff. Seventy-seven employees, this time including some of "the girls," volunteered for the services, and those left behind had to work long hours to make up for their absence. Even when the company was able to engage new employees who seemed to have adequate qualifications, they did not always fit the Huron & Erie mould. Walter Mills joined the company in London in 1924 but put in most of his forty-one years' service in Hamilton. He recalled that the Hamilton branch once hired a teller whose husband was a serviceman newly stationed in the area. When the office closed one day, she put on her coat and prepared to go home. Her male supervisor protested, "Your books aren't balanced—you can't leave yet." Incredulous, the woman said, "I *can't*?"—and to emphasize her point swung her purse at the supervisor and hit him in the face before stalking out. The branch manager was spared the unpleasant duty of firing her because she never came back. "We had an awful time with help here," Mills said, chuckling in recollection.

Revolt such as this was not part of the Huron & Erie tradition, but in 1943 the directors finally rebelled against their autocratic chairman and president, T.G. Meredith, and forced him out. Incredibly, he had clung to his position into his ninetieth year. Longtime director Col. Ibbotson Leonard replaced him as chairman and Morley Aylsworth took over as president. Since he retained his post of general manager, Aylsworth now became what

---

1. In response to the government's wishes, the Huron & Erie directors sanctioned a move that within a few years would come back to haunt them: they agreed to close their savings branch in Vancouver and hand its business over to the Bank of Toronto (now the Toronto-Dominion) in exchange for the modest business being done by a Bank of Toronto branch in east London.

would today be styled president and chief executive officer; and one of his first acts in that capacity would turn out to be one of the most important of his many services to the company.

When Aylsworth took over, Canada Trust—even though it had paid a ten-per-cent dividend throughout the depression, contributing a welcome $100,000 a year to its parent company's coffers—was still very much a poor relation. The rest of the Horsemen, and certainly Meredith, considered it merely an adjunct to their main business, the "intermediary" operation of gathering in savings and putting them to work in mortgages and other investments. They had done little to develop the "fiduciary" side of the business, the administration of estates, trusts, and various agency functions, since fiduciary operations were, and still are, far less profitable than their intermediary counterpart. Aylsworth, however, realized that the Huron & Erie might gain valuable, if sometimes intangible, benefits by beefing up Canada Trust's fiduciary operations.

The candidate he chose to undertake this task was John Allyn Taylor, an outwardly unassuming but inwardly determined man in his mid-thirties, who had until then been ploughing a somewhat lonely furrow as the sole representative of Canada Trust in Winnipeg. Whether or not he knew it at the time, Aylsworth had chosen his eventual successor, the man who would lead the company to heights Aylsworth himself could hardly have dreamed of.

Allyn Taylor was born in Winnipeg in 1907, son of an English immigrant father and an Irish-Canadian mother. The senior Taylor, who managed a group of coal-mines in southeastern Saskatchewan, suffered from heart trouble, and in the hope that it would help his health the family moved to the milder climate of Victoria, B.C. Young Allyn attended St. Michael's prep school there, but when his father died in 1919 his mother took him back to Winnipeg, where he attended high school and earned his B.A. at the University of Manitoba in 1928.

Short in stature and virtually blind in one eye as the result of a childhood accident, Allyn Taylor nevertheless radiated a cheerful warmth and genuine concern for other people that won him the affection and admiration of all who met him. After a few weeks in his first job, as an apprentice in an accounting firm, he decided he would rather work with people than figures and moved into an insurance company. He found this no more congenial, and in 1929 he was lucky enough to find his niche as a trust officer with the Royal Trust company in Winnipeg.

The corporate trust function has acquired more importance in modern times, but the old-style trust officers were attracted by the personal side of the business. Their job has sometimes been too casually dismissed as managing other people's money, but it is actually much more. Certainly it calls for knowledge and experience in both legal and financial matters, but essentially it boils down to rendering service to people in an endless variety of ways, often in distressing circumstances. One day a trust officer might find himself consoling bereaved relatives or trying to mediate a dispute among family members. On another day he might have to negotiate the sale of a business whose proprietor has bequeathed it to his widow, or arrange for its continuing operation. On yet another he may be arranging for the financial security and care of an orphaned child. Often he is called upon to fulfil strange provisions in wills: someone's cat has to be cared for as long as it lives; someone's ashes have to be scattered over a favourite lake; ducks must regularly be fed on a certain pond; and in one celebrated example of a trust officer's responsibility in a western city, an aged family retainer had to be supplied with a pint of ale every day for the rest of his life.

The personal trust officer's job calls for qualities that are difficult to spell out in a resumé: compassion, the ability to inspire confidence in people, often at a low point in their lives, judgment, prudence, integrity—in short, trustworthiness. Allyn Taylor conspicuously possessed all these qualities; he was also a man of great drive and initiative, with a capacity not only for generating ideas of his own but for welcoming and encouraging those of others. In the Winnipeg branch of the Royal Trust he quickly rose to the position of chief clerk, where he found himself supervising the activities of much older men.

One day, in the depth of the depression, the Winnipeg manager received notification that he must give out no salary increases that year. Taylor was making a hundred dollars a month at the time. This was less than the men he supervised were being paid, since salaries in those days tended to be based on years of service with the company and not on merit, and he protested that an exception should be made in his case. The manager agreed and wrote to head office in Montreal. A letter came back authorizing him to grant Taylor a raise—of $100 a year. So when Taylor saw an advertisement seeking a trust officer for Canada Trust in 1935, he applied for the job, and was taken on by the Huron & Erie's manager, William Whyte, at a salary of $1,800 a year.[2]

About a year after he joined the company, Taylor was invited by a friend to fly with him to New York, where they could stay with his brother and take in a few Broadway shows. Since Taylor was not yet married and was still living at home with his mother, he could afford the trip—his first aboard an airplane. On the way home, on his own initiative, he stopped off in London to get better acquainted with his new company. He was greeted warmly by Charlie Clarke, the treasurer, who said, "I'd like you to come in and meet the chairman of the board."

T.G. Meredith was sitting at the boardroom table signing documents when Clarke said, "Mr. Meredith, this is Allyn Taylor, who joined the company last year in Winnipeg." Meredith wasted no time on social amenities. After a gruff "Hello" he turned to Clarke and said, "Charlie, why don't we close that damn office? It's never been anything but a headache for us." Clarke and Aylsworth spent most of the rest of the day persuading the irate Taylor not to quit.

Back in Winnipeg Taylor set about doing whatever he could to alleviate Meredith's headache by developing the trust side of the company's business. This was no easy task. The Huron & Erie had had an office on a prominent corner in Winnipeg for years and was well known. But Canada Trust, which consisted of Taylor and his secretary, was virtually unknown, and little had been done to develop its business. Taylor's boss, Whyte, like the rest of the Huron & Erie people during the depression, was preoccupied with problem mortgages, and while he knew and was popular with all the city's leading lights, he could not bring himself to use his social connections to drum up business.

So Taylor began to write letters and to make "cold calls" on people, expatiating upon the excellent variety of services that Canada Trust could perform for them. Gradually, his patent sincerity and peristence began to bring results. Gradually, too, his talents were becoming recognized back at head office, though he

2. When Taylor handed in his resignation from the Royal Trust, his boss warned him darkly that the Huron & Erie was in such trouble that it would probably soon be bankrupt.

came to the attention of Richard Cronyn, the company's trust executive, in embarrassing circumstances.

One day in the summer of 1939 Whyte told Taylor that Cronyn would be in the office on the following Saturday on a swing through the west, and since he was not booked to leave the city until Sunday someone would have to entertain him after the office closed. Since he himself was tied up, would Taylor mind taking Cronyn under his wing? By now, Taylor had married Betty Haig, daughter of one of the city's prominent lawyers, but she was away visiting her parents' cottage for the weekend, so Taylor agreed to look after Cronyn and entertain him.

Throughout his long life Allyn Taylor has always been strongly involved in local causes and activities, both social and charitable. At that time he was, as he puts it, "involved in tennis," and that Saturday afternoon the finals of the Western Canada Tennis Tournament were being held in Winnipeg. Cronyn was himself a tennis enthusiast, so they spent an enjoyable afternoon in the stands, after which Taylor invited Cronyn to dinner. Then he realized to his horror that he had only two dollars in his pocket.

One of the first things Taylor had done when he married was to put ten dollars in an envelope and tell his bride, "If ever we're stuck, there's ten dollars in this envelope in the top drawer of my bureau." He now remembered this act of prudence with intense relief, and as he and Cronyn drove off to dinner he made some excuse to stop off at his home, where he dashed upstairs to retrieve the blessed envelope—only to find that it contained an I.O.U. from his wife, who had borrowed the money and forgotten to tell him about it.

That honesty is not only the best but the only acceptable policy is a maxim in any properly run trust company, and so when Taylor rejoined Cronyn he confessed his plight and told him the story. Cronyn roared with laughter, sympathized with his host, and cheerfully paid for dinner. The episode began a close friendship between the two men, and it seems likely that Cronyn, though he had not done much to develop the trust side of the business himself, may have influenced Morley Aylsworth's decision in 1943 to move Taylor into London with the newly minted title of "trust superintendent."

As soon as Taylor and his family had settled in London, Aylsworth assigned him to visit Toronto and report on the company's activities there. The new trust superintendent was appalled at what he found. The Canada Trust office was hidden away at the rear of a dingy building on the fringe of the city's financial district, with seemingly little business to disturb its somnolent atmosphere. Taylor was so concerned at the inadequacy of its operations in such a potentially rich market that he submitted a scathing report in which at one point he said, "You can't do business in Toronto from a peanut stand." In recollection, he told the author, "It was indiscreet on my part. I think I could have said it in a more diplomatic way."

Though the report certainly startled and probably offended Aylsworth's colleagues, Aylsworth himself supported Taylor's initiatives from the start. In Taylor's words, "We started to pull and haul at it." But developing business in a field that depends so much on establishing confidence and making the right connections is not something that can be accomplished overnight.

Allyn Taylor had become a popular and respected citizen of Winnipeg by virtue of his gift for friendship and his unfailing willingness to put his energy and talents at the disposal of various civic endeavours. He now realized that to succeed in his new position he would have to broaden the range of his connections, not only in London but on the national scene. He accordingly welcomed another chore Aylsworth assigned to him soon after his arrival in London. John W. Hobbs, who was a director of the Huron & Erie and vice-president of Canada Trust at the time, was also a Toronto director of the Canadian Pacific Railway. He told Aylsworth one day that D.C. Coleman, the legendary president of the CPR, was going to be in London soon and that he thought it would be nice if the Huron & Erie gave a reception for him. Aylsworth agreed, and asked Taylor to arrange it.

One immediate snag Taylor encountered was in trying to procure a supply of the appropriate refreshments. Under wartime liquor-rationing regulations, only one bottle could be bought at a time, and then only on a personal permit. Taylor was quite willing to sacrifice his own permit in the common weal, and when he approached them so were Aylsworth, Clarke, and Baker. But when he suggested to the teetotaller Dan McEachern that he apply for a liquor permit, McEachern was outraged. "He just about threw me out of his office," Taylor recalled. "But I said, 'Well, sir, I simply came to ask you and I respect your views. But I've been charged with this responsibility and there it is.' I had the feeling that he and

I became better friends after that. We had levelled with each other and it sort of cleared the air, and whereas he never had any use for the trust business I always felt he had for me."

Taylor's considerable powers of persuasion made no dent in McEachern's determination to have no truck with the Devil, but one way or another he managed to round up adequate supplies and the reception was a great success. And Allyn Taylor had begun to broaden the range of his connections. Charlie Clarke's son Bob, who would eventually become the company's general counsel and secretary, left the University of Western Ontario for the army and served overseas for five years before returning to complete his law degree. "I had never heard of Allyn Taylor when I went overseas," he recalled, "but by the time I got home in 1946 he was a going concern. He had only been in town a few years but he knew more people than others who had lived here for fifty years."

Along with his gift for making friends, Taylor clearly had administrative ability and a capacity for leadership. Richard Cronyn retired as trust executive in 1945, though he remained a director and vice-president of the company until shortly before his death from a heart attack in 1948 at the age of fifty-four. Taylor replaced him as trust executive, the top trust department job, and as soon as the young Huron & Erie men began to return from the war he started sizing them up as potential recruits for his assigned task of beefing up the fiduciary side of the business.

On a visit with Aylsworth to the Windsor branch toward the end of 1945, he stopped by a desk and introduced himself to a mortgage clerk he had not met before, Arthur Mingay. Mingay had joined the Windsor branch in 1938, enlisted in the Royal Canadian Air Force in 1941, served four years overseas, and had just returned as a flight lieutenant. When Taylor asked him if he was happy in his job, he did not retreat into affable platitudes. No, he replied; in fact, he was thinking of leaving. He felt his experience and ability justified a more challenging job, and the $1,500 annual salary awarded to all returning servicemen was less than he had been making in the air force. Impressed by his frankness, Taylor had Mingay transferred to head office as a trust understudy, a position in which young trust officers learned their trade under an older man. Like Aylsworth before him, he probably did not realize that he had set his eventual successor's foot on the upward ladder.

Another ex-serviceman, Jack Wilson, who eventually became a director of the company and vice-president in charge of all western branches, had joined the company in 1928 and before enlisting in the army had been assistant mortgage manager in head office. When he returned, as a major, he was put in the debenture department, and Bob Baker could not tell him how long he would be condemned to what Wilson considered penal servitude there. Frustrated, Wilson was contemplating going into business for himself. One day, when he was talking to Bert Blackwell, manager of Canada Trust's main branch, he showed him a list he had compiled of senior officers he had met in the army, men who had returned to their own or their families' businesses and who seemed to him to be potential customers. Allyn Taylor happened to drop in to Blackwell's office during the conversation, and within days Wilson was transferred into the administration and trust department, to his great delight. When he assumed his new duties, Taylor told him, "Look on this as a training ground. What I have in mind is for you eventually to go into developing business for us." And several retired company veterans told the author that Wilson was the best salesman the company ever had.

Charles O'Hara joined the company as a junior straight from high school in the early 1930s and had worked his way up to the post of assistant manager in the debenture department when he left to join the army. He landed in Normandy on D-Day as a forward observation officer for an artillery regiment and came home as a major. Baker put him in to manage the debenture department, and O'Hara was surprised when Allyn Taylor asked him to transfer to Canada Trust, since all his experience had been on the intermediary side. He went to Dan McEachern to ask his advice. McEachern told him to accept the transfer, and if he didn't like the work he would always be welcome to return to the Huron & Erie. "You see, Charlie," he said, "these days, the tail is wagging the dog."

Thus Taylor went about assembling his troops for the campaign ahead. But he found progress disappointingly slow. In 1943, when he arrived in London, Canada Trust's net profit had slumped to $68,163, less than half what it had been in 1939, and the dividend it passed along to its parent company had fallen from its prewar ten per cent to six per cent. By 1946 Taylor's efforts had increased the net profits, but only slightly—to $87,565. The dividend remained at six per cent. Taylor concluded that if the company was going to grow the way he wanted it to, it would have to do so by acquiring other trust companies with worthwhile business volumes.

12

Allyn Taylor Looks to the Future

BEFORE Allyn Taylor moved to London, Canada Trust had bought two smaller trust companies: Consolidated Trusts Corporation, of London, in 1930, and Community Trusts Corporation, of Chatham, in 1938. But these were such modest operations that their absorption passed almost without notice. Taylor had bigger things in mind, and so he was immediately excited when Morley Aylsworth said one day in 1946, "Doug Weldon[1] tells me the London & Western is for sale."

The London & Western Trusts Ltd. had been a neighbour of the Huron & Erie since 1896, and its original board of directors included, as well as John Labatt, the Huron & Erie's president at the time, John Little, and his successor, T.G. Meredith. By 1946, besides its head office in London, it had branches in Toronto, Winnipeg, Saskatoon, Vancouver, and Victoria. But it was purely a fiduciary operation, with no supporting intermediary arm, and it had never fully recovered from the unwise purchase in the mid-1930s of a local trust company in Winnipeg that was widely known

1. Lt. Col. Douglas Black Weldon began life as a newspaperman in his native Maritimes. Legend has it that one night in Halifax when he was left in charge of the office, he found things dull and quit early. Next morning his paper was the only one not to carry the news of the sinking of the *Titanic*. Whether or not that was his reason for abandoning journalism, after winning a Military Cross at Vimy Ridge he turned his attention to the business world, with conspicuous success. He arrived in London in 1922 and became one of the city's leading investment dealers, founding Midland Securities Corporation Ltd. (now Midland Doherty Ltd.) in 1925. He was a mainstay of the University of Western Ontario's board of governors for many years, and his service, and family benefactions, are commemorated in the university's excellent D.B. Weldon library, to which the author owes a special debt of gratitude.

to be floundering at the time the London & Western invested heavily in it. Its net profit in 1945 had been less than $60,000, barely three-quarters of Canada Trust's, and way below the Huron & Erie's. When Aylsworth broached the idea of buying it, his colleagues McEachern, Clarke, and Baker gave it a unanimous thumbs down; they had had enough of the tail wagging the dog. Nor was there any apparent enthusiasm for the purchase among the Huron & Erie directors.

Taylor, however, saw enormous possibilities in the deal. Of course, it would expand Canada Trust's business volume, which he had so far been unable to do with much success. But even more important in his eyes, it would open the door to a vastly enhanced range of those all-important connections, influential men who could direct business his way. London & Western's president was Arthur Meighen, who had gone into the financial world after his second crushing defeat as Conservative prime minister in 1926, and he had recruited a blue-ribbon gallery of the country's business leaders to his board of directors and to the advisory boards that trust companies traditionally maintained in the various centres where they had branches, to give guidance on local conditions and investments.

Vancouver was a particular London & Western stronghold. Meighen's associates there were the cream of the city's business elite. They included the timber magnate H.R. MacMillan, Gordon Farrell, financier and longtime president of B.C. Telephone, and Col. Clarence Wallace, president of Burrard Dry Dock Company Ltd. and a director of numerous other companies, who would soon become lieutenant governor of the province. Even in London, where the Huron & Erie had been ensconced much longer, Meighen had powerful associates, chief among them being London & Western's vice-president, Ray Lawson,[2] who had recently been appointed lieutenant governor of Ontario.

---

2. Ray Lawson's father, a reporter on the old *London Advertiser*, had joined forces with a printer, Harry Jones, to form the printing firm of Lawson & Jones Ltd. Ray was only twenty-four when his father died in 1911, but he took over the company, soon buying out the Jones family and expanding into the packaging and paper-box business. During his long career he accumulated a substantial fortune and numerous directorships, including a vice-presidency of the Royal Bank. In 1953, when his son, Lt. Col. Tom Lawson, was president, an English company, Mardon Son & Hall, bought fifty per cent of the shares of Lawson & Jones, thus acquiring technical control, though in practice it was a partnership

Taylor ached to harness this illustrious team to Canada Trust's wagon, and he pleaded with Aylsworth to overrule his colleagues and take the leap into what he was sure would be a bright future. While the Four Horsemen always worked closely together, there was never any doubt as to who was the boss. On one occasion recalled by a retired employee, McEachern, Clarke, and Baker, while Aylsworth was out of town, sanctioned the expenditure of eight hundred dollars for the long overdue renovation of a dilapidated lunch room in the Winnipeg office. Aylsworth saw the minutes of their meeting on his return and scrawled an emphatic "No" across them. Fortunately for Taylor, and the future of the company, he once again overrode his colleagues and supported Taylor in his several presentations to the board on the merits of the purchase of London & Western.

Just before Christmas 1946 it was announced that the Huron & Erie and Canada Trust had agreed to buy all 12,137 outstanding shares of the London & Western for $175 each, a total of just over $2.1 million. The deal was ratified by the shareholders the following February; it more than doubled Canada Trust's assets—to $107.8 million—and almost tripled the value of the accounts under its administration, from $36.1 million to $92.5 million. This was the first of a string of postwar acquisitions by both the Huron & Erie and Canada Trust, and many retired members of those companies believe it was the most important, in that it laid the groundwork for the tremendous expansion, both in size and sophistication, that eventually enabled what had been a small, albeit solid, regional company to challenge the nation's chartered banks on their own turf.

As Taylor had hoped, the deal brought a group of valuable new directors to Canada Trust. Ray Lawson and Arthur Meighen joined the board as vice-presidents and a couple of years later Lawson also joined the Huron & Erie board. Other London recruits included A.E. Silverwood, head of the famous dairy company, Col. J. Gordon Thompson, founder of Supertest, a gasoline distribution company with several hundred service stations in

---

agreement. In a complex $560 million transaction in 1985 the Canadian branch of the company bought out its English parent, and the Lawson Mardon Group Ltd. is now an international packaging and commercial printing company with more than two-thirds of its assets overseas, in Britain, Ireland, West Germany, and France.

Ontario and Quebec, and Col. J.E. Smallman, whose family had founded a dry-goods store in 1877 which became the city's leading department store. But when Aylsworth and Taylor visited Vancouver to enlist the support of Meighen's associates there, they received a nasty shock.

Their first approach was to Gordon Farrell, who was chairman of the London & Western's advisory board in Vancouver. When Aylsworth said he hoped Farrell would agree to join the Canada Trust board, Farrell replied, "Aylsworth, why should I? Why do you think I would be interested in doing that? You people gave the back of your hand to Vancouver five years ago, and you have no business here now." He was referring, of course, to the Huron & Erie's withdrawal from Vancouver in favour of the Bank of Toronto. Aylsworth hastily explained that that move had been made at government behest, and Taylor joined him in pleading for a second chance and promising that henceforth Canada Trust would consider Vancouver one of its most important priorities. Farrell remained unconvinced, and Taylor saw the golden connections he had envisaged turning to dross. But after more persuasion Farrell agreed to reconsider his decision after a few months, if he detected any signs that the Huron & Erie intended to honour its promise.

When the Huron & Erie had closed its Vancouver office, it had transferred its modest volume of trust business to the Victoria branch. Now it had suddenly inherited a much larger volume of business from the London & Western, including agency accounts such as the management of the considerable assets of H.R. MacMillan and Meighen's other eminent associates in the city. So Canada Trust retained the London & Western's Vancouver staff, including its manager, Col. E.B. Westby, a transplanted Londoner, and in addition it sent out one of its most experienced estate administrators, Bill Baxter, to reinforce them. And, of course, the Huron & Erie reopened its savings business. Within a few months Farrell was satisfied that his and his associates' affairs were still in good hands, and he and H.R. MacMillan both joined the Canada Trust board, where they were joined some years later by their good friend the Honourable Clarence Wallace.

The crisis had passed, and it rapidly became apparent that Aylsworth had backed the right horse in Allyn Taylor. By 1948 Canada Trust's net profit had risen to $125,719, almost double what it had been when Taylor had arrived in London, and the six-per-cent dividend it had paid for the previous seven years had risen to seven. It was clear that Taylor was now the dominant force in Canada Trust, and the title of assistant general manager was added to his previous designation as trust executive.

By 1948 the Huron & Erie had also begun to recover its momentum. The previous year the "real estate in hand" item on its balance sheet had read "Nil" for the first time in many years: the company had finally managed to shed all the properties it had inherited during the depression. Its 1948 profit was $414,014, the highest it had been since 1934, but still a far cry from 1930's record $593,495. In fact, it is an indication of how close the company had come to disaster that the 1948 figure was only a few thousand dollars higher than it had been in 1914, though the company's total assets had grown since then from $16.4 million to $52 million. Nevertheless, in 1948 it managed to pay its first five-per-cent dividend since 1936.

Allyn Taylor had been brought to London to develop Canada Trust's fiduciary business, and until then he had had no experience on the intermediary side of the business. But it was clear by now that Morley Aylsworth set great store by his advice. And Taylor, much younger than the Horsemen and more of a go-getter, was convinced that if the company was going to prosper it must grow, and that the quickest way to grow was by carefully chosen acquisitions in areas where it was so far not represented. Aylsworth evidently accepted his view, because in the summer of 1948 he entered into negotiations for the purchase of the Guelph and Ontario Investment and Savings Society.

Incorporated in 1876, the Guelph and Ontario, though much smaller than the Huron & Erie, was very similar: it owned eighty-six per cent of a subsidiary, the Guelph Trust Company, and it had built up an excellent reputation in its own rich area. It had $6.5 million in assets and had paid a six-per-cent dividend for some years. Curiously enough, it too had almost gone under during the depression, at which time it had $750,000 invested in Saskatchewan, and almost the same amount split between Alberta and Manitoba. Its position became so precarious that one day in September 1927, its president, George D. Forbes, telephoned Hume Cronyn seeking an interview. Cronyn agreed to receive him that same day and Dan McEachern was present at their meeting. Morley Aylsworth was out of town but McEachern wrote to him that evening saying that Forbes "acted in a most canny manner but I think he wants to do business with us." Forbes had admitted to Cronyn that his company had "problem cases" in the west, and McEachern told Aylsworth, "The Guelph and Ontario board are prepared to take a trimming on their western stuff—it's just a matter of amount. Apparently there has been much slackness in their investment management."

As the negotiations progressed, Aylsworth and Charlie Clarke were despatched to examine the Guelph and Ontario's western loans. Aylsworth was so disturbed by what he found that he called off the inspection and wrote to McEachern saying, "We thought the Hamilton Provident business was perhaps below the mark, but their investments were really gilt edge bonds compared with these." Company records do not show whether Forbes, after his approach to the Huron & Erie was rebuffed, tried unsuccessfully to find other suitors. But at any rate the company survived, and the Huron & Erie bought it for $2.2 million in 1949.

The Huron & Erie always tried to retain the staffs of any companies it acquired, partly for humanitarian reasons but also to preserve the continuity of the business. Accordingly, the Guelph and Ontario's manager, H.L. Benallick, and his staff became part of the Huron & Erie, and its directors were invited to constitute an advisory board for the area. But meshing one company's activities into another's can be difficult, because of what has today come to be called the "corporate culture," which differs from one organization to another. Aylsworth had probably never heard that phrase, but he was not impressed with what he perceived to be a laxity in the Guelph and Ontario's operation that was quite foreign to the ethos of the Huron & Erie. So Benallick for a while had to suffer frequent incursions into his territory by "visiting firemen" from head office, one of whom was Charlie O'Hara.

Morley Aylsworth seemed from his outward appearance to be a formidable, rather stern man. But those who came to know him well ascribed his forbidding exterior and apparent aloofness to an innate shyness. Certainly he hated to have to exercise his undoubted authority in personal confrontations. One day he called in O'Hara and said, "Charlie, I want you to go up to Guelph and lay down the law. When I was there last week there were papers all over the floor of their vault. Tell them to get it cleaned up." O'Hara felt like replying, "You're the boss. If you were there last week, why didn't *you* tell 'em?" But no one talked like that to Mr. Aylsworth.

Even with the addition of what now became the Guelph branch, the Huron & Erie still had only sixteen branches across the country, far fewer than Allyn Taylor thought it should have. He found an ally in Jack Wilson, who had been appointed manager of the Hamilton branch in 1949. Taylor had recruited Wilson to Canada Trust after the war with the idea that he would be assigned to developing new business, and once installed in his new post that is exactly what Wilson started to do, not only for Canada Trust but also for the parent Huron & Erie. Always alert to opportunities, he saw no reason to confine his sales effort to Hamilton, and he began to expand the company's activities to the east, into the Niagara Peninsula. Recognizing that this area occupied a strategic position between the United States and Ontario's developing "Golden Triangle," he foresaw a huge expansion of industry and influx of population.

As he circulated around the area, Wilson's finely tuned antennae detected signals that a couple of major Toronto-based trust companies had also recognized the potential of the Niagara Peninsula and were planning to open branches in St. Catharines to garner its business. He recommended to head office that the Huron & Erie forestall them and, encouraged by the volume of business he had already generated thereabouts, Aylsworth and the board agreed with his assessment and sanctioned the opening of the company's first branch in St. Catharines in 1951.

Four years before this, a well drilled by the old London company Imperial Oil in a wheat-field at Leduc, just south of Edmonton, had struck it rich and had catapulted Alberta into its postwar oil boom. By 1951 liquid gold looked like a better bet than the golden wheat that had almost brought the Huron & Erie down a couple of decades earlier; so in the same year that it opened in St. Catharines in the east, the company supplemented its old-established Edmonton branch with a new office in Calgary.

A year later Dan McEachern finally retired, after fifty years' service with the company. Charlie Clarke had gone three years earlier. Bob Baker was nearing the customary retiring age of sixty-five; Morley Aylsworth was long past it. An infusion of new blood was clearly overdue, and Allyn Taylor was made assistant general manager of the Huron & Erie as well as Canada Trust. In that capacity he relied closely on McEachern's successor as secretary, a brilliant lawyer named Percy Collyer who had become his confidant as he struggled without much encouragement from the old guard to develop the trust side of the business. Younger associates marvelled at Collyer's ability to sit at his desk for a while in silent contemplation, then summon his secretary and dictate a complicated legal document as though he were reading it from a book. He died tragically early from cancer, but those who remember him say he could easily have held his own with any of the leading corporate lawyers in Toronto; however, he preferred to remain in his native London.

In his new capacity one of Taylor's first recommendations to Morley Aylsworth was that they send Jack Wilson out to take hold of the Vancouver branch. The business there had not developed as much as Ayslworth and Taylor had hoped it would when they pleaded with Meighen's associates to join their board. Colonel Westby, the London & Western's manager, had resented the advent on the scene of the Huron & Erie, and despite an attempt to placate him by making him superintendent of B.C. branches, of which there were only two at that time, he seemed to Taylor to be dragging his feet. As manager of the Vancouver branch, Bill Baxter was doing his best to develop the business, but he was an intensely religious, mild-mannered man who was no match for Colonel Westby in the kind of in-fighting that the old soldier seemed to enjoy. Westby still had considerable influence with the advisory board and H.R. MacMillan, in particular, whose account was the biggest the company had anywhere, was becoming restive.

Baxter welcomed Wilson's arrival with relief and willingly relinquished the title of manager to him, working on happily under him until his retirement. One of the first things Wilson noticed in his new job was that no one on the staff ever entered or left the office through the front door. Puzzled, he asked the accountant why. The accountant explained that Westby had had a rule that only he was to use the front door; the staff were to use the back door opening on to the lobby of the building. Baxter had apparently thought it unwise to provoke a confrontation by revoking this rule, but Wilson told the accountant to draft a memorandum right away telling the staff he didn't want them to use the lobby door unless they were going to the washroom. "Let's make this place look as though there's some life around here," he said.

Under Wilson's forceful direction, new life there certainly was. He rapidly won the confidence of the advisory board, and with the business looking up he was able to persuade Aylsworth in 1953 that the company should put up a new building on a site he had found across Howe Street from the location it had inherited from the London & Western. The branch moved into it before the end of the year; and the staff continued to use its front door.

When Wilson arrived in Vancouver, the Huron & Erie had only 105 savings accounts and $1.4 million in mortgage investments in British Columbia. Six years later, by which time he was assistant general manager in charge of all western branches, it had $14 million in savings deposits and more than $15 million in mortgage investments. And the value of the estates, trusts, and agencies being administered by Canada Trust in the province exceeded $63 million—more than twenty-three per cent of the company's entire business across the country.

Taylor next turned his attention to the Toronto branch which, while it had now outgrown the "peanut stand" status he had accorded it a decade earlier, was still in his view far from living up to its full potential. Toronto had not yet displaced Montreal as the undisputed centre of financial power in Canada, but it was obvious that there was plenty of trust business there to be tapped. Canada Trust's operations were still largely confined to the personal trust business; it was unable to break into the corporate trust field because it lacked the close ties with the chartered banks enjoyed by its larger rivals.

At that time probably half of all the trust business in Canada was handled by the Royal Trust and the Montreal Trust. Though not owned by the banks, both these companies had close links with them through a system of interlocking directorships—the Royal Trust, confusingly enough to outsiders, with the Bank of Montreal, and the Montreal Trust with the Royal Bank. Similarly, the Toronto-Dominion Bank had effective control of Canada Permanent, and the Commerce Bank, with allies, controlled National Trust. Bank directors formed powerful contingents on the boards of these favoured trust companies and often served as their chairmen and presidents. And naturally enough, given the old-boy network that was an even more potent force then than now, they were willing and able to bring huge chunks of business with them.[3]

---

3. This cosy arrangement was brought to an end, formally at least, by the 1967 Bank Act, which prevented chartered banks from owning more than ten per cent of a trust company and prohibited bank directors from sitting on trust companies' boards.

Lacking a high-powered bank connection to feed Canada Trust lucrative corporate business, Taylor nevertheless thought he scented an opportunity to develop a field that had not so far seemed to interest most trust companies: acting as trustees for and administering corporate pension funds and investing their assets so as to ensure their growth. The Huron & Erie had established its own pension fund years before, in 1913, but in 1954 many otherwise quite reputable companies either made no provision at all for their employees' old age or relied on joint employer-employee contributions to an annuity scheme run by the federal government. Taylor therefore called in Arthur Mingay, who had graduated from his understudy role and was now a full-fledged trust officer in Chatham, and asked him to move to Toronto and head the company's embryo pension trust division. Mingay protested that he didn't know anything about pensions, but Taylor replied, "I know you don't, but spend two or three months learning what it's all about and then go to work."

Mingay spent his first three months in Toronto talking to actuaries, insurance people, investment managers—anyone who knew anything about pensions. Then he set out to look for business. It did not come easily. He knew that the "establishment" companies such as Montreal Trust had already landed the big fish, the pension funds of major corporations such as General Motors, General Electric, and Stelco, and so he concentrated his effort on smaller companies with perhaps two or three hundred employees. But his first success, when it came in 1955, was with a union rather than a company: he won the account of the newly formed Toronto Printing Pressmen's Fund, and after that the business started to roll in.

Originally, Mingay's job was to generate the business, not to administer it: if he obtained an account in Chatham, say, it would be administered by the Chatham trust department. But the trust officers in the branches could not be expected to master all the intricacies of what was at that time a rapidly developing field, and as Mingay brought in more and more accounts it was decided to centralize all pension business in Toronto.

Mingay next introduced to the industry what became known as the pooled fund concept, though he credits the idea to a pension consultant now retired in Vancouver, Cyril Woods. When a small or medium-sized company decided to introduce a pension plan, the amount of money available for investment in its first year might be only a few thousand dollars. This did not permit those managing it to observe one of the cardinal principles of safe investment: diversification. Mingay suggested to Aylsworth and Taylor that the company should offer smaller companies the opportunity to pool their funds with those of other companies to form an accumulation of capital that could be put to better use than merely buying a trust company certificate. His plan was attended by a variety of complications, both legal and financial, and at first the directors were reluctant to approve it. But when Morley Aylsworth decided he wanted to do something he usually won the day, and within a short time Arthur Mingay had a new vehicle to sell to his potential clients.

In 1956 the federal government let it be known that it was considering legislation to introduce tax incentives to encourage the self-employed and others not covered by group pension plans to accumulate savings for their retirement. The Trust Companies Association, among other bodies, was invited to submit its views on the proposed legislation. By now Mingay's expertise in the pension field was widely acknowledged, and he and Fraser Coate, head of the Montreal Trust's pension department, journeyed to Ottawa to present the Association's views to the Minister of Finance, Walter Harris.

Although they were competitors, Coate and Mingay were good friends, and Coate had been one of Mingay's tutors when he set about learning the pension business. But they disagreed about the potential for what became known as Registered Retirement Savings Plans. Coate felt that the coming legislation would be of more interest to professional associations than to individuals. The Canadian public, he thought, was slow to adopt new ideas, preferring to stick with what was tried and true. Mingay thought otherwise. He saw enormous potential in the government's plan and was so sure the legislation would be passed that he went to London and told Percy Collyer he wanted to jump into the race as soon as the starting gun was fired.

As a result of his discussions with officials in Ottawa and his own study of the subject, Mingay was able to make an educated guess about the shape the government's scheme would eventually take, and he spent a couple of days explaining his ideas to Collyer. His briefing completed, Collyer leaned back in his chair, his eyes closed in contemplation, while Mingay waited impatiently for some reaction. Suddenly Collyer summoned his secretary and dictated the legal text for a Canada Trust individual retirement plan. The company was thus able to introduce RRSPs as soon as the legislation was passed—so quickly, indeed, that some of Mingay's competitors mistakenly assumed he had been privy to inside information from Ottawa.

At first it seemed that Fraser Coate's reservations had been justified. Even though Canada Trust had been first in the field with its plan, Canadians were slow to sign up for RRSPs. For several years the company opened only four or five hundred plans across the country each year. But eventually the idea caught on, and by 1988 Canada Trust could boast that it had more RRSP accounts than any other financial institution in the country: 571,700 plans totalling $6.8 billion.

When Arthur Mingay entered the field in 1954, the pension assets administered by Canada Trust totalled only $17 million. By 1958, thanks to his efforts, they totalled $40 million, and no one was surprised in 1959 when Mingay was appointed assistant general manager in charge of all the company's activities in the Toronto area.

13

The Old Order Changes

BOB Baker, as the youngest of the Horsemen, the four-man team that had nursed the Huron & Erie through the depression and the difficult war years, might reasonably have expected to cap his career with a term as president. But Morley Aylsworth, his senior by ten years, showed no disposition to relinquish the reins. And when Aylsworth was finally persuaded by his fellow directors to bow out at the age of seventy-five, early in 1958,[1] Baker had already retired. As a sort of consolation prize, he spent his last year with the company, 1956, as one of two "joint general managers," the other being Allyn Taylor, and he was later appointed to the board of directors.

It had long been obvious that Allyn Taylor was Aylsworth's heir-apparent, and when he took over as president and general manager he was already becoming known on the national scene. He had been president of the Trust Companies Association of Ontario in 1949 and of the Trust Companies Association of Canada in 1955, and the work he did for both these bodies, and the speeches he made while in office, had won him considerable respect in business circles.

Aylsworth's retirement provided the new president with an appropriate opportunity to review the company's recent progress. He told the shareholders early in 1958 that in the ten years between 1947 and 1957 the money deposited by the public with the Huron & Erie and Canada Trust had increased from $56 million to $135 million. Mortgage investments made possible by

1. Colonel Ibbotson Leonard retired from the chairmanship of both companies at the same time, at the age of seventy-eight. He was succeeded in both posts by Verschoyle Cronyn, who had joined the board twenty-four years earlier.

those deposits had increased from $27 million to $107 million, and the personal trust business had increased from $92 million to $267 million. The combined assets of the two companies now exceeded $157 million. The Huron & Erie's net profit for 1957 was $703,343, and Canada Trust's had risen to a satisfying $335,450—a combined total of more than a million dollars.

It was a firm base on which to build, and Taylor was determined so to do. One of his first acts as president was to summon the first management meeting in the company's history. In May 1958 senior managers from head office and all seventeen branches across the country gathered in London and were greeted by a pep talk from their new boss, in which he nevertheless sounded a note of caution. "It should be our basic resolve," he told his troops, "to constantly improve our standard of performance and not to place undue emphasis on growth as such. One of the great North American heresies is that what is bigger is *ipso facto* better. Bigger and better are not synonymous terms and unless the group of us around this table are constantly on guard, we're going to find ourselves growing constantly bigger without the improvement in standards of service to the public and dollar returns to ourselves and the shareholders that are really what we are working toward."

In 1957 the company had become the first financial institution in the country to introduce a management incentive plan. Explaining it in his last annual report, Aylsworth had said "it should not be confused with a bonus or profit-sharing plan in the ordinary sense." Its purpose was "to provide incentive for senior employees who, through the exercise of initiative and responsibility, are in a position to make decisions which will have a direct bearing upon the companies' net profits. . . . No employee, no matter how senior his position may be, will share in the plan as a matter of right."

The two companies now had 650 employees across the country, and during the first year of the plan's operation 93 of them had shared incentive payments amounting to $75,304. Taylor now gave his assembled senior managers a new incentive to excel. "We are going to give increased emphasis to branch office autonomy," he told them, "because only by doing this can we ensure the highest calibre of branch management. Within the framework of general company policy, we are going to give increasing authority to branch office managers, but that can only run on a two-way track, and on the other track in return we are entitled to a certain standard of results."

As to junior staff, the company was beginning to replace the old haphazard system of having experienced employees show newcomers the ropes. It had recently introduced a training program that included regular lecture periods, formalized teller training, study courses, and staff conferences. To emphasize the importance attached to this new departure Taylor had invited Bill Hall, the personnel administrator, to explain his plans to the assembled managers. Through the years ahead, the program Hall initiated was constantly developed and refined until its competitors generally conceded that one of Canada Trust's major strengths was its excellently trained staff.

In his welcoming address to his managers Taylor set out some new corporate policies he was introducing. One of these was a change in the company's method of generating funds for investment. Hitherto its borrowings from the public had been approximately evenly divided between "call money," or savings and deposit accounts that could be withdrawn on demand, and "term money," funds locked up in debentures and guaranteed trust certificates for specified periods, in return for higher interest rates. "Our costing figures," Taylor said, "show that call money is by far the more profitable form of borrowing and we intend to shape a course in future that will provide two-thirds of our borrowings from this source."

In other words, the company was going to become even more like the banks. Taylor had realized for some time that, since the company's intermediary operation was the most profitable segment of its business, his real competitors were the banks, not the other large trust companies; some of these latter did not even have intermediary operations at that time, lest they impinge on the activities of their bank allies. Taylor knew full well, of course, that the banks were formidable competitors, because of their thousands of branches across the country—hence his determination to increase the coverage of his own branch network.

In any financial institution, garnering in money from the public is only one aspect of the business. That money must also be promptly and profitably invested to create the all-important "spread." Here again, Taylor had some words of caution for his managers. "I am convinced," he said, "that one of our biggest problems in the years ahead is going to be that of finding an outlet for our funds."

Badly stung during the depression, the company had virtually stopped making farm loans, particularly out west. And as farmers recovered from the depression and paid off their debts, the proportion of the company's funds invested in farm mortgages had dwindled. By 1958 it was down to only $2 million, and ninety per cent of the company's investments were in housing. But by that time, also, the tremendous demand for new housing created by the suspension of building during the war and the wave of postwar immigration was showing signs of being met. In the years ahead, Taylor said, "mortgage competition will increase, our borrowings will continue to increase, and mortgage funds available in pension accounts and various other accounts in the personal trust department will also increase. We shall have to intensify our aggressiveness in the loaning field accordingly."

Consequently, he went on, "we are going to actively seek larger loans than has been our policy in the past. I believe that provided a loan meets all standards of quality, we can consider it in size up to a maximum of half of one per cent of our total loaning volume. In other words, we today have over a hundred million dollars in mortgage investments and therefore I believe we are entirely sound in considering loans up to half a million dollars without offending the principle of diversification."

There are obviously enormous economies to be gained from lending half a million dollars in one transaction, rather than, say, in fifty smaller mortgages of ten thousand dollars each. And Taylor disclosed that only the previous week the company had agreed to make the largest single loan in its history: $400,000 for a shopping centre near St. Catharines. That this new corporate policy proved successful is indicated by his decision a year or so later to set up a separate commercial and industrial division in Canada Trust "to formalize activity in the purchase and sale of businesses and in the development of real estate investment situations of all descriptions."

As another part of the new policy, Taylor said, "We intend to seek new loaning fields in promising centres where we are not doing business, such as Ottawa, Kingston, Peterborough and the Head of the Lakes." The idea here was that the company could set up offices that were not "full-service" branches, in that they would not have savings departments and full trust services but would

The first president of the Huron & Erie Savings and Loan Society, the little company formed in 1864 which became today's giant Canada Trust, was Adam Hope. A wholesaler of dry goods, hardware, and groceries in London, Canada West, Hope later moved to Hamilton and established a similar business – and another trust company – in the city. In later life he became a senator.

UWO LIBRARY

The Cronyn connection. Typical of the continuity prized by the old Huron & Erie and the present Canada Trust, four generations of London's eminent Cronyn family have maintained an unbroken connection on the board of directors. Family patriarch, the Reverend Benjamin Cronyn (opposite, top left), arrived in London from Ireland in 1832. Thanks to his energetic proselytizing, and some shrewd real estate deals, his church prospered and he was chosen the first bishop of the Anglican diocese of Huron in 1857. Benjamin's son Verschoyle (opposite, top right), a lawyer born just a few months after the family arrived in London, was the moving spirit behind the company's formation and served on its board for more than forty years. Verschoyle's son Hume (opposite, bottom), gave up his law career to become first general manager and later president of the company, a position which he held until his death in 1933. One of Hume's sons, Verschoyle Philip (above left), a World War I fighter pilot and World War II RCAF administrative officer, was first elected to the board in 1929 and retired as its chairman in 1968. His son, John B. Cronyn (above right), after wartime army service in Europe, became a qualified brewmaster and long-time executive of another famous London company, John Labatt Limited. He has been a director of Canada Trust since 1972.

This farmhouse near Bayfield, on the eastern shore of Lake Huron, incorporates the original log cabin occupied by Edward Talbott, who took out the first mortgage ever granted by the Huron & Erie. The seventy acres on which the house stands were bought from John Galt's Canada Company in 1860 by a settler named Niniam Woods. Two years later, Woods sold the property to Talbott, who applied to the newly formed Huron & Erie for a mortgage on it in 1864. The society's valuator estimated the property was worth $1,250, and the directors, establishing the conservative policy that would characterize the company in future years, granted Talbott's loan of $400, repayable in five annual instalments of $144.32 – a total of $571.60. Talbott paid off the mortgage on the due date, in 1869, and farmed the property until he sold it in 1882. It has passed through several hands since then, and a local real estate agent estimates that, had it not become part of a much larger farm, it would now be worth about $100,000.

UWO LIBRARY

The most remarkably versatile man ever to hold the post, William Saunders was president of the Huron & Erie from 1879 to 1886. Apprenticed to a London druggist as a boy, Saunders taught himself science, became Canada's foremost authority on agriculture and horticulture, and was chosen by the federal government to establish the country's experimental farm system.

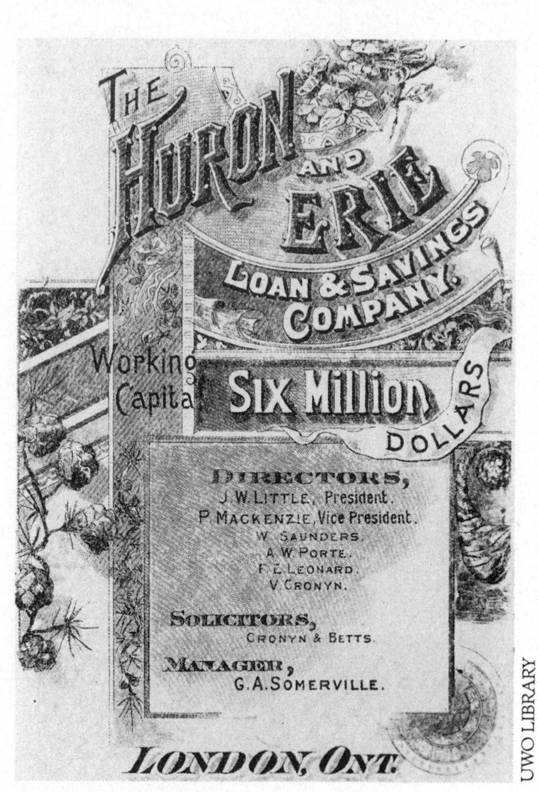

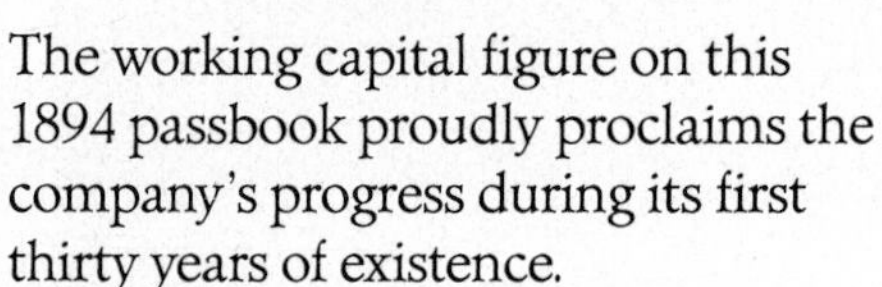
The working capital figure on this 1894 passbook proudly proclaims the company's progress during its first thirty years of existence.

UWO LIBRARY

Detail taken from a 1895 staff photograph shows George Somerville (seated), general manager of the Huron & Erie for eighteen years. Standing behind him is Harry Givins, who would later open the company's second branch office, in Regina, and go on to be superintendent of all western branches.

UWO LIBRARY

Autocratic Thomas Graves Meredith, London's city solicitor for fifty-one years, headed the Huron & Erie almost as long. First elected president in 1909, he occupied that post, or the chairmanship, until the directors forced him out in 1943, in his ninetieth year.

The building on London's Richmond Street (right) was occupied by the Huron & Erie from 1871 to 1931. A contemporary photograph of another stretch of Richmond Street (below) shows how London looked at the time. This building was replaced in 1931 by the new headquarters, shown here in an aerial view (opposite, top) and a contemporary drawing (opposite, bottom).

THE HURON & ERIE MORTGAGE CORPORATION
HURON & ERIE BLDG

By 1912, when this staff photograph was taken, women employees were no longer quite the novelty they had been only a few years earlier, and their responsibilities were to increase during the Great War that would soon follow.

Three of the "Four Horsemen" who shepherded the Huron & Erie through the difficult years of the Depression and World War II, photographed at an anniversary party in 1942. Morley Aylsworth (centre), then general manager and later president, cuts a cake commemorating his first forty years with the company. Dan McEachern (left) joined the company two weeks after Aylsworth. Charlie Clarke (right) joined two years earlier, in 1900.

With mutton-chop whiskers donned for the day, president Allyn Taylor (right) hoists a toast with savings supervisor Milton Templeman at the company's 1964 centennial celebrations.

Canada Trust marketers drew attention to the opening of a new Toronto headquarters building in 1967 by wrapping it with a broad ribbon. President Allyn Taylor (right) and Arthur Mingay, then assistant general manager in charge of the Toronto region, permitted themselves to be hoisted in a crane bucket to perform the ceremony of cutting the ribbon.

At the 1973 annual meeting, retiring president Allyn Taylor (left) raises the hand of his successor, Arthur Mingay.

The changing of the guard: early in 1978, Allyn Taylor (right) retired as chairman, and Walter Bean (left) retired as deputy chairman and vice-president. Arthur Mingay (second from left) became chairman and Merv Lahn took over as president.

Canada Trust's gung-ho marketing gimmicks raised eyebrows in more sedate financial circles. Johnny Cash was persuaded to lend his name to the company's electronic banking machines, and as they were introduced to the various branches in the early 1980s, the singer gave cut-rate concerts for employees and customers. He and his wife June Carter also posed happily for photographs with staff members and guests.

Twin towers housing the London head office (above) opened for business in November 1974. Model of projected BCE Place in the heart of Toronto's financial district (opposite) shows Canada Trust Tower (on left), scheduled for occupation in mid-1990.

YONGE STREET

Dynamic team at the helm of today's still-growing Canada Trust: Merv Lahn (centre), chairman and chief executive officer of the parent CT Financial Services Inc., is flanked by chief lieutenant Peter Maurice (right), president and chief operating officer, CT Financial Services Inc., and Jack Speake (left), president, the Canada Trust Company.

restrict themselves to making mortgage loans. These could be accommodated in lower-rent upstairs offices without the expense of building and staffing full-service branches.

Taylor also announced that the company was considering extending this policy— the establishment of what might be termed "part-service" branches—to its borrowing operations. The expense of building and staffing full-service branches obviously limited the rate at which the company could grow. Its experienced comptroller, Hugh Hutton, Taylor told the other managers, had done some extremely valuable work examining what it cost to operate a branch office and what such an office could reasonably expect to earn. "These figures," he went on, "show that if we handle the expense problem realistically and if we choose our locations properly so as to insure a minimum borrowing volume, we can establish simplified borrowing offices that will be on an almost immediate paying basis." These would be headed by "a manager who can intelligently discuss our other departments in a general way but with no attempt at facilities for loaning, trust development or even safe deposit boxes." The offices would be set up in rented premises "at least until their operation over a period of years has established the wisdom of purchasing our own premises."

Plans were at that moment being completed for an office of that kind at New Westminster in British Columbia, "on the strong recommendation of Jack Wilson and the Vancouver advisory board." It did not take Wilson long to get his advisory board on side, and the office opened a year later. Harold Clark, soon to be replaced as assistant general manager in Toronto by Arthur Mingay, was seeking a site for a similar office there.

Work was also under way on a new office which had been Taylor's idea, but which he had had great difficulty persuading Aylsworth and the board to accept. Some time before Aylsworth's retirement, Taylor had heard that there was a building site for sale near his home—and even nearer to the main gates of the University of Western Ontario's campus. He immediately realized that it was a prime site for a new branch. He knew that there was no bank branch within easy each of the campus, and that the university's enrolment was approaching the forty-five hundred mark, which meant that a thousand or fifteen hundred students would be graduating every year and fanning out across the country to begin their careers. If the Huron & Erie could establish a satisfactory connection with them during their student years, and if it took pains to follow up that connection, they could become valuable customers for years into the future.

For some reason, on this occasion Taylor's enthusiasm failed to win over Aylsworth. "I just don't see it, Allyn," he said. Neither, when he approached them, did Charlie Clarke or Bob Baker, who, while now retired, still kept closely in touch with the company's business. Help came from an unexpected quarter: Dan McEachern. McEachern had long since forgotten his outrage at Taylor's audacious suggestion that he take out a liquor permit, and he immediately recognized the validity of Taylor's case. He was an exceptionally shrewd investor himself, and even though he too had retired and hated to leave his beloved garden, he journeyed down town to exercise his considerable influence with Aylsworth on Taylor's behalf. The new building opened in 1958, and before long the London-University branch amply justified Taylor's hopes for it.

Another initiative Taylor exercised when he took the helm was to set about changing the company's "signature," the name by which it was known to the public. The Huron & Erie, of course, had been a familiar name to the people of southwestern Ontario for almost a hundred years now. But Taylor privately tended to agree with Dorothy Harvie, wife of Calgary Canada Trust director Eric Harvie, who once complained to him that "it sounds like a railroad—the Atchson, Topeka and Santa Fe, or something."

The annual reports of both the parent company and its subsidiary had for some years now been combined in one document, but its cover always spelled out their names in full: The Huron & Erie Mortgage Corporation and The Canada Trust Company. The two companies could not be merged into one without great and costly internal and legal difficulties. Taylor decided instead to try to meld the two names into one corporate image. The first annual report under his presidency, for the year 1957, bore the much shorter name "Huron & Erie–Canada Trust." His idea was that once the public became accustomed to this format, the order in which the two companies were listed could be reversed. The process took a few years, but in 1962 the company began billing itself as "Canada Trust–Huron & Erie," a more fitting reflection of its now national scope. Very soon it became known everywhere as simply "Canada Trust."

The annual reports for those years reflect Taylor's campaign to give the staid old Huron & Erie a more modern, dynamic image. Under Aylsworth the shareholders were presented with nothing more by way of a report than a small booklet containing a few pages of figures, printed in black and white and unembellished with photographs, illustrations, or explanatory charts. It did not even include explanatory remarks by the president, and any remarks Aylsworth considered the shareholders were entitled to at their annual meetings he kept brief.

The first report under Taylor's new regime, in contrast, was much larger and was printed in colour on glossy paper. It contained coloured charts showing the company's progress, an itemized and illustrated list of the many services it offered to the public, photographs of some of the new Canada Trust buildings that were already beginning to spring up all over the place, and an explanation of the company's new staff training program, accompanied by photographs of some of the classes at work. The following year's report contained samples of lively advertisements that were appearing across the country to familiarize the public with the new "Canada Trust-Huron & Erie" name and to solicit business. Later still, imaginative illustrative methods were adopted to further explain the company's business—drawings showing graduated stacks of coins, for instance, graphically depicting "Where each dollar came from" and "Where each dollar went." Before many years had gone by, the Canada Trust annual reports began to earn a long string of national awards for their informative and attractive presentations.

From the first, Taylor included in his reports a message to the shareholders, outlining and explaining the salient developments of the year under review. He expanded on the printed text at the annual meetings, not confining himself to company affairs but making general comments on the country's economic condition and prospects. Many of these comments, which were not always complimentary to the government of the day, dealt with taxation. "We learn a lot about taxes in the trust business," he once said. But rather than indulge in a blanket condemnation of taxes in general and of profligate government spending, as some businessmen liked to do, Taylor preferred to point out in his reasonable way various specific tax anomalies and inequities that the government could, and often did, correct. In 1961, for example, he pointed out that an unintended result of new federal estate-tax legislation introduced a couple of years earlier was to subject some Canadian residents to double taxation in the United States and Canada.

Some of his comments have the same validity today as when he made them, almost thirty years ago. Early in 1960 he told the shareholders: "Highly favourable expectations for Canadian business activity in 1960 are overshadowed by one enormous problem that confronts Canada in the next decade. That problem is export markets. Despite our recent growth and development we are still an export nation, directly dependent for our continued prosperity on our ability to meet international competition in the sale of raw materials and surplus goods in world markets. . . . To the extent that we indulge in inflation and increase production costs we make the export problem more difficult. In our individual affairs we know we can't do business if we price ourselves out of a market, and yet collectively as a nation that is just what we have been doing. We need better general understanding of the dangers inherent in such a course."

By the end of 1962, five years after Taylor took over as president, the number of company branches across the country had doubled, to thirty-four, the largest number maintained by any company in the trust industry. There were now four branches doing business at the old "peanut stand" in Toronto and three in Vancouver, and with the addition of a branch in Halifax in 1961 the company could for the first time boast that its activities extended from coast to coast.

Two of those branches, in southern Alberta, had been brought into the company by Taylor himself, in a deal he particularly likes to recall. The British Canadian Trust Company had received its charter in 1901, before Alberta became a province. Headquartered in Lethbridge, 225 kilometres south of Calgary, it had one branch office, at Medicine Hat, a little over 160 kilometres to the east. Though it had no savings department, it had a virtual monopoly of the personal trust business in southern Alberta and was considered the "crown jewel" of regional trust companies in the west. Its reputation and popularity were such that several national companies had tried to buy it, but its president and majority owner, Roy Davidson, had rebuffed all offers.

One day toward the end of 1960 Taylor was having lunch in Calgary with one of Canada Trust's directors, the lawyer and oil millionaire Eric Harvie. The company had just opened another branch in Red Deer, between Calgary and Edmonton, and Taylor figured that if only it could break into southern Alberta it would have blanket coverage of the province. As they chatted, he told Harvie, "I'd love to meet that character Davidson in Lethbridge." Harvie excused himself to go to the phone, returned a few minutes later, and said, "He'll see you tomorrow." The following afternoon Taylor presented himself at Davidson's imposing white house in Lethbridge, to be greeted by a lean, straight-backed man standing over six feet tall who, when his white hair was covered by the ten-gallon hat he invariably wore, looked every inch the Hollywood cowboy. In fact, Roy Davidson was one of the most respected lawyers in Alberta and a rich man; he ran British Canadian as a hobby.

As he ushered Taylor into his den, Davidson asked, "What do you drink?" Taylor saw a table bearing a decanter, some glasses, and a few bottles, and had a sudden inspiration. "Do I see a little bourbon there?" he asked. Davidson looked at him keenly and said, "I thought you were another damn easterner." The drinks poured, the two sat and chatted for a while. Then Davidson suddenly said, "So, Taylor, you want to buy my trust company?" Taylor admitted that he would certainly like to discuss merging it with Canada Trust. "You don't mean merging—you mean buying it," said his host, in his no-nonsense way. "I suppose you know all your competitors have tried and they haven't succeeded. What makes you think *you* will?"

By now Taylor was not at all sure that he would, but he made his pitch. Davidson rose to pour another round and when he sat down again he said, "Well, I guess the timing is right"—he was in his seventies. "It's got to happen sooner or later. I'd sooner deal with a westerner than somebody else, so if you'll make me a fair offer, I'll accept it. I'll open my books to you, but if you make me an offer that is trying to steal this company from me, then you'll never hear from me again. That's it."

Taylor almost floated away from the house, partly because of the bourbons—few ordinary men could keep up with Roy Davidson in that department—and partly because of his excitement at the prospect of making a deal. The examination of British Canadian's books was completed by mid-December and Taylor took the figures to his executive committee, where he ran into some unexpected opposition. When he told the committee what he thought the company was worth, one director asked, "So what are you going to offer?" Taylor replied, "Just that." Incredulous, the director said, "Surely your last figure isn't going to be your first?", and there were murmurs of agreement around the board table. Doggedly, Taylor stuck to his guns. "I know the man I'm dealing with," he said. "If we don't make him the offer he's expecting, we'll never hear from him again."

Somewhat reluctantly the committee sanctioned the offer. Davidson was spending Christmas at the Empress Hotel in Victoria when Taylor reached him by telephone and quoted the price the company was prepared to pay. There was a long silence, and then Davidson said, "You've kept your word, so I'll keep mine. When do you want to close?" Early in January 1961 it was announced that Canada Trust had bought all 2,000 outstanding shares of British Canadian for $303 each, a total of $606,000.

Recalling Davidson with obvious affection, Taylor told the author: "He told me later, not once but several times, that if we had attempted to play footsie with him and had offered ten or fifteen per cent less, even though we were prepared to go up, we would never have heard from him again. And I knew that was true, because he was independent and he didn't care." At that point, Taylor excused himself to go into another room and returned with a huge bottle on a wooden stand. "He went down to Montana before we closed the deal and brought this back for me," he explained. It was a bottle of Old Taylor bourbon—still more than half full, since Taylor never much cared for bourbon.

As it always tried to do in mergers, Canada Trust took over the staffs of British Canadian's two branches,[2] thus augmenting its burgeoning payroll by a little over thirty employees. By 1963 the company's staff across the country numbered 1,037—a sixty-per-cent increase in Taylor's five years as president. Besides creating new jobs, all the expansion and opening of new branches provided plenty of opportunity for promotion to existing employees. In 1961, for example, there were fifty-four promotions within the

---

2. Whenever one company is absorbed by another, its employees always feel a quite natural apprehension about their future, and often bitter resentment. Most of British Canadian's staff apparently welcomed the wider horizons opened by the deal. One who did not was the company's young accountant, Bob Redgwell. He wondered if he would find a place in the much bigger, national company for which he now found himself working. He need not have worried: today, he is at head office as vice-president in charge of audit services for Canada Trust.

company; in 1962, fifty-three; and in 1963, sixty-five. Canada Trust's management and staff thus headed for the company's hundredth anniversary in 1964 with morale as high as it had ever been.

Long before "management by objectives" became a widely publicized business technique, Allyn Taylor had always tried in his own mind to work toward set goals. Whether it concerned family financial affairs or corporate objectives, he sat down at the beginning of each year and asked himself, "Where do I want to be a year from now, or two years?" Then he would work toward that goal. At the beginning of 1962 he set an objective for Canada Trust's employees: by its hundredth anniversary in 1964, "the old Huron & Erie" would be a company doing a billion dollars' worth of business a year.

14

Raising Eyebrows

GRANDMA'S cooking, it seems, is often better in fond recollection than it actually was in her own kitchen. That, at any rate, was the conclusion of a committee of the Huron & Erie's women employees charged with unearthing some authentic 1864 recipes to provide the menus for the company's hundredth anniversary celebrations. The committee members searched old cookbooks and magazines and even came up with some tattered hand-written "receipts" from family archives. But when the old recipes were tried by modern cooks the resultant dishes fell sadly short of gourmet standards.

A food consultant hired for the occasion, Jean McKinley, suggested some reasons for the disappointing results. Cooks in the good old days, she said, tended to overcook everything, particularly vegetables. Temperature controls, in outdoor ovens or on the hearth, were by no means accurate, and the old-time cooks were no more precise with their measurements; a "pinch" of that or a "handful" of the other served their purposes. Also, ingredients in 1864 differed considerably from those of a century later. Chickens were scrawny beasts suited only to stews or pot pies; flour was stone-ground and coarse; and milk was used with its natural fat content, being neither homogenized nor pasteurized. But by a process of trial and error, and with the aid of experiments carried out by Georges Jacot, maître d'hôtel of the Hotel London, the committee eventually came up with an 1864 menu suited to a 1964 palate.

The company's annual meeting was postponed from the usual February date until 18 March, the anniversary of the filing of the declaration establishing the company, and on the evening of 17

March more than a thousand staff members and their spouses from across the country sat down to sample the fruits of the committee's researches, served by waitresses in a reasonable facsimile of 1864 dress. They began their meal with hot spiced cider, then worked their way through cabbage salad with hot bacon dressing, Sunday-Go-To-Meeting bread, and Johnny cake to a helping of chicken and oyster pot pie, followed by hot savouries, including sausage and bacon, baked beans on toast, and "baby Welsh rabbit." Finally came hot buttered apple-chunk pie with Wensleydale and old Canadian cheese.

Anticipating that the diners might not relish physical exertion after this repast, the company had laid on buses to take them to the Grand Theatre, a few blocks away, where they were treated to the anniversary entertainments. There was a "Victorian Variety" show, the high point of which was elocutionist Lucille Walker's rendition of "Father, Dear Father, Come Home With Me Now," from the "immortal" temperance play "Ten Nights In A Bar Room." The company had also commissioned the local historian, the Reverend Orlo Miller, to write a one-act play re-enacting the founding meeting above Daniel Macfie's store. Since no minutes of that meeting survive and the dramatic possibilities inherent in the spectacle of twenty-five business worthies signing their names to a document are somewhat limited, Miller ingeniously had the actors representing the founding fathers discuss among themselves topics that might have preoccupied them at that time. Some of those topics were local, such as the depredations of Frank Cornish's bully boys and the ramifications for London of the American Civil War; some of them are still being discussed today, such as the assorted delinquencies of youth and the danger of Canada being gobbled up by the Goliath to the south.

So many shareholders had signified their intention to attend the annual meeting next day that the Hotel London had to serve them their old-time lunch in staggered sittings in two separate dining rooms. A fleet of buses then took them to the theatre for a repeat performance of the entertainments and for the meeting, where they listened contentedly to Allyn Taylor's account of yet another record year. Savings deposits and mortgage investments were both up by twenty per cent during the year, and there was a ten-per-cent increase in the volume of assets under administration. To everyone's great pride, Canada Trust–Huron & Erie had indeed become a billion-dollar company, with half a million customers across the country, almost twice as many as it had had just three years earlier.

At the end of that year the annual report included a chart detailing progress during the previous ten years. The net profit registered by the two companies, just under $600,000 in 1954, had tripled to $1.8 million in 1964, and no doubt that figure would have been even higher had it not been for the expense of the continuing expansion program. Soon after the anniversary celebrations, the company's main Vancouver branch moved into a new seven-storey office building, and three new branches opened in British Columbia during the year: one in Nanaimo and two in Vancouver itself. Five new building sites had been bought, in Prince George, B.C., Niagara Falls, Sarnia, and two residential areas in London. And a site had been bought for a new building at Yonge and Adelaide streets to house the Toronto branch.

The value of the savings deposits, debentures, and trust certificates lodged with the two companies had more than quadrupled, from $110.5 million in 1954 to $450.4 million, and the estates, trusts, and agencies business had increased by an even larger margin, from $184.8 million in 1954 to almost $700 million. The largest increase of all was in the company's mortgage portfolio, which had grown more than fivefold during the ten-year period, from $72.1 million in 1954 to $365 million.

Mortgage lending, of course, had been the core of the company's business throughout its century of existence, but its portfolio was now beginning to become more diversified. The old dependence on farm mortgages had long since disappeared, to be replaced by loans on urban properties. Now only seventy-four per cent of those loans were on single-family homes; the rest, reflecting a change in the country itself, were on apartment buildings and a few commercial and industrial properties.

The company was beginning to branch out in other directions, too. In 1962 it had joined two of the chartered banks and two other trust companies as a partner in Roynat Ltd., of Montreal, a company set up to provide term financing for medium-sized Canadian businesses. And in 1959 its pension division had launched the Canada Trust Investment Fund, the first mutual fund run by a trust company, which proved so popular with the public that by 1964 it was growing at the rate of a million dollars a month.

All in all, everyone connected with the company—directors,

staff, and shareholders—had good reason for satisfaction; it was healthy, more profitable than it had ever been, and still as solidly based and well regarded as the old Huron & Erie. Better still, far from showing the creaking joints and decrepitude of old age, it seemed to be moving with the times as vigorously as any youngster.

But 1964 was more than just an occasion for nostalgia and self-congratulation. It was a watershed year, marked by two developments which in just a few years would change the company in ways that no one could yet imagine, far more than it had changed during all the previous century. Those two developments, separate but in a way complementary, were the harnessing to the company cause of that technological novelty, the computer, and—equally a novelty for a financial institution in those days—the hiring of the company's first professional marketing expert.

In its essentials, the office work performed by the company's employees in the early 1960s differed little from that of their frock-coated predecessors in the quill-pen era. Paper was still king. The advent of the telephone and the typewriter in the late Victorian era—and, much later, of the adding machine[1]—had speeded things up somewhat. But no one had yet figured out how to adapt modern technological advances to the time-consuming and often dreary routine work behind a trust company's counter. Jet planes were now flying overhead, and the first satellites were circling the earth in space, but at Canada Trust, as at all the other banks and trust companies, everything was still done in the time-honoured way, by hand. Transactions with customers were recorded on slips of paper by hand; the information on the slips was transferred, again by hand, into cash-books, which had to be balanced every night after the office closed; and the information in the cash-books was then laboriously entered into massive general ledgers, which had to be balanced every month. The preparation of customers' receipts, the calculation of interest paid or payable—everything was done by hand. And every veteran employee has a

---

1. The Huron & Erie directors did not exactly fall over themselves to embrace the technological advance represented by the adding machine. Retired employees who joined the company as juniors in the early 1930s chuckled as they described to the author the embarrassment caused them by one of their regular chores: loading the main branch's only adding machine on to a child's wagon and trundling it over to the Market branch, which did not yet have one.

horror story about the unpaid overtime this often entailed, sometimes even on Sundays.

The company's first tentative step into mechanization occurred in the pension division in the late 1950s. When it was decided to centralize all the pension trust business in Toronto, Arthur Mingay invited a friend from his Chatham days to come aboard and oversee what was bound to be a complicated process. Eric Minns was an eager young man from Bracebridge, Ontario, who had graduated from high school at the age of seventeen and apprenticed with a Toronto accounting firm. Posted to the firm's Chatham branch, he met Mingay when both were ushers in their local church. About a year after Mingay left for Toronto, Minns, too, was transferred to his company's head office, and they used to meet occasionally for lunch. It was at one of these lunches that Minns, by then working in the internal audit department at the Robert Simpson company, agreed to switch to Canada Trust.

By this time the company's pension business was booming, and to keep track of the voluminous records its growth entailed it was decided to acquire an IBM 402 accounting machine which, though it operated mechanically rather than electronically, was a precursor of the computer. Pre-programmed with wired boards, the machine could "read" and print out information from holes punched in cards. As the operational guru to handle this newfangled device, Minns hired Norman White, a young Englishman who had emigrated to Canada a couple of years earlier. Finding jobs in their own field was not always easy for the wave of immigrants arriving in this country at that time, but White was fortunate. He had learned to work with punched cards in England, a skill few Canadians had yet acquired, and when he was recruited by Canada Trust it was from a job as data-processing supervisor at Woolworth's.

After familiarizing himself with the workings of the pension division and the information required on the periodic statements issued to clients, White designed and wired his boards and set up the punched cards. Gradually all the pension trust accounting was transferred from the venerable, and hitherto venerated, ledgers to the machine. The machine eliminated so much donkey-work and so many reams of paper, and saved so much time, that Minns was soon able to persuade management that it could handle the company payroll as well. There was some reluctance to hand over this function at first, since the employees were still paid in cash and it was an unheard-of thing for comparatively junior employees like White to know what anyone else was earning.

Though the machine was hopelessly primitive by today's standards, it came through again. A few people within the company now began to suspect that if a mechanical device could perform so many functions which had always before been the exclusive domain of human hands, there might well be a place within the organization for the electronic computers that had begun to make their appearance in the business world. One of those people was Eric Minns, who was transferred to head office in London in 1960 to take over as comptroller. Canada Trust had expanded so fast, and the volume of its business had increased so enormously, that Minns concluded that the company was in danger of foundering in a sea of paper; at the very least, the proliferating paper threatened to put a crimp in any plans for further expansion. He therefore recommended to Allyn Taylor that the company investigate the possibility of converting its operations to the computer.

In Taylor he found a receptive listener. The London Life Insurance Company, faced with a paper problem more daunting even than Canada Trust's, had begun to computerize its operations several years earlier, in 1958, and Taylor, as a member of its board of directors, had seen the benefits. So in 1961 he established a task force of senior executives to look into ways in which the computer might be applied to Canada Trust's business.[2]

The task force visited computer companies and financial institutions in the United States that had already introduced computers into their operations, and a management consultant firm, Woods Gordon, was commissioned to examine the question. The Woods Gordon report recommended that the company acquire an IBM 1401 computer and use it to keep the records for three of the company's important functions: its mortgage accounting, term borrowings (debentures and certificates), and its personal trust business.

When the computer was first being introduced to the business world, its advocates tended to emphasize how many jobs it could eliminate, thus saving labour costs, rather than how it could facili-

---

2. Headed by Minns, the task force included Hugh Hutton, his predecessor as comptroller, who had recently been named executive assistant to the president; John Sherlock, the company's treasurer; Arthur Steele, a veteran of the trust side of the business; and Norman White, as head of data processing.

tate existing operations and, in its later evolution, make entirely new operations possible. At one of the senior management meetings convened to hear a Woods Gordon progress report, one of the consultants, probably a graduate of the old time-and-motion-study school, gave a branch-by-branch review of the staff savings the computer could be expected to accomplish. At one branch, he said, the staff could be cut by decimal eight of a person.

Allyn Taylor, who had been becoming increasingly restless as the presentation wore on, broke in to say, "If a computer comes into this company, there will be no loss of jobs. Let's get that straight from the start." Then, musing aloud, he added: "And I for one would be at a loss to know how to eliminate decimal eight of a person."

Eventually, with the company's own task force supporting the Woods Gordon recommendation, Taylor took the computerization plan to the executive committee of the board for its approval. He knew it was going to be an expensive proposition: one estimate was that during its first year it would cost a quarter of a million dollars for the equipment alone—the "hardware"—quite apart from the additional cost of staff and programming. (Actually, the first-year hardware costs amounted to $150,000.)

As Taylor had expected, one of the committee members said, "This is a big expenditure, Taylor. Why are you doing it? Are you going to improve the service?" Taylor replied, honestly enough at that stage, "I don't know." The member persisted: "Are you going to save money?" Again Taylor confessed that he did not really know. "Well, why in the name of the Great White Father are you doing it?" his questioner asked. "Because," Taylor replied, "if we don't, we're going to be up to our ass in paperwork."

It was not only the cost of the computer program that gave some of the directors pause; like many of the company's veteran staff members, they feared that automation would somehow destroy the warm personal contacts with customers that had always been considered so important to the company's success. But in the end the directors realized that if Allyn Taylor had decided the computer was necessary, they could not oppose him. To do so would have been tantamount to voting no confidence in his management, when in fact he had earned their utmost confidence.

And so the decision was made in 1963 to embark on what was christened "Operation Mayflower." The implication that the company was sailing into uncharted seas was clear, and as the voyage progressed the pilgrims tried to introduce a note of levity into what was for many old-timers a wrenching experience by elaborating on that theme. As each new corporate function was transferred to the computer, the ship was reported to have "taken on cargo," branches were referred to as "ports of call," and the steering committee set up under Eric Minns to supervise the operation was known as "the Admiralty."

The project manager chosen to supervise the computerization program was a man whose enviable physical and mental energy and capacity for innovative thinking would prove invaluable to the company in the years ahead. Jack Speake was born in London in 1928, son of an amateur artist employed as a sign-painter by the London Transportation Commission. His mother was a devout Methodist who believed the Sabbath should be observed with a reverent silence and respectful decorum that Jack and his two brothers found unbearably cramping on hot summer Sundays. To head off any potential family strife, their father used to take the boys out into the country on weekend hikes, when they would camp by the Thames River, fish, swim, and cook their meals on wood fires. These outings inspired in Jack a love of the outdoors which he has never lost. A few years ago, in his mid-fifties, he took five days off and canoed and camped his way along the 210-kilometre length of the Rideau Canal system, from Kingston to Ottawa.

Speake senior had been a keen Boy Scout in his native England, and as soon as Jack was old enough he joined the Wolf Cubs. From there he went on into the Boy Scouts, with a shirt that gradually filled up with badges. When he reached the age at which boys customarily put that sort of thing behind them for the workaday world, Jack was too fervent a believer in the Boy Scout philosophy to turn his back on it. He set up his own Scout troop at his local church and was its leader for eighteen years. After that, he graduated to the management side of the organization, holding positions of advancing authority, first on the London scene and then on the provincial and national councils.

When he graduated from the University of Western Ontario with an honours degree in general arts, Jack—uncharacteristically, in view of his later career—was undecided about what he wanted to do. He thought he might like to practice law, and his father was able to arrange an interview for him with a local lawyer named Livermore, a partner in the city's leading law firm, Ivey, Livermore

& Dowler. In a fatherly chat, Livermore suggested that before enrolling in law school he should take a job for a year, preferably with a trust company, where he would be exposed to various practical aspects of the law. Among the Speakes' neighbours was Charlie O'Hara, and when he heard that young Jack was looking for a job in a trust company he directed his footsteps to the Huron & Erie. With his brilliant scholastic achievements and his record, already at that early stage of his life, of community involvement as a Boy Scout leader, Jack was clearly prime material for the company's trust department, and he began work as a trust understudy in 1950. By the end of his first year he had abandoned all thought of becoming a lawyer, and in 1955 he was posted to Windsor as manager of the trust department there.

Like Allyn Taylor and most other sucessful men, Jack Speake always worked to objectives; his own strategy was to try to plan his life in five-year segments. He went to Windsor with the idea that he would spend five more years in the trust department but would then seek some administrative position closer to where the executive decisions were made. So after his five years at Windsor he approached head office with a request for a transfer to some other stream of the business. That led to a short spell as an assistant branch manager, followed by his assignment to Toronto as manager of the pension administration department.

This was Speake's first exposure to mechanization, and his fascination with what Norm White had achieved with the IBM 402 turned him into an immediate enthusiast for the computer, at a time when many of his colleagues had profound reservations about its practicality for their purposes. Always a voracious reader, he learned all he could about computers and their capabilities, attended courses given by computer manufacturers, and when head office cast about for someone to supervise Operation Mayflower he was the logical choice. He moved back to London in 1963 as manager of data processing, taking the indispensable White with him.

Most companies, when they first converted to computer systems, tended to begin with their comptroller's department; in other words, with their own internal accounting. But Canada Trust decided at the outset to begin in areas where the computer would have most impact on its business operations and would be of most benefit to its customers. The area chosen to be first was term deposits, and Speake and White began to design programs that would enable the computer to replace most of the paperwork these had formerly involved. They had advertised within the company for staff members who thought they might have the skills needed to become computer programmers, or systems analysts, which now became a new job description in the personnel department. From the couple of hundred applicants, they chose three who seemed suitable, and hired one experienced programmer from outside. The department thus started out with a staff of five; within ten years it had burgeoned to a hundred, and today it employs nearly four hundred people.

Before the arrival of their own rented computer, an IBM 1401, the designing of appropriate systems involved the new staff in the burning of much midnight oil. The AVCO loan company had agreed to act as IBM's test centre in London, and the time allotted for non-AVCO people to try out their programs was between midnight and 3 a.m. Nevertheless, by the time the computer was set up in head office, Speake and White had evolved a workable program, and one by one the managers of the various London branches brought in the cards on which all the records of their term-money transactions with customers had been recorded manually. A team of six experienced key-punchers recruited from outside the company then transferred the records on to cards in a form that could be interpreted by the computer, and all the relevant information was recorded on magnetic tape.

Hitherto, holders of debentures or savings certificates had received parchment-like bonds, signed by hand by the president and company secretary, and bearing dated coupons signifying the interest due on them during their term. On those due dates, the customers had to go in to the branch office, perhaps retrieve their bonds from their safety-deposit boxes, if they did not keep them at home, and take them to a teller, who would clip off the relevant coupon and credit the interest to the customer's account. The coupons would later be cancelled and stuck on the record cards kept in the branch to show that they had been cashed. Now, however, once the records were all stored in the computer, the coupon-clipping was no longer necessary. Interest was credited automatically on the due date; the computer printed out all the customers' quarterly and annual statements and such other documents as maturity notices (all of which had previously had to be typewritten); and as existing debentures matured, the new ones, instead of being printed on bond paper, were issued by the computer.

When the records of all the London branches had been put into the computer, the company's other branch offices began to send in theirs. And once a branch's existing records had been stored on tape, notification of any new transactions would be either taken or mailed in overnight, so that eventually the computer at head office had complete, up-to-date records of all the term money in the company's possession. By June 1964 the operation was complete, and the data-processing department moved on to the next stage: the computerization of the company's mortgage records.

In the design of this program, the computer had to be "taught" to recognize how much of each mortgage payment was interest and how much went to paying down the principal, and to calculate automatically how much the reduction of principal would lower the interest component of the next payment—all of which had previously involved long hours of manual calculation. The machine was also programmed to send out renewal and arrears notices automatically and produce any required statistical reports. It was a complex operation, but when it was completed in 1965 Canada Trust became the first trust company able to supply its clients with annual "full-disclosure" mortgage statements telling them exactly how much they had paid during the year, how much of their payment had gone to paying down their principal, and how much of it was interest. These statements were more detailed than any produced in pre-computer times: they showed all transactions that had occurred during the previous year, including late payments, if any, and their effect on the balance.

By the end of 1965, when the expanding data-processing team was preparing to "capture" the company's payroll and personal trust operations[3] on the computer, all but the most hidebound had

---

3. It was never the intention, nor indeed would it have been possible, for the computer to replace the intimate dealings with clients that had always been the core of the personal trust business. But the administration of estates and agencies for individuals was the most paper-intensive of all the company's activities. Three separate sets of ledgers had to be kept, covering cash, unrealized assets, and investments; detailed statements had to be prepared for beneficiaries and trustees; taxes had to be calculated and statements produced for surrogate courts—all by hand. By the end of 1967 the computer had taken over all these functions.

forgotten their original misgivings about automation. The reservations felt by some directors and many veteran employees about the other break with tradition in 1964, the hiring of a marketing professional, perhaps took longer to overcome.

The company, of course, had always done some advertising, though in the decorous fashion customary among financial institutions in earlier days. The advertising manager, Doug Paddell, while he had no prior experience in the field, having graduated from the teller's cage, had also pioneered some tentative ventures in sales promotion, with Allyn Taylor's encouragement. These did not always prove popular with his more conservative colleagues.

Bob Clarke, for example, recalled his indignation at one of Paddell's schemes in which he reluctantly became involved early in 1963. As manager of the Hamilton branch, Clarke was preparing to move his staff into a new building the company had erected on the site of the premises it had occupied ever since its acquisition of the Hamilton Provident in 1926. Paddell came up with the idea of marking the opening with a "give-away" promotion: anyone opening a new savings account with ten dollars or more would have the choice of receiving as a free gift a Brownie Hawkeye camera or a Cory glass coffee-maker.

Clarke was so horrified when he heard of this plan that he drove to London to protest to Allyn Taylor. "Here I am," he complained, "trying to build a trust-company image in Hamilton, and we're going to look like some crummy five-and-dime store." Mindful of his stated policy of giving branch managers maximum authority, Taylor replied, "Well, you're the manager, Bob, and if you don't like this scheme, that's it. But Doug tells me it will probably bring us fifteen hundred new accounts." Clarke knew he was licked when Taylor went on to add, innocently, "If you can come up with something else that will bring us fifteen hundred new accounts, you don't have to go along with this."

When the branch opened in its new premises, Clarke had a table set up in the corner for people wishing to open new accounts. Before the day was out he had to set up another table to handle the crush, and as the new customers' friends and neighbours saw the gifts they were receiving the lines at the tables grew until there were six of them, and Clarke had to scramble to get new supplies of cameras and coffee-pots. The branch "opening" eventually lasted three weeks, and one day the trust officer poked his head into Clarke's office and told him that a widow whose husband's estate the company was administering wanted to open an account for each of her eight grandchildren, and wanted eight cameras. "Okay," said Clarke, "let her have 'em." Privately, he felt it was a waste of the company's money—until he checked up on the accounts a few months later and found that together they amounted to about $30,000. The children's grandmother was in the habit of giving them substantial cash gifts for Christmas and on their birthdays.

"Of course," Clarke recalled, "some of the new accounts never amounted to a hill of beans. But I think over the long run we kept about sixty-five per cent of them, and the promotion brought in more than six thousand new accounts."

In the light of this success, Canada Trust's decision to hire a professional marketing manager was not as surprising as its competitors considered it to be. There had always been a crippling constraint on what the company could accomplish with its advertising. The banks, with their thousands of branches across the country, could afford the substantial expense of national advertising campaigns; Canada Trust could not. Even taking into account its recent expansion, the greater part of any advertising dollar it spent on a national campaign would be wasted on people who were not within reach of any Canada Trust branch. New-branch promotions, such as the one mounted in Hamilton, had proved their worth, but they did little for existing branches.

In 1964 Arthur Mingay had been elected to the company's board of directors and was clearly emerging as Allyn Taylor's right-hand man. They were discussing the advertising problem one day and decided that the solution, even though no other financial institution had yet tried it, was to move into the aggressive kind of marketing practised by other commercial companies to sell everything from breakfast cereals to cars.

As with some other modern techniques that were finding their way into the business world in those days, there was some dispute as to whether marketing was an art or a science. Certainly it involved the familiar elements of advertising and promotion, but as practised at its higher levels it went further; its credo might have been summed up as "Find out what the customers want, and give it to them." It was a credo that had not yet disturbed the serenity of the country's banks and financial institutions.

The classified advertisement in the Toronto newspapers seeking a marketing manager, while it mentioned neither the company nor the location of the job, attracted dozens of applicants. From his vantage point in Toronto Mingay interviewed those whose credentials sounded most promising, and eventually introduced the man he considered the likeliest candidate to Allyn Taylor for his approval.

Don McLean knew nothing about the financial business. In fact he was surprised when he discovered the identity of the anonymous advertiser, and dismayed when he learned that the job was in London: after several career moves he had promised his wife they would henceforth live in Toronto. McLean, who was born in Montreal, had begun work in an advertising agency, from which he moved first to a tire company's marketing department and then to the Glidden Paint company, which soon transferred him to Cleveland, Ohio. After some years there, he and his family began to hanker after the old life in Toronto, and he returned to Canada as head of communications and advertising for O'Keefe Breweries. He had responded to Canada Trust's advertisement because he was "not too happy" in the beer business, for what he describes today as "philosophical reasons."

Allyn Taylor was impressed with McLean at their first meeting, when he questioned him about his definition of marketing. "Hard work," McLean replied. "Roll up your sleeves and interface with the consumer." Rather than shying off nervously, Taylor was further impressed when it became clear that McLean would only take the job if he were given his head. That accorded well with Taylor's philosophy of management, and McLean and his family soon moved again, this time to London.

The first campaign McLean initiated went sadly awry. He had concluded that many customers opening savings accounts had some particular objective in mind: a boat, a vacation, or perhaps the down payment on a house. So the idea of a "target savings" account was devised, with the slogan "Start something with us." Continuing that theme, counter staff were given buttons to wear bearing the legend, "Start something with me." It was an unfortunate choice of invitation; so many women employees were upset by the leering response of some jocular male customers that the slogan was quickly jettisoned.

The nay-sayers among the old guard had a field day. What could you expect from a guy who knew nothing about the finance business? And a *beer* salesman, for God's sake! There was just no place in a decent trust company for Madison Avenue hucksterism.

The eyebrow-raising at Canada Trust's sortie into the marketing field was not confined to the company itself. One day, Arnold Hart, chairman of the Bank of Montreal, was visiting London and Allyn Taylor joined him at a lunch given by the bank's local manager. Chatting afterward, Hart ventured a gentlemanly reproof. "I know it's none of my business, Allyn," he said, "but you're doing an awful lot of harm to the image of your company with these give-aways and things." Taylor, whose support of McLean never wavered even in the face of the button imbroglio, replied, "Just you wait, Arnold. It's only a matter of time before the Bank of Montreal will have to do something similar if it wants to compete."

Not very many years later, after McLean had familiarized himself with the business, built up his staff, and initiated a whole string of imaginative marketing campaigns that helped to establish Canada Trust's leadership in the industry, the Bank of Montreal wooed him away to become its vice-president of marketing.

15

Getting the Wagons in a Circle

ONE of the most audacious con men ever to cut a destructive swath through the field of Canadian finance died of leukemia soon after testifying from his hospital bed to investigators from the Royal Commission set up by the Ontario government to try to unravel the intricacies of his depredations. Campbell Powell Morgan, an ambitious accountant, had founded a finance company called Atlantic Acceptance Corporation Ltd. in 1953, ostensibly to make consumer loans on such things as television sets and automobiles. After a meteoric rise Atlantic Acceptance collapsed in 1965 in Canada's worst financial shambles since the Home Bank fiasco more than forty years earlier.

It is a truism in the lending business that one sure, though perilous, way to grow is to make loans that more conservative companies won't touch, and that is what Atlantic Acceptance proceeded to do. It soon expanded its lending field from the consumer market, making huge unsecured loans to, among others, a web of companies connected in some way or other with Atlantic Acceptance itself. The capital from which these loans were made came not just from the proverbial "widows and orphans": Morgan and his associates managed to gull some of the supposedly most astute institutional investors on Wall Street. The influential financial house Kuhn, Loeb and Company agreed to become their U.S. agent, and among the roster of institutional investors that bought their "paper" (Atlantic Acceptance shares, bonds and notes) were such heavyweights in the business as the Ford Foundation and the $1.6 billion U.S. Steel and Carnegie Pension Fund.

Not surprisingly, the company's growth was phenomenal. It reported sales in 1960 amounting to more than $24 million. That volume almost doubled in each of the next two years and in 1963 it was no less than $176 million. By 1965 Atlantic Acceptance was the sixth largest finance company in Canada. Then on 14 June that year the Toronto-Dominion Bank refused to honour $5 million worth of its cheques supposedly covering notes that had matured. After a few days of frantic behind-the-scenes attempts to mount a rescue operation, Atlantic Acceptance went into receivership; the house of cards had collapsed.

The Ford Foundation gritted its teeth and wrote off $4.7 million of its investment in Atlantic Acceptance; Massachusetts Mutual Life waved farewell to $4.4 million in the company's notes. And there were lots of other losers: when the Royal Commission submitted its four-volume report at the end of 1969 it put the total losses by the company's investors and creditors at more than $77 million.

The debacle, besides resulting in criminal charges against a dozen of those involved, sent shock-waves through the whole Canadian economy, and one of the tremors rocked the city of Stratford, Ontario. Occupying the same position of trust and prestige in Stratford that the Huron & Erie had always had in London, the eighty-eight-year-old British Mortgage and Trust Company had been run by the much-respected Gregory family since 1914. Its chairman, W.H. Gregory, had handed over the reins of the company eight years earlier to his lawyer son, Wilfred P. Gregory, and under Wilfred's presidency the company seemed to prosper as never before. Its assets, $30 million when Wilfred took over, had multiplied by 1964 to almost $107 million; its original single office had been supplemented by fifteen new branches in the surrounding area; and its head office was now housed in a palatial new stone building perched above the Avon River and dominating Stratford's main street.

Wilf Gregory was a young man in a hurry, and these were the Swinging Sixties, the Go-Go years. Like many another young man in that era, and indeed in any other, he saw no reason to follow slavishly in the conservative footsteps of his father and grandfather. In fact, discussing mortgage lending, he once told the president of a substantial regional trust company who belonged to the old school, "You don't do business that way any more. Times have changed. You have to be aggressive, run much closer to the limits, take on more risks."

Unfortunately for British Mortgage's shareholders, Wilfred

Gregory ran very close indeed to the limits—evidence before the Royal Commission suggested that he had frequently exceeded them—and the unwise risks he took ultimately brought him down. Among the cardinal principles of the trust business that he seemed to have considered outmoded in the Go-Go years was that of diversification of investments. Within days of Atlantic Acceptance's collapse, it emerged that he had invested more than $7 million of British Mortgage's money in Atlantic paper, and had lent several more millions to individuals and companies in the Atlantic network. This news drove British Mortgage's shares down from $25 to $8 in one day. And to further complicate Gregory's problems, the company's "aggressive" mortgage lending had backfired: twelve per cent of its $85 million mortgage portfolio was in arrears.

Gregory was forced to resign and auditors called in by the company's directors estimated British Mortgage's loss at more than $10 million. It later turned out to be only $7 million, but that was still enough to sink the company, unless someone could be found to rescue it. An appeal was made to the Trust Companies Association without success, although there were those among its members who feared that if British Mortgage was permitted to collapse there would be a domino effect that might well undermine public confidence in the whole trust industry and perhaps topple some other fragile companies.

Among those particularly concerned at this prospect were Allyn Taylor and Walter Bean, president of the Waterloo Trust and Savings Company in Kitchener. Neither had any reason to fear for the stability of his own company. Waterloo Trust was if anything more of an institution in its own area than Canada Trust was in London. But Stratford was only about fifty kilometres from Kitchener and sixty-five from London, and to have a trust company go under so close to home would certainly not be good for business. It might not cause a "run on the banks," and in any case both their companies were strong enough to survive one if it did. But it might certainly make some people nervous about entrusting new deposits to them.

So Taylor and Bean joined forces and approached the premier of Ontario, John Robarts, with an offer to salvage British Mortgage and guarantee all its customers' deposits in full. They wanted only one assurance from the government: no one yet knew exactly how large British Mortgage's losses would turn out to be, but Taylor and

Bean offered to bear the first $5 million if the government would undertake to protect them against any liabilities beyond that. To their surprise—since there was a widespread feeling that British Mortgage's troubles had arisen in part because of the failure of the government's regulatory watchdogs to ensure that it complied with the rules governing trust companies—that undertaking was not forthcoming.

Whether the government changed its mind, or whether the management of the then little-known Victoria and Grey Trust Company ventured to tread where others feared to go, was never made clear. But eventually the Victoria and Grey bought British Mortgage and continued its operations, so that its depositors never lost a cent. Its shareholders, though, suffered badly, since the price Victoria and Grey paid, in a deal that doubled its size, was only a fraction of what British Mortgage had been worth before its collapse. And Taylor and Bean have always found it hard to believe that the small Victoria and Grey could have taken such a gamble without an assurance of some undisclosed government backing.

The ripple effect of the Atlantic Acceptance affair persisted for some time. Several other companies found themselves in difficulties, including some that had been permitted to call themselves "trust" companies although they never carried on trust operations in the accepted sense. Among those that went to the wall was a finance company that used the word "Prudential" in its title, presumably to the discomfiture of the famous Prudential Insurance Company, with which it had no connection. The widespread public concern ultimately persuaded the federal government to set up an organization in 1967 that insured depositors in its member financial companies against losses up to a maximum of $20,000. Since the scheme was financed by a compulsory levy on the industry, there was some grumbling by the most responsible financial institutions that they were in effect being forced to subsidize less responsible and even unethical companies, those most likely to have need of the protection. But the establishment of the Canada Deposit Insurance Corporation was naturally popular with small investors, and it probably benefited the whole industry by restoring public confidence in the system.

The British Mortgage scare prompted Allyn Taylor to repair what he had for some time considered a deficiency in the way financial institutions, including Canada Trust, reported information about their affairs to their shareholders. For more than a century it had been customary practice to set aside part of each year's earnings in undisclosed reserves, which did not show up in the annual balance sheet. This was done with the best of intentions, namely, to add to the company's strength and to afford extra protection to its depositors. It was perfectly legal and in accordance with general accounting practice, but Taylor felt it was unfair to the shareholders, since it did not fully reflect the company's financial position. Instead of revealing the inevitable swings in earnings from year to year, a company could show a steady pattern of upward progress by the simple expedient of adjusting transfers to or from the undisclosed reserves.

In his annual report for 1965 Taylor announced, in a move that was widely praised by financial analysts and columnists as a long overdue "first" for the financial industry, that Canada Trust would henceforth abandon this practice, thereby enabling shareholders and potential investors to form a more accurate picture of the true worth of the company's shares. At the end of 1964, he said in the report, Canada Trust's undisclosed reserves, exclusive of its mortgage reserves, had amounted to $6.9 million. This sum was now brought into the published figures under the customary heading of the "general reserve." With the addition of just over $1 million out of 1965 earnings, and $4.6 million paid by the shareholders in premiums in a 1965 stock issue, the company's general reserve now stood at the substantial figure of $29.7 million.

The 1965 stock issue was one of several made necessary during the preceding decade by the company's continuing expansion: it now had a total of fifty branches across the country, including no fewer than eight new ones opened that year. As the volume of its business kept on increasing by millions of dollars every year, it had to keep on increasing its capital and reserves to remain within its mandatory "multiple."

In February 1956 there was a rights issue, with shareholders being given one right for each share they held, and permitted to buy one new share for $30 plus five rights, in other words, for each five shares they held. (Those not wishing or unable to buy the new shares could, of course, sell their rights on the open market.) In February 1963 they were given the opportunity to buy one new share for $45 plus five rights. And two years later they were permitted to buy one new share for nine rights and $50.

During the same period there were also several stock splits. In

1954 there had been 40,000 fully-paid shares of the company outstanding—in other words, in the hands of shareholders—and their par value was still, as it had been for years, $100. In addition, the old "accumulating shares" which had existed from the beginning, and for which the shareholders had only had to put up twenty per cent of the full price, were still in existence, and there were 50,000 of them outstanding.

The par value of the shares, of course, bore no relationship to their price on the open market. This had sunk from a high of $211 early in World War I to a high of only $55 in 1942, after the buffeting of the depression. By 1954 the high was back up to $158, and in an attempt to make the stock more readily available to small investors, it was split in 1955. Holders of fully-paid shares received five new shares with a par value of $20 for each old share they held. At the same time legislative approval was obtained to eliminate the old "twenty per cent" shares, and their holders received one new share for each old one.

The effect of the split, as intended, was to bring down the price of the shares on the market; during 1955 they traded at a low of $34 and a high of $42. But as the company continued to grow and report record profits, the price of its shares once again began to rise. By 1960 the high had reached $65, and in 1961 there was another split, with shareholders receiving two shares with a par value of $10 for each one held. This brought down the market price to $37 for a while, but by 1964 the high had again risen—to $70. In 1965 there was yet another split, with shareholders receiving five new shares, for which the par value was now $2, in return for each share they already held. The necessity for periodic injections of new capital was temporarily eased that same year by legislation which raised the company's multiple from twelve and a half to fifteen times its capital and reserve.

An enthusiastic purchaser of the shares and rights issues during that period was Colonel Maxwell G.C. Meighen, O.B.E., who had been elected a vice-president of the Huron & Erie after his father, Arthur Meighen, died in 1960.[1] An engineer who had served over-

1. Arthur Meighen's close friend and fellow vice-president of Canada Trust since its acquisition of the London & Western, the Honourable Ray Lawson, had retired from the board in 1956. He too was replaced as vice-president by his son, Lt. Col. Tom Lawson, who was for many years a valued member of the Huron & Erie's executive committee.

seas with distinction during World War II, Max Meighen had also taken over the direction of two investment companies controlled by his father, Canadian General Investments and Third Canadian General Investment Trust. In 1963 Allyn Taylor learned that through these companies Meighen had gradually accumulated about fifteen per cent of the Huron & Erie's outstanding shares. This made him by far the largest single shareholder and raised an uncomfortable question in Taylor's mind: could it be that he was trying to take control of the company?

Taylor, his board of directors, and his fellow executives had always been proud of the fact that the Huron & Erie, by virtue of the widely held ownership of its shares, was one of the few independent trust companies in Canada. They felt that independence was vital to the public interest; in fact, they believed that no institution taking deposits from the public should be controlled by any one individual or commercial interest because of the potential this created for "self-dealing," that is, the use of customers' funds to further private interests. The government appeared to recognize this danger in the 1967 Bank Act, which stipulated that no individual or commercial interest could own more than ten per cent of a bank's shares, and for years Taylor and his successors campaigned to persuade successive governments that similar legislation should apply to trust companies. Strangely, despite periodic scandals involving privately held trust companies, they were never able to convince legislators that their concerns were valid.

When he was told the extent of Meighen's shareholding, Taylor sought him out and explained this philosophy. "Max," he said, "you may tell me it's none of my business, but I'd like to know what your intentions are." Meighen immediately disavowed any ambition to take over the company; he had merely thought his companies should have an interest in a trust company in their portfolios, and what better trust company than the Huron & Erie? Taylor persisted. No one had ever accumulated such a large percentage of the company's shares before, he said, and since he considered it so important that the company retain the independence it had always had, he would like Meighen to be content with the percentage he had already acquired and not buy any more shares. Meighen thought for a few moments and then said, "Okay, I'll agree to that."

Taylor was considerably relieved by the conversation; he knew Max Meighen was a man of his word. But a couple of years later he became concerned again when he began to receive inquiries about the company from investment dealers. "The impression was left with me," he recalled to the author, "that perhaps there was somebody in the wings thinking of making a run at us." Then the rumours began: the Montreal Trust, it was said, was about to make a takeover bid for the Huron & Erie. They were only rumours, but they alarmed Taylor and he asked his friend John Harrison, a London lawyer, and a member of the company's executive committee, what he might do to protect the company from an unwanted advance. Harrison suggested they should see J.S.D. Tory, a formidable eminence in Toronto legal circles who was regarded as the authority on takeovers.

After Taylor had explained to Tory the reasons for his concern, he went on: "Mind you, I'm not too worried, because we have a group of very loyal shareholders—some of them the second and third generation of Huron & Erie shareholders. And we have one major shareholder in Max Meighen, and I know his stock won't be moved. So we have a pretty firm base."

Taylor never forgot Tory's response. He wagged his finger at his visitor and said: "If you don't take anything else away from this conversation, Mr. Taylor, just remember I told you there is no such thing as a loyal shareholder, and there's no reason why there should be. Shareholders are there to buy and sell a commodity, and if they can make a profit on their shares, why should you expect them to have loyalty to you and the company?"

It was not exactly a cheering interview, and Taylor was relieved when no takeover bid materialized. Perhaps none had ever been considered: the takeover mania that would convulse the financial world in later years had not yet developed. The fear that the company might fall into unfriendly or undesirable hands nevertheless remained at the back of Taylor's mind, and in the spring of 1969 he thought he saw an opportunity to protect it against raiders. One morning he received a telephone call from Ian Sinclair, president of the Canadian Pacific Railway, an old friend from his Winnipeg days. Sinclair told him he would be in London a couple of days later with Norris "Buck" Crump, the CPR's chairman, and he invited Taylor to lunch with them.

Taylor knew, of course, that the CPR's pension fund was a major shareholder of the Huron & Erie, with about ten per cent of its shares. Over lunch, Sinclair and Crump told him they had decided to sell their holding, because they felt it no longer suited their investment strategy as a company involved in the transportation and resources business. But they were in no hurry, and they would certainly not sell to anyone Taylor and his board considered undesirable. Had Taylor any suggestions?

Taylor thanked them for their consideration and promised to try to find an acceptable buyer for their shares. He already had one prospective purchaser in mind, the London Life Insurance Company. When Taylor had arrived in London he had been surprised to find that the relationship between the city's two leading financial institutions was decidedly distant. Some time during the 1930s, Ed Reid, London Life's longtime president, had become so incensed by some cavalier treatment he had received at the hands of the Huron & Erie's imperious T.G. Meredith that he had stormed out of a Huron & Erie board meeting and severed all connections between the two companies.

Through the years Taylor had become a close friend of Reid's son Bob, who had succeeded to the London Life presidency, and between them the two men set out to heal the breach between their respective organizations. By 1969 Taylor had been on the London Life board for several years, and Reid had joined the Huron & Erie board. Also, London Life had begun to buy Huron & Erie stock for its investment portfolio in 1965, and by 1969 had accumulated a holding of 65,000 shares. This was only a tiny fraction of the total number of shares outstanding, and Taylor thought Reid might well consider a substantial addition to it. Certainly, from Taylor's point of view, any shares in the hands of his friend Bob Reid would be safely parked out of reach of any raider.

The CPR holding amounted to almost half a million shares, and while the London Life financial people were considering the ramifications of this substantial addition to their portfolio—at the going rate it represented an investment of more than $9 million—Taylor learned that there was another potential purchaser in the wings. He received a visit one day from Ken MacGregor, who had resigned as the federal government's superintendent of insurance in 1964 to become president of Mutual Life of Canada in Waterloo.

Mutual Life, like London Life, had a small holding of Huron & Erie shares in its investment portfolio. MacGregor, with his wide knowledge of the various loan and trust companies, rated the Huron & Erie as tops in the field and recommended to his board of directors that Mutual should take a much more significant interest in it. He believed a substantial holding would not only be a good investment but might also pave the way for Mutual to collaborate with the Huron & Erie to their common advantage in some areas, particularly data processing. He was aware of the Meighen and CPR shareholdings, which were public knowledge, but did not yet know that the CPR shares might be for sale. Before making any move to increase Mutual's holding he felt it only proper to get in touch with Taylor to make sure that his approach would not be unwelcome.

Taylor had come to know MacGregor well in his dealings with him as superintendent of insurance, the trust companies' federal regulator, and in fact when MacGregor left the government to become president of Mutual he had tried to persuade him to join the Huron & Erie's board of directors. MacGregor had felt he had to refuse since it was traditional at that time for the president of Mutual to sit on the board of its neighbouring company, the Waterloo Trust. Certainly, from Taylor's point of view, MacGregor and Mutual would be eminently acceptable as a "friendly" shareholder and as an ally against any potential raider, and he told MacGregor so.

With this assurance, when he heard that the CPR shares were for sale, MacGregor began to negotiate for them. He found the CPR's vice-president, finance, Dutch-born Gijsbertus van den Berg, a hard bargainer, but eventually it was agreed that CPR would sell its interest in the Huron & Erie to Mutual at $18.50 per share, the stock's high for the year. When Bob Reid of London Life became aware of the impending transaction, through Allyn Taylor, he immediately expressed an interest in joining Mutual in the purchase. Knowing of Taylor's desire to have London Life involved, MacGregor agreed to split the purchase approximately equally, and so in May 1969 Mutual Life bought 264,580 Huron & Erie shares from the CPR and London Life took the remaining 226,580. The price in each case was $18.50 per share.

The two insurance companies also agreed that they would take turns buying more shares on the open market to bring their holdings up to almost ten per cent each. Neither company wished to exceed that percentage—the result would have been to denude their boards of any directors who were also directors of banks, since under the legislation governing insurance companies, bank directors were not permitted to sit on the boards of any insurance company owning more than ten per cent of a trust company.

Eventually, therefore, Taylor and his colleagues could relax in the knowledge that, with the addition of the Meighen shares, almost thirty-five per cent of their company's ownership was in the hands of what became known as the "friendly shareholder" group. This arrangement was thought to provide protection against raiders, since the rest of the company's ownership was in the hands of almost five thousand individual shareholders; it was reinforced by an informal gentleman's agreement among the three friendly parties. Ken MacGregor, for Mutual, Bob Reid, for London Life, and Alex Barron, Max Meighen's right-hand man, agreed that no member of the group would sell its shares without offering right of first refusal to the other members.

It was a cosy arrangement, one that would no doubt be considered altogether too cosy in today's vastly changed business environment. But in the eyes of the friendly shareholders it seemed only logical to try to protect the independence of a company they considered a gilt-edged investment, run by a management team having their complete confidence. For his part, Taylor welcomed the support of a group he considered excellent shareholders, men he trusted implicitly and whose advice he valued, good men to have on his side if any battle for control of the company developed in the years ahead.

16

Two Mergers Quicken the Pace

THE revision of the federal Bank Act in 1967 was thought by some in the industry to have sounded the death knell for loan and trust companies. The Porter Royal Commission on Banking and Finance which had studied Canada's financial institutions in the early years of the decade had recommended that the government establish "a more open and competitive banking system." To that end, it also recommended that some of the restrictions on loan and trust companies be removed and that they be given full banking powers and brought under the authority of the Bank of Canada.

The government shied away from this undoubtedly radical recommendation, possibly because most loan and trust companies were incorporated under provincial rather than federal charters, and an attempt to bring them all under federal control might have offended various provincial sensitivities. But in trying to foster the competition the Porter Commission had favoured, the government removed a number of constraints on the banks, and by so doing gave them an added advantage over the much less powerful loan and trust companies. For instance, until 1967 the banks had been forbidden to charge more than six-per-cent interest on loans. This ceiling was removed and for the first time they were permitted to make conventional mortgage loans on real estate. This, of course, directly encroached on the loan and trust companies' traditional business, and the banks took full advantage of their new freedom; within three years their mortgage portfolios jumped from $825 million to $18.6 billion.

Allyn Taylor mentioned the new situation—"the most vigorous competition we have had from the banks in our 104-year history"—at Canada Trust's annual meeting in February 1968. He also voiced another warning to the shareholders. "We have no illusions that the pressure will ease," he said, "but tough as it may be, competition is not our chief concern in 1968. We worry more about the unpredictable vagaries of the economic weather. There have been gales in recent months which blew interest rates to the highest levels of the century, and there still are storm clouds all around us."

During the thirteen years from the end of the Korean War until 1965, the consumer price index in Canada, the traditional barometer of inflation, rose only modestly, at an average rate of 1.3 per cent per year. Then, in 1966, longshoremen in St. Lawrence ports and workers on the Seaway went on strike for higher wages. Fearful that they would disrupt important wheat shipments to the Soviet Union and give the country a symbolic black eye by preventing completion of the Expo 67 construction in Montreal on time, Prime Minister Lester Pearson intervened and the workers received two-year contracts giving them wage increases of fifteen per cent each year. "The Pearson Formula," as it was called, was taken by union leaders and the press to mean that henceforth all Canadian workers could look forward to fifteen-per-cent raises every year, and a round of large wage settlements followed. There were international inflationary factors at work, too, and in 1966 the consumer price index rose by 3.7 per cent, more than double the annual rate of the previous thirteen years. By 1968 it had risen to four-per-cent.

The mounting inflation naturally drove up the price all businesses had to pay for their raw materials—in Canada Trust's case, money. For many years, the company had been accustomed to paying its savings depositors four-per-cent interest. By March of 1968 inflation had driven that rate up to five per cent; two months later it was up to five and a half per cent; and to attract long-term money, in the form of debentures or savings certificates, the company had to offer even higher rates.

True, on the other side of the ledger, mortgage rates were also rising. In the late 1940s and through the 1950s they had averaged five and a half or six per cent. When they hit eight per cent in the 1960s, Don Miller, Canada Trust's treasurer, blurted out to a colleague, "My God, that's *usury*!" But usurious or not, the rising rates could not shield the company from damaging inroads on its all-important "spread." Since mortgages in those days traditionally extended over five-year terms at fixed rates of interest, there was a time-lag potentially disastrous to the company's balance sheet: the price that market forces compelled it to pay for its borrowings was fast approaching the return it was making on money invested in earlier years.

There was nothing Taylor or his colleagues could do at that stage about the first of the twin threats he perceived at the beginning of 1968—inflation. As to the second, he had long believed that the way to meet the competition of the banks was to grow. And providentially, only days after his cautionary words to the shareholders, he was offered two separate deals which, if they could be brought off, would greatly enlarge Canada Trust and enhance its presence in two rich and fast-growing parts of Ontario.

The first offer came in a telephone call from Brigadier Walter A. Bean, C.B.E., president and general manager of the Waterloo Trust and Savings Company, based in Kitchener. Bean and Taylor had become good friends as a result of their activities within the Trust Companies Association, and had worked easily together in their abortive attempt to rescue British Mortgage a few years earlier. Now Bean told Taylor that his directors had decided the time had come to sell their company to a larger group, and he was inviting three major trust companies to bid for it. Was Taylor interested? Taylor assured him he most certainly was, as Bean had known he would be; they had talked casually about merging their two companies years before, but the time had not then seemed ripe.

Founded in 1913, the Waterloo Trust had grown to the point at which it had twelve branches in and around Kitchener and Waterloo, twin cities that started out as hamlets about three kilometres apart but had long since grown into each other so completely that the only way a visitor could tell when he was leaving one and entering the other was from signs posted on the busy streets. The Waterloo Trust was so well regarded that it had more accounts than there were households in the rich market area it served in Waterloo and Wellington counties. Its customers ranged from workers in the hundreds of factories in its area, many of them descended from pioneer German settlers, to farmers on the productive agricultural land around the cities. Its Elmira branch had a hitching post at the rear where its thrifty Amish and Mennonite customers could park their horses and buggies while they went inside to transact their business.

Walter Bean himself stemmed from pioneer stock. His forebears, from the German-speaking part of Switzerland (the family name was originally Biehn) were among the first settlers in Waterloo county in 1800. Young Walter joined "the trust company," as everyone in the area called it, in 1930, with a Bachelor of Commerce degree from the University of Toronto and a reputation as an athlete. As a lineman on the university's football team he had played in the Grey Cup and was the only college player named to the 1929 Canadian All Star team. Starting out as a ledger keeper, he quickly made his mark and was the company's treasurer from 1934 until 1940 when, with ten years' service as a militia officer, he volunteered to go overseas with the Highland Light Infantry. He held a variety of staff appointments, including one at British army headquarters in North Africa. Later he was attached to Admiral Nimitz's United States headquarters in the Pacific as a brigadier involved in planning Canada's contribution to the Pacific campaign, until the need for it was removed by the sudden end of the war.

Back at Waterloo Trust, Bean held positions of increasing responsibility as the company grew, becoming its general manager in 1957 and its president in 1964. By the time he made his call to Allyn Taylor, Waterloo Trust had assets under administration of $302 million and almost three hundred employees. It was a progressive, well-run company, ahead of the rest of the financial industry in that it was the first company to install an "on-line" banking system, linking its whole network by computer so that its customers could cash cheques, make deposits, and have their passbooks updated at any branch they found convenient.

But Waterloo Trust was essentially a savings operation, and Bean felt it had not developed its trust side as much as it might have done. He believed that to offer its customers all the fiduciary expertise they could get from larger companies it would have to expand, and that would probably mean moving out of its traditional area into Toronto. One way of doing that would have been to buy a smaller company, but there did not seem to be a suitable candidate available. Bean knew that whatever expansionary course was adopted would be expensive, and he sensed that there was little enthusiasm among either his directors or shareholders for the sacrifice of earnings this would entail, if only in the short term. Also, the installation of the computer system had been costly, and one of the shareholders, disturbed at the impact of this cost on the company's earnings, had lately caused an unseemly disturbance at the annual meeting by demanding changes on the board of directors. The answer, Bean decided, was to join with a larger competitor, and the directors agreed with him.

When he called Taylor he did not disclose the identities of the other two companies he was inviting to submit bids. But Taylor guessed, correctly as it turned out, that they were the Royal Trust, which he knew would like a foothold on Canada Trust's home turf of southwestern Ontario, and National Trust which, while he did not regard it as particularly expansion-minded at that time, had personal ties with at least one Waterloo Trust director. So when Taylor put his financial people to work examining the information Bean provided, he knew they were entering a poker game with very high stakes.

The game had hardly begun when Taylor received a call from another old friend, Oswald Earl Manning, known to one and all as "Oz." Born in Woodville, Ontario, just before the turn of the century, Oz Manning began his career with the Dominion Bank in Toronto. In 1933 he was put in charge of the troubled Grey & Bruce Trust and Savings Company at Owen Sound, which, seventeen years later, after he had turned its fortunes around, joined forces with a larger company based in Lindsay, Ontario, to form the Victoria and Grey Trust Company. He then worked for a time for the Canada Permanent before taking charge of the Trust Company of the Bahamas in Nassau.

One day in 1955 Manning told his friend Taylor that he had enlisted the support of several prominent businessmen in the fast-growing "Golden Triangle" west of Toronto and was about to open his own trust company. Taylor congratulated him on his choice of location, wished him luck, and said, "If you ever get into trouble, call on me." In 1967, by which time Manning's Halton & Peel Trust & Savings Company had more than $75 million in assets under administration and nine branches, a Toronto investment company, Security Capital Corporation, made a takeover bid for it. The price offered was seven dollars cash and three Security shares for each Halton & Peel share. Manning and his board of directors considered this too low and managed to organize a majority of their shareholders into a voting trust which successfully resisted the offer.

Early in 1968, however, with the voting trust arrangement due to expire later in the year, Oz Manning decided that in order to fend off any other unwanted advance he should find a friendly buyer and negotiate a satisfactory deal. Remembering his conversation with Taylor years before, he was not prepared to deal with any company other than Canada Trust, though this made him unpopular with some of his directors, who thought he should put the company up for bids, as Walter Bean had done with Waterloo Trust. Though he never held financial control of the Halton & Peel, Manning had founded it entirely on his own initiative and it had been considered "his" company all along. Indeed, there were some who thought he was unduly autocratic in his conduct of its affairs. So even though he did not have all his directors behind him, he went ahead and called Taylor and invited him to make an offer.

The spring of 1968 was thus a busy and tension-filled time for Taylor and his lieutenants. In deciding how much to bid for Waterloo Trust they had to do more than merely analyze the voluminous financial reports supplied to them. That same information was available to their rivals, and after expert scrutiny all three bidders might be expected to come up with comparable offers. The imponderable was the "goodwill factor," that is, the enormous loyalty of Waterloo Trust's customers, which Taylor hoped to inherit by continuing to operate its branch network, with its existing staffs, as a new region of Canada Trust. Eventually it was decided to make a complicated package offer, estimated to be worth in all $22 million. Waterloo Trust shareholders would be offered three choices: they could sell their shares to the Huron & Erie for $27.25 each; or they could elect to receive one and a half shares of Huron & Erie stock plus $10.75 cash, or one and a quarter Huron & Erie shares plus $13.50 cash, for each of their Waterloo Trust shares.

The Waterloo Trust's board of directors met to open the tenders on 28 May, and the Huron & Erie's bid was the highest—by how much, Taylor never learned, though he was told the Royal Trust's bid was very close and the National's well below. After the meeting, at which the board agreed unanimously to recommend the Huron & Erie's offer to the shareholders, Walter Bean called Taylor and said, "I guess you want us pretty badly, don't you?" Taylor admitted that indeed he did. "Well," said Bean, "you've got us."

Setting a price on the Halton & Peel was no less difficult. Even though the Huron & Erie was the only company invited to bid, it would certainly not retain that status unless its offer was judged fair by the Halton & Peel's directors and shareholders. Though much newer than the Waterloo Trust, the Halton & Peel was nevertheless a valuable property. Oz Manning had chosen his territory well. Oakville, where he sited his head office, was strategically located on the shore of Lake Ontario between Toronto and Hamilton, and it regularly figured in national statistical tables as the city with the highest per capita income in the country. And he had established his branches in places like Brampton, Milton, and Georgetown at a time when the farmers there were making fortunes selling their land for factories and housing estates as the "Golden Triangle" burgeoned and its population grew by the thousands every year.

Eventually the offer was made: one Huron & Erie share and eight dollars cash for each Halton & Peel share. On the day it was to be considered by the Halton & Peel directors, Allyn Taylor waited anxiously in his office until after 7 p.m. before Manning called him. It had, Manning told him, been a stormy meeting, but after much argument a majority of the board had voted in favour of accepting the offer.

By the end of 1968 the shareholders concerned had taken up their shares and both acquisitions had been approved by the Treasury Board.[1] They increased Canada Trust's total assets under administration by $400 million, bringing them to $2.2 billion—more than twice the billion dollars Taylor had been so proud to announce to the anniversary meeting four years earlier. The two deals brought the company almost 400 new employees and more than 165,000 new customers. Its branch network grew from fifty-seven offices to seventy-seven, the largest number maintained by any trust company in the country.

This major expansion naturally called for some changes in the company's management structure. Allyn Taylor, as chairman and president, invited Walter Bean to become deputy chairman and to join him on the Corporate Planning and Policy Committee, a sort of three-man office of the president, whose third member was Arthur Mingay. Mingay, fresh from his successes in Toronto,

1. As provincially chartered companies, Waterloo Trust and Halton & Peel could not at that time be legally merged with the federally chartered Canada Trust. They were operated as subsidiaries until legislation by both the Ontario and federal governments streamlined procedures and paved the way for the complete merger, which took place in 1971.

where the old peanut stand now had ten branches and he had lately presided over the construction of a spanking new eighteen-storey building at Yonge and Adelaide, was now at head office in day-to-day charge of the company's operations as vice-president and general manager.

Two new regions were created, bringing the total to eight. John S. Beatty, general manager of the Halton & Peel, continued to operate its nine existing branches as assistant general manager, Halton & Peel region. The Waterloo Trust's twelve existing branches were combined with four that had previously been operated in its area by Canada Trust to form the Central Ontario region. (It was decided later to close the Canada Trust branch in Kitchener, where there were already six Waterloo Trust branches.) The assistant general manager appointed for the Central Ontario region was Mervyn L. Lahn, who had previously held the same title in Waterloo Trust.

Bob Knighton, who was Canada Trust's secretary at the time of the merger, recalled that when the time came to prepare the formal offer to the Waterloo Trust's shareholders he consulted the relevant statutes and journeyed to Kitchener with a list of the official documents he would require, such as an up-to-date list of the company's shareholders and the constitution of its pension plan. He had expected to spend the whole day in the Waterloo Trust's offices while the young man he had been told to see, Merv Lahn, dug all the documents from the files. Instead, he found that Lahn had obviously consulted the statutes too and had all the required material ready on his desk. Knighton was greatly impressed by Lahn's thoroughness and efficiency. It was an impression that would come to be widely shared in the years ahead.[2]

---

2. It was an open secret that had Waterloo Trust not been sold, Lahn, though only thirty-five, would have soon been made its general manager, and everyone expected that he would in due course inherit the presidency from Walter Bean. It is also no secret that when two companies merge, the worst fallout is at the top: no department of any company can have two vice-presidents, and the one who retains the job tends to be the incumbent in the larger company. Lahn knew that Allyn Taylor was acknowledged as the dean of trust company executives in this country; Arthur Mingay was probably going to be his successor, but if not, there was no shortage of management talent and experience at Canada Trust. So where did that leave Lahn? One day he expressed concern about his future to Eric Brown, a senior executive at Canada Permanent. Brown reassured him. He himself, he said, had been "taken over" twice: he had worked for a company that

Before the merger negotiations began, the Huron & Erie's authorized capital was 5 million shares, of which 4 million were outstanding. A further 911,856 were issued in the offers to Waterloo Trust and Halton & Peel shareholders. This left the company with virtually no unissued capital, an obvious constraint on its continued growth. It therefore applied to Parliament for permission to double its authorized capital to 10 million shares, which it was granted in 1969. Canada Trust was granted an increase in its capitalization at the same time, which enabled the Huron & Erie to supply it with new funds to complete the merger; and in 1970 the Huron & Erie raised $7.5 million in new capital by issuing a further 609,232 shares, shareholders being given the right to buy one new share at $12.50 for every eight shares they already held.

The company's ability to grow without constantly bumping its head on the ceiling of the multiple was further assured that same year, when long-awaited amendments to the federal Trust and Loan Acts sanctioned an increase of a company's multiple from fifteen to twenty times its capital and reserve, subject to Treasury Board approval. Canada Trust quickly applied for, and was granted, the increase.

This relaxation of the limits on the loan and trust companies' capacity for growth met one of two requests the companies had been making of the government ever since the 1967 Bank Act tilted the somewhat precarious competitive balance among the country's financial institutions in favour of the banks. The other legislative amendment to which they felt they were entitled was one giving them the authority—or more precisely confirming the authority they had already begun to assume—to make personal, or consumer, loans. Until the 1967 Act freed the banks to enter the lists, the public demand for consumer loans had been filled by the finance companies. The loan and trust companies had not ventured into this business, for two reasons. First, there was the matter of tradition. Lending money to people for such perishable assets as automobiles and stoves rather than on the good solid

---

was merged into another that was later absorbed into the Permanent, and he had not suffered. Indeed, soon afterward he became president of the Permanent. He advised Lahn to "stay where you are and just play the game," and promised him that if things didn't work out he could always get a job at "the Perm." As chairman of Canada Trust today, Merv Lahn would doubtless agree that it was good advice.

security of land and bricks and mortar was considered not only foolhardy but somehow undignified. Second, it was not at all clear that the regulations under which they operated permitted them to do so.

But in the new competitive environment after the 1967 Act some trust companies began to venture tentatively into the personal loan field. After all, it was a lucrative one, earning more interest than mortgage loans, and the banks had entered it with enthusiasm, bidding fair to bring about the demise of the finance companies. Also, the trust companies felt that by not offering personal loans they were depriving their customers of a service they should have: no matter how much credit a customer had established with a trust company, if he wanted a loan to buy a chesterfield or car he had to go to a bank or a finance company where he was not known at all. Moreover, the trust companies thought they could get into the business under the umbrella of what was called in the regulations governing insurance companies the "basket clause."[3]

Canada Trust began what it called a pilot project in the consumer loan field in 1968. Allyn Taylor was reluctant at first to sanction the new departure. He feared it might damage the image of the old Huron & Erie and turn it into a mere finance company. But he was eventually persuaded that it was essential if the company was to avoid losing customers to the banks. His doubts were widely shared among the staff. Bob Overholt, one of a small group of three experienced finance company people hired to get the project under way, recalled that when he and his colleagues sat in the company cafeteria in the early days they were greeted by leery looks from fellow employees: "Someone would say, 'Who are those people?' and the reply would be, 'Oh, those are the guys who do the repossession of the stoves and fridges.' The perception was that we were getting into the dirty end of the business and we'd better watch out because we were going to own every stove, fridge and chesterfield across the country."

---

3. The term "basket clause" did not actually exist in the legislation governing loan and trust companies. That legislation, however, explicitly stipulated in percentages how the companies could invest their funds: so much must be in specifically defined liquid assets, so much in mortgages, and so on. When the categories were added up, they totalled ninety-three per cent. The remaining seven per cent became known as the basket into which investments neither specifically permitted nor forbidden by the regulations could fall.

Allyn Taylor recalled: "We started it in a very small way. I said, 'Let's go at it easily. We'll have it *available* for our customers, but we won't promote it.'" Beginning slowly, branch by branch, by the end of 1969 the company had made more than 1,500 personal loans totalling $1.8 million—and had only one delinquent account. Arthur Mingay celebrated when the total loan volume passed the million-dollar mark by inviting the three "repossession guys" and their wives to dinner at his home. By the end of 1970, the year in which the government confirmed that consumer loans could be made under the basket provision, the company's total volume of these loans had reached $6 million.

17

The "Stunts" Begin to Pay Off

ARTHUR Hammond Mingay was born in Windsor, Ontario, in 1919, son of a Canadian National Railways yard master. At school his best subject was mathematics, with basketball a close second. In his high school years he worked on Saturdays and in the evenings as a parcel packer and stocker of shelves for Loblaw's, a company of which many years later he would become a director. Perhaps this early contact with merchandising accounted for his later success. Certainly he was interested in business in his youth and after high school he enrolled full time in the Windsor Business School.

Jobs were still scarce in Canada in the late 1930s, but one day the minister at his family's church, Chalmers United, told him the local branch of the Huron & Erie was looking for a bright young man. Mingay presented himself for interview and was engaged as a junior clerk and messenger boy. He was soon promoted to teller, and then to clerk, first in the mortgage department, then in the trust department. When he joined the Royal Canadian Air Force in 1941 he wanted to train for air crew, but the powers-that-be had decreed that air crew were not needed at that stage of the war and he was assigned to administrative duties. Overseas after only six months' service, he was attached to the Royal Air Force records office in Ruislip, near London, and later in Gloucester, until the RCAF set up its own records office in London.

Back home in the Windsor branch he was introduced to a wartime recruit to the company, Florence Carmichael, who would eventually become his wife. After Allyn Taylor had rescued him from what Mingay had begun to think was a dead-end job, he rose steadily through the company, becoming familiar with all aspects of its operation. During his years in Toronto, in addition to vastly increasing the company's scope and its business, he made many close friends and wide contacts, and plunged deeply into community endeavours. Among the many institutions that benefited from his hard work and business acumen was the Ontario Heart Foundation.

Mingay was so well ensconced in the Queen City, in fact, that he was hesitant when Allyn Taylor asked him to return to London as vice-president and general manager in 1968. Taylor wooed him by reminding him that London offered excellent facilities for one of his favourite sports, golf. Mingay laughed as he told the author it was years before he ever managed to get in a single round.

Faced with his new responsibility for the day-to-day operation of the company, he realized that while he had plenty of administrative experience he had not paid much attention to the sophisticated new management techniques that were beginning to be adopted by some of the more progressive Canadian companies—things like management by objectives, formal corporate planning, and personal development, which went a step beyond the training programs for new employees the company had introduced years earlier. Jack Speake had just returned full of enthusiasm from a sojourn in the United States on an American Management Association course. So Mingay went back to school and spent a stimulating two weeks on an AMA course in Florida.

He returned as a preacher of the gospel and began to undertake a thorough transformation of the company's administration that would stand it in good stead in the turbulent decade that lay ahead. When he took over, the company had grown to such an extent that he had fifteen department heads reporting directly to him. It was an impossibly large number and so he named George Whitaker, a company veteran and its former secretary, as deputy general manager to coordinate the activities of all the assistant general managers in charge of the regions. This reduced the number of people reporting directly to him to a more manageable seven.

Several years earlier Allyn Taylor had begun to include a set of general objectives for the year ahead in his remarks at the annual meeting. Mingay took this practice a major step further early in 1969, when he instituted a program under which, twice a year, department heads were required to spell out their objectives for the six months ahead. Much time was spent in planning these objectives, but once they were established the staff knew what was expected of them and less time was spent in discussions about what they might or should do next. Mingay left no doubt that he was serious about the program, that it was not just some hare-brained notion he had picked up on his AMA course. "Standards of performance are required for each objective," he said in the annual report for that year, "and the results of the performance reviews will be a key factor in consideration of future merit increases in salary."

This "review of performance" process led naturally to the personal development program. In the old days, as in so many other companies, bosses seldom praised people for a job well done; employees were left to assume that they must be doing their jobs adequately so long as no one lowered the boom on them. Under the new program they sat down individually with their bosses every year for a candid discussion of their strengths and weaknesses. If there were any weaknesses they were given advice on what additional training they might take to improve their performance. They were also encouraged to discuss where they would like to go in the company in the future, and efforts were made to promote those whose performance showed promise into positions that would further their ambitions.

Mingay's next move was to summon more than a hundred of his management people to a conference in the fall of 1969 at which he announced a formal program of corporate planning and the appointment of a coordinator for it, Don Hughes, the first corporate planner the company had ever hired. One of the most important fruits of the new emphasis on planning, however, came not from outside but from within the company, with Mingay's enthusiastic sponsorship of an idea put forward by Jack Speake and Don McLean: the product manager concept.

Speake had welcomed the marketing initiatives brought to the company by McLean, and he had gradually come to believe that the same sort of professional attention should be given to the design, not just the marketing, of every product—in other words, service—that the company offered its customers, whether it was RSPs, savings accounts, guaranteed investment certificates, or anything else. The ultimate point of sale for all the company's services, of course, was the branch office. But now specialist managers were appointed at head office for each product the branches had to offer. The product manager's assigned responsibility was to make that product the best in the business. The job entailed keeping abreast of what the competition was doing, to make sure the product was up to date; consulting with branch staffs to find out what customers wanted; examining the implications of any tax changes; and ensuring that the product met all the legislative requirements under which the company operated.

It was a revolutionary concept in the financial industry, and as the product managers began to work hand in hand with McLean's marketers, Canada Trust pioneered a whole range of innovative services that would have bewildered consumers only a few years before. Both product managers and marketers worked closely with the data-processing team, and as each generation of computers surpassed the last in sophistication they began to use them to gather useful information as well as to store it.

In 1963, when the company embarked on its computerization program, everyone thought that once the three types of record-keeping activities seemingly adapted to automation—mortgage accounting, term borrowings and personal trust—had been captured on magnetic tape, that would be it: the computer would have made its contribution and the company would proceed on its course as before. The prevailing opinion was reflected in a sentence in Allyn Taylor's remarks to the shareholders at the beginning of 1965: "The installation of the electronic data-processing system continues well on schedule and will be close to completion by the end of the calendar year."

Two years later so many other aspects of the business were being computerized that the original IBM 1401 model had to be replaced by a more powerful and up-to-date IBM 360/30. The following year, with its annual expenditure on computer hardware approaching the million-dollar mark, the company had to add another 360/30. But in 1967, when head office in London was linked with all ten Toronto branches in an on-line teller system that enabled each customer to treat any branch as his own, the company used the services of a computer in the IBM data centre in Toronto rather than its own equipment.

Waterloo Trust, in contrast, had built its own on-line, any-branch banking system "in house," using its own computer. Fortunately, it was IBM equipment compatible with Canada Trust's 360/30s, and so when the time came to integrate the Waterloo Trust's branches into Canada Trust the transfer was accomplished literally overnight. All the savings records of the twelve Waterloo Trust branches were gathered together after close of business one day and Norm White drove them back to London in the trunk of his car; they amounted to just two disk packs. He arrived in London at 5 a.m., in time to plug the Waterloo Trust records into Canada Trust's system before the branches opened for business that morning. Soon afterward, with the benefit of Waterloo Trust's experience, the company set up its own on-line system and the Toronto branches' records were transferred to London from the IBM data centre in Toronto. In a gradual process extending over the next few years, every Canada Trust branch in the country was plugged into the any-branch banking network, an enormous convenience to travelling customers.

The convenience of the customer, of course, had been a key consideration in the computerization program from the beginning. But as computers became more powerful and sophisticated, and the staff began to realize how many apparently miraculous tasks they could perform, they began to be used more and more in the planning of the company's business, not just its day-to-day operation. A product manager charged with responsibility, say, for promoting the sale of debentures might find it useful to know who was buying them, and where the money was coming from. Was it "old money," for example, being transferred from one of the company's own savings accounts? Or was it "new money"? If so, where was it coming from? Was it being withdrawn from the Toronto-Dominion, or the Royal Bank, or some other competitor? Properly programmed, the computer could come up with answers to these questions and assist the product manager in his planning.

The new emphasis on planning and technology was not permitted to obscure the essential fact that the company's business, as it had been for more than a century, was to provide financial services for *people*. The "people factor" was heavily stressed in the company's advertising and public relations. "People serving People" was the theme of the annual report for 1970, in which the chairman's remarks and the pages of figures were sandwiched between pages of coloured photographs showing happy families at play, attractive young women skiing on both water and snow, and businessmen convening with the ever-helpful Canada Trust people.

When Don McLean took on the marketing job he realized that to market the company's products he would also have to "market" the company itself, to raise people's awareness of its presence on the financial scene. When the new building housing the main Toronto office opened at the corner of Yonge and Adelaide in 1967, he conducted an experiment. He sent staff members out for half a block in all four directions with instructions to ask passers-by, "Can you tell me where the Canada Trust is?" So few people knew, that McLean began to mount what he describes as "events" at the branch. "We had steel bands in," he recalled. "We even put a small aeroplane in the branch one day. We got all sorts of calls from people who didn't like it, but we soon identified the location."

The entrance to the building at 110 Yonge Street sits well back from the sidewalk, far enough back to allow a couple of cars to be parked outside it. McLean knew that the Ford Motor Company was about to launch a new line, its Fairlane model. He sought out his counterpart at Ford and asked him, "How would you like to have your cars displayed in downtown Toronto?" From there it was only a small step to deciding to give away one of the cars in a contest, with customers getting a chance to win with every deposit they made above a certain minimum. Car "give-aways" have been a successful part of the company's promotional effort ever since.

To raise public awareness of the company on the national scene, it was decided to commission the acknowledged leader in his field, Chris Yaneff, to design a new logo, or corporate symbol. Most financial institutions in those days, when they used colour at all, favoured blue or green. McLean considered those colours "cold," and persuaded Taylor that the new logo should be a "warm" colour, orange. The design ultimately selected was a rectangular C overturned on its side, open end down, with the white area inside it forming the T for trust. With its orange colour, the new logo had a brick-like appearance thought to convey the reliability and solidity of the company it represented. It was something of a departure in the financial community, and once again there was some eyebrow-raising. The first sign incorporating the logo was installed on the former head office of the Halton & Peel in Oakville, and Arthur Mingay and McLean went down late one afternoon and stood on a corner opposite to view the result in both daylight and dark. McLean chuckled as he recalled that some of the old Halton & Peel staff shook their fists at them, as if to say, "You can't do this to us."

Individually, Huron & Erie employees had always been encouraged to be good citizens, to give their time freely to community service. Now McLean set out to establish a public awareness that collectively, too, the organization they represented was a good corporate citizen. In the early 1970s there was a growing interest across Canada in ecological issues, a widespread concern that the environment was being polluted in all sorts of ways. One of the first uses for the new logo was on a series of stamps customers were invited to stick on their mail to express their concern. Given out free at the branches—a few sheets were even included in the 1971 annual report—the stamps featured attractive coloured illustrations with the theme, perhaps intentionally subliminal, of "Save." One showed a fish leaping for a fly, unattached to any hook, and bore the legend, "Save our lakes." A pair of appealing Bambi-like fawns illustrated the "Save our forests" stamps, and a couple of monarch butterflies perched on a flower carried the message "Save our air."

The following year, the illustrations on the "savings" stamps were replaced by reproductions of paintings by the Group of Seven. At the same time the company made the first corporate donation, a canvas by Tom Thomson titled "Pinecleft Rocks," to the McMichael Canadian collection, a gallery established in their home at Kleinburg, near Toronto, by Group of Seven enthusiasts Robert and Signe McMichael. The environment as a corporate cause proved popular, and the company followed up by sponsoring a series of television nature programs—"To the Wild Country," starring John and Janet Foster, with Lorne Greene as narrator—which won it national exposure on the Canadian Broadcasting Corporation network.

The promotions, or "stunts," as some still scornfully described them, followed each other in rapid succession. The 1974 annual report featured photographs of a longtime Canada Trust shareholder and customer, Toronto columnist and TV panelist Gordon Sinclair, famous, indeed notorious, for his curiosity about other people's money. Under a photograph of Gordon fishing contentedly from his boat was the caption "Start using the government's own rules and save a bundle on taxes"—an invitation to participate in the company's RSP program. In kilt and tam-o'-shanter, Gordon posed outside his cottage in the Muskoka Lakes country, assuring people in the caption "Whatever your needs, Canada Trust can help you."

Then there was the year that coach Punch Imlach and the local sports writers decided it was time for the Maple Leafs' ebullient Eddie Shack to hang up his skates. This suggested to the lively minds at Canada Trust that Eddie would be a good man to enlist in the corporate cause, with some theme such as, "If you're going to retire, make sure you have a Canada Trust RSP." Eddie proved amenable to the suggestion that he should make some TV commercials promoting the company's retirement plans and even managed to talk crusty old Harold Ballard, the Maple Leafs' owner, into permitting Maple Leaf Gardens to be the locale for the filming.

McLean and his marketers knew the importance of winning the support of the staff in the branches for their promotional efforts, and so the popular Shack was taken around to a variety of staff functions. McLean recalled a skating party at the Cambridge arena, when staff members were provided with sweaters bearing their names and Shack's number: 23. When the "mystery guest," the grinning Eddie, made his appearance on the ice, the employees roared with laughter and leaped up on to their seats to cheer him. "We had an organization in the branches," McLean said, "of people who were just exciting for any marketing person to run promotions with—they always added to them. They got excited about them and we made sure we told them why we were doing them and went around and got their support."

Naturally, with so many promotional balls in the air, some would occasionally drop to the floor. There was the year when the product manager and marketers crafted a campaign to drum up public enthusiasm for the company's investment fund. As the time approached for its launch, a rash of headlines proclaimed the ignominious collapse of Investors Overseas Services, a much-touted multi-billion-dollar American "offshore" mutual fund organization. The time was clearly not propitious for selling mutual funds, and the "abort take-off" button was pressed. Another program at about the same time drew a reproachful letter from John Turner, then the Liberal government's minister of finance. A TV commercial designed to sell RSPs was built round the theme of "Beat the tax man," and in its closing scene someone offscreen dumped a bucket of water over that unfortunate bureaucrat. Mr. Turner wrote to say he thought the whole thing rather undignified.

There was another, potentially more damaging, backfire involving an RSP campaign. That year's selling slogan was "The income tax problem—How to lick it," and to drive it home the marketers mailed out bulky envelopes containing children's suckers—just at a time when it was reported in the press that a Jewish resident of southwestern Ontario had received a letter-bomb in his mail. Jack

Wilson in Vancouver was so concerned about the possibly disastrous publicity this might entail that he somehow managed to talk his way into the Post Office to intercept the mailing.

Such embarrassments and setbacks notwithstanding, the marketing and promotional efforts were triumphantly successful. The company's assets under administration, $2.2 billion at the time of the merger in 1968, had mounted to $3.2 billion by 1971; only two years later they had grown by a further $1 billion.

As the company grew and its operations became more sophisticated, Allyn Taylor decided that the advisory boards across the country no longer served any useful function. In the old days these boards, composed of prominent local businessmen in cities such as Toronto, Hamilton, Winnipeg, and Vancouver, had been able to offer management valuable advice on mortgages in their areas. But by the early 1970s Taylor decided that the company's own "mortgage machine" had become so efficient that they were no longer necessary. There were by now almost a hundred members on the advisory boards across the country, and Taylor felt they were being treated as second-class citizens, in that very few of them were also directors of the company. They thus in a sense had responsibility but no authority, no opportunity to participate in the decision-making process.[1]

It was a delicate mission, but Walter Bean, deputy chairman, joined Taylor and they set out across the country to disband these committees of distinguished elder statesmen of the business world. They expected to run into what Taylor described as "a lot of flak." But the businessmen—at that point there was only one women member, Margaret P. Hyndman, a Toronto lawyer who had been a director of the old London & Western—accepted their fate with equanimity. "They realized we were just being honest," Taylor recalled. To his relief, only two of the advisory board members were disgruntled enough to withdraw their business from the company.

---

1. Taylor was perhaps influenced in his decision by the fact that his own board had now reached a rather impractical size, fifty-five members, since all directors of the Waterloo Trust and three Halton & Peel directors had been invited to join the Canada Trust board after the merger. Though this meant that extra tables had to be set up in the boardroom, it had one compensation for Taylor; his friend Ken MacGregor of Mutual finally became a member of the board, as a director of Waterloo Trust.

The old order was about to change in another way too. Years before, there had been general agreement that the irascible T.G. Meredith, and later Morley Aylsworth, had clung to the reins of power too long. Consequently, it was decided that no one should remain president after the age of sixty-five or chairman after the age of seventy. In 1973 Allyn Taylor, though still as vigorous as anyone in the company, reached the age of sixty-five and relinquished the role of president to Arthur Mingay. He retained the title of chairman of the board and the executive committee. Mingay, as president, also assumed the new designation of chief executive officer. Merv Lahn, who had been brought to head office from Kitchener as deputy general manager a year before, took over the responsibility for day-to-day operations as senior vice-president and general manager.

18

The Challenge of Inflation

MERVYN Lloyd Lahn was born in 1933 in Hanover, 105 kilometres north of Kitchener. His father and mother were both descended from hard-working German immigrant families who took up homesteads in that area in the 1880s. Shortly before Merv was born his father left the family farm and took his wife to Hanover, where he founded a construction business that soon began to prosper. A strapping youngster, Merv worked at any part-time job he could lay his hands on during his school years. He once had the biggest *Toronto Star* paper route in the area. He worked in grocery stores and ran a buzz-saw in a furniture factory. He even worked on the chicken-killing line at a local meat-packing plant, where he acquired an equanimity about blood on the floor that would come in useful in his later career.

With the money he earned Merv dabbled in the stock market, but he still found time to earn good grades, take part in the usual high school sports, and play cornet in the Hanover town band, which picked up its share of gold medals at exhibitions, including one from the celebrated Canadian National Exhibition in Toronto. Though he did not continue with his music in later life, he was good enough as a teen-ager to play in a dance band of some local renown, Frankie Banks' Orchestra.

When he graduated from high school, young Merv was accepted in an apprenticeship course which would have led to a job as an Ontario Land Surveyor. While waiting to join a crew headed for the north country, he mixed mortar and carried bricks for his father's company, which was at that time building a women's dormitory at Waterloo College. As the students began to arrive at the college in the fall, Merv decided he would like to join them, and even though he was late in applying he was accepted.

Waterloo College, which had been founded by the Lutheran church, was at that time affiliated with the University of Western Ontario.[1] Merv's best subjects as he worked toward his bachelor's degree in general arts were those related to business, such as economics and accounting; in one of his economics courses he earned the highest marks in the whole University of Western Ontario. After his graduation in 1954 he travelled for a while in the United States and planned to enter Columbia University on a scholarship in the fall of 1955. To fill in the time until then, he went to the Kitchener-Waterloo area looking for a job. He was offered three—times were good in those days—and he chose the one that paid the lowest wage since it sounded the most interesting. So at the beginning of 1955 he joined Waterloo Trust as a clerk in the investment department, where his duties included keeping charts on bond and stock prices and preparing statements of account by categories of investments. His immediate superior, like Merv himself, dabbled in the stock market and soon left for a job in a brokerage house. Thus fortuitously presented with the opportunity to move up on to the first rung of the ladder, Lahn abandoned the thought of enrolling at Columbia and began to look for the next rung.

His boss, Walter Bean, recognized his potential and encouraged him in his quest, sending him off to courses given by the Trust Companies Association and at universities in both Canada and the United States. Three years after joining Waterloo Trust he was made assistant treasurer; two years later he became treasurer, and in 1967 assistant general manager. As Bean's heir-apparent, he was a logical choice to take over Canada Trust's new region after the merger, and it was not long before Allyn Taylor and Arthur Mingay came to share their new colleague Water Bean's admiration for Lahn's qualities.

For years before he retired from the presidency, Allyn Taylor had kept under his blotter a memo to the board of directors containing his recommendation for the corporate succession should he, as he says, "get hit by a truck." Arthur Mingay had long headed that list as his choice of president; and when Mingay

1. Waterloo College, to take advantage of provincial grants, later became a non-denominational university, initially called Waterloo Lutheran University and subsequently Wilfrid Laurier University. Lahn was a member of its board of governors years later when WLU gave birth to the University of Waterloo.

persuaded Lahn to move from Kitchener to head office in 1972, both he and Taylor were clear in their minds that they were ensuring the continuation of that orderly succession process. Going all the way back to the days of Morley Aylsworth, changes in command at the Huron & Erie were free of the upheavals and purges that sometimes accompany them in less ordered organizations.

When he arrived in London, Lahn was in the prime of life: thirty-nine years old, tall, straight-backed, and broad-shouldered. He had an easy air of authority guaranteed to attract attention in any room. His active mind had been honed by wide experience, and he was blessed with energy, a passion for efficiency, and, like Taylor and Mingay before him, a capacity for inspiring others to follow his leadership. He could be tough, very tough, when he thought circumstances required it, a quality often revealed in the stream of numbered memos that poured from his office. Precisely because they were numbered, his lieutenants could marvel at how many hundreds of these he despatched each month. But though demanding, he was always fair. His philosophy of management was to set out clearly what had to be done and then try to obtain a consensus on it by thrashing it out with his senior management group; once unanimity on the goal was attained, he believed, everyone would have a shared commitment to achieving it.

Lahn took over responsibility for day-to-day operations at a difficult time. The inflation that had worried Allyn Taylor in the late 1960s had pushed mortgage interest rates up far past levels considered usurious not so long before. By the end of 1969 they averaged ten and a half per cent, and other rates rose to match. The company found it had to pay eight and three-quarters per cent to attract term deposits, and interest on savings accounts rose to six and three-quarters per cent. Inflation eased in the early 1970s—in 1971 the consumer price index rose by less than three per cent, the smallest increase for years—and interest rates returned to more normal levels. The company's net operating earnings that year rocketed up to $10.1 million, an increase of more than $4 million from the year before; and they rose again in 1972, by almost $3 million.

But in 1973, the year Lahn took over, the Organization of Petroleum Exporting Countries quadrupled the international price of oil, from $3 a barrel to almost $12. In an attempt to shield

Canadians from the worst effects of the worldwide economic chaos that followed, the federal government instituted a policy—perceived as unwise by some at the time and by virtually everyone in retrospect—of controlling domestic oil and natural gas prices at much lower than international levels. As so often before, Canada could not insulate itself from what was happening in the outside world: in 1974 the consumer price index rose by 10.9 per cent. Double-digit inflation had arrived.

The effect on Canada Trust was dramatic—and not at all what Merv Lahn would have liked to report at the end of his first year as general manager. Even though the assets under its administration increased by sixteen per cent during the year, to just under $5 billion, the company's net operating earnings fell by thirty per cent, from $12.9 million to $8.9 million. Translated into earnings per common share, this was a drop from $2.33 to $1.60. Inflation remained above ten per cent in 1975, and with every indication that it would continue, something clearly had to be done.

As the head-office staff settled into new quarters,[2] Mingay and Lahn exhorted them to new efforts. The reason for the loss of earnings in 1974 was that the "spread," which had stood at 2.15 per cent in 1972 and 1.98 per cent in 1973, had slumped all the way down to 1.37 per cent. In the old days, when interest rates were relatively stable, the company could survive by gathering in savings deposits, subject to short-term interest-rate fluctuations, and lending them out in mortgages, at interest rates set for five years. If the interest rate went up or down, it would be only by a small percentage, and what the company lost on the swings one year it would gain back on the roundabouts the following year.

But when double-digit inflation arrived and interest rates kept on rising, the price the company had to pay for new money came perilously close to what it was earning on mortgages made in earlier, more settled, years. In other words, its assets and liabilities—what it owned and what it owed—were becoming badly

---

2. The Canada Trust Tower, occupied at the end of 1974, is part of the City Centre development in downtown London, which consists of two high-rise office towers, a twenty-two-storey Holiday Inn, restaurants and stores. Canada Trust is a twenty-five-per-cent partner in the company that built it. The branch and vaults in the company's former head-office building, opened with such fanfare in 1931, continue in use, and among the building's tenants is Bishop Cronyn's Anglican diocese.

mismatched, to the detriment of the spread. One of the first attempts to cure the mismatch in order to achieve a better balance between the maturity dates of the company's assets and liabilities came in 1975, with the introduction of variable-term mortgages. Instead of the traditional five-year term, customers were now offered mortgages for periods varying from one to five years, and in the unsettled economic climate many of them began to choose one-year terms.

That was only the first of a whole series of new departures from the traditional way of doing business that followed during the next few years, as inflation raged on and management battled to cope with its ravages. It had always been recognized that the company's intermediary, or retail banking, operation was by far its most profitable. In fact, studies during the 1960s had shown that the margin of profit on its personal trust business was only about one-twentieth of one per cent per year. That meant a return to the shareholders of about $50 for every $100,000 in the volume of its assets under administration.

The company had been in the retail banking business ever since its formation, of course, and despite 1974's disappointing financial results it passed an encouraging milestone that year with more than $2 billion in deposits. Unimaginable as this would have been to Adam Hope, Daniel Macfie, and the rest of the founders, it was only a tiny fraction of the country's total retail banking business, ninety per cent of which was transacted at the thousands of branches of the chartered banks. In Lahn's view, that left plenty of room for Canada Trust to increase its market share, and he took dead aim at the banks. The company had been trying for some time to be "more like the banks." Now the focus changed: the strategy became to be *different* from the banks, by offering more and better services.

One of the first moves in the new competitive strategy was the decision in 1976 to introduce extended banking hours. Banks in those days were open only from 10 a.m. to 3 p.m. Canada Trust was open longer: from 9 a.m. to 5 p.m. But Eric Minns, as senior product manager in the savings area, thought these hours were still too short to suit many customers. More and more, husbands and wives both worked outside the home, and for many of them "nine to five" was the workday. So it was decided that one way to be different from the banks, and to offer better service, would be to keep longer hours.

Minns and a group of product managers and marketers met one day to "brainstorm" this concept. How long should the branches be open, and how should the new service be advertised to the customers? The phrase "extended banking hours" had no appeal to the marketers, and someone threw out the suggestion that the hours should be "nine to nine, all the time." Minns did not think he had a chance of winning approval for such a revolutionary change. The next contribution came from Frank Pratt, a graduate of the University of Western Ontario who had been working in Colgate-Palmolive's marketing department when Don McLean hired him as his assistant in 1967. Pratt came up with "Eight to eight, six days straight." Someone repeated it, and they tossed it back and forth across the room. It would certainly make a catchy slogan, and with those hours most people would be able to do their banking before they went to work or on their way home. But it was such a radical concept, would it "fly" with the powers-that-be?

Eric Minns took the idea to the general manager. "It was the only time I ever saw Merv Lahn hesitate on a decision," he recalled. It would certainly be a revolutionary break with tradition. How would it be accepted by the staffs of the branches? Could enough part-time people be recruited and trained? Could the new hours be managed effectively without lowering the standards of service and perhaps incurring lawsuits because of people who lacked adequate training? Above all, would it pay for itself?

As usual, Lahn thrashed it out with his top lieutenants and it was decided to suggest to the board that the new concept be tried for a year in London and St. Thomas; if enough new business resulted it should then be gradually introduced across the country. The board, though no doubt with some qualms, sanctioned the pilot project.

London was already the scene of another pilot project that proved as important to the company's future sucess as "Eight to Eight" would turn out to be. When Merv Lahn first moved to London and was driving around getting to know the city, he told his wife, Myra, "Obviously we have to duplicate here what we have in Kitchener-Waterloo." At that time there were nine Canada Trust branches in Kitchener-Waterloo. London, with a population probably half as large again, had only six. Lahn figured that to match the blanket coverage that existed in Kitchener-Waterloo,

London should probably have as many as eighteen branches. So what became known as the "cell concept" was born. Instead of, as previously, trying to be represented in as many communities as possible across the country, if only by one branch, the company now began to target specific cities; by establishing more branches in strategic locations it would try to achieve blanket coverage.

Jack Biggs, vice-president of the southwestern region, with London as his headquarters, embraced the cell concept enthusiastically. He pinned a huge map of the city on his office wall and, area by area, set out to study traffic flows, shopping patterns, population densities, and possible branch sites. Within five years the number of branches in London grew from six to fourteen.

Biggs was just as enthusiastic about the "Eight to Eight" project, though not all his branch managers shared his enthusiasm. As Minns put it, "They could see their comfort zone being eroded." The advertisements for part-time staff drew several hundred applications, many from former tellers who had left their jobs to marry and have children and were delighted at the prospect of perhaps being able to work at a time when their husbands could look after the kids. The logistical problems of training so many new employees and fitting them into the branches were overcome, and the target figure of 15,000 new accounts for the year was exceeded in the first five months of the "Eight to Eight" operation.

When the year-long pilot project was completed it was unanimously judged a resounding success, having exceeded all its objectives. Its cost, including all marketing expenses and extra salaries, was less than half a million dollars. It brought in more than 18,000 new accounts and $24 million in new demand deposits, and a satisfying increase in the company's other business, such as term deposits and RSPs.

Before the "Eight to Eight" campaign in London and St. Thomas, Archie Kerr, who had replaced Merv Lahn in Kitchener, was proud of his region's position as No. 1 in the company. By the end of the campaign, the southwestern region had usurped his lead. Kerr did not like being No. 2 and grumbled about it to Minns. Minns told him the answer was simple: go "Eight to Eight." Kerr did, and Minns proved right. From then on both the "Eight to Eight" hours and the cell concept were gradually introduced across the system.

In 1976,[3] even before the London "cell" was completed, the company substantially increased its branch coverage in Ontario by acquiring two smaller but flourishing regional companies, the Lincoln Trust and Savings Company and the Ontario Trust Company. Lincoln Trust had been founded in 1964 by a young Niagara Falls lawyer, Jack Burnett, one-time campaign manager for Judy LaMarsh, a fellow lawyer and feisty federal cabinet minister during the 1960s. Burnett felt that the trust services available to residents of the Niagara Peninsula were inadequate, and with the backing of a group of local businessmen he organized a series of public meetings to enlist support for his application to the provincial government for a charter. At that time anyone seeking to found a trust company had to demonstrate that he had potential shareholders committed to subscribe at least $500,000 for its shares. By the time Burnett applied for his charter, almost 400 potential shareholders had subscribed $1.1 million.

Lincoln Trust's first employee was Leo P. Sauvé, a young accountant born in Foresters Falls, west of Ottawa, who was at that time the resident partner in Niagara Falls for a Toronto firm of chartered accountants. He went to work in May 1964 in a small room above a liquor store in Niagara Falls, but by the end of the year Lincoln Trust had opened five branches. It grew rapidly, until it had ten branches in the Niagara Peninsula and assets under administration amounting to more than $215 million.

Sauvé, by now Lincoln Trust's president, was in Montreal early in 1976 for a meeting of the Trust Companies Association at which Arthur Mingay was elected president. During one of the sessions he was handed a note: could he meet Michael deGroote, president of Laidlaw Transportation Ltd., in deGroote's hotel room after the meeting? Sauvé had no idea what lay behind the summons, and when he answered it he received an unpleasant jolt: deGroote told him he had asked the regulatory authorities to take Lincoln Trust's shares off the market, since one of his companies, Hamilton Trust, had made a takeover bid for them. Sauvé returned to his own room immediately and got on the phone to summon a meeting of Lincoln Trust's directors for the next morning. He had taken his

3. By that time, the long process of shedding the original name of the old Huron & Erie had been completed: the company formally changed its name to the Canada Trustco Mortgage Company in April 1976.

wife and daughter with him to Montreal and he rounded them up and drove home overnight.

That same evening deGroote told Arthur Mingay about his takeover bid. The two men were not unacquainted; Mingay had tried to buy Hamilton Trust as part of Canada Trust's expansion program. He had also tried to buy Lincoln Trust, and when he heard the price deGroote was offering for it—$15 cash per share—he realized it was worth considerably more to Canada Trust.

When Lincoln Trust's directors met on the morning after deGroote's offer, they also considered the price far too low. They did not want to sell at all, but they could not muster enough of the widely-held shares to be certain of fighting off deGroote's bid. So when Arthur Mingay donned the armour of a white knight and offered to counter it with a straight share-for-share exchange—Canada Trustco shares were selling for $23 at the time—the directors unanimously recommended that their shareholders accept it.

The ten Lincoln Trust branches and the ten Canada Trust branches already operating in the area were combined into a new "cell," the Hamilton-Niagara region, with Leo Sauvé as vice-president in charge, and most of Lincoln Trust's 135 employees stayed with the new organization. Some senior managers left for other jobs, and Sauvé in retrospect thinks they made a mistake. He himself went on to become Canada Trust's senior vice-president for western Canada.

The other company acquired in 1976, Ontario Trust, had been formed in Toronto in 1971 as an amalgamation of three smaller companies operating largely in northern Ontario. When it was purchased by Canada Trust it had sixteen branches and assets under administration of more than $271 million. It was controlled by Dr. Kenneth Roberts, a physician who had found his hobby of playing the stock market so profitable that he had abandoned medicine for a full-time career as an entrepreneur. Once again, the purchase was accomplished by an exchange of shares—three Canada Trustco shares for every five shares of Ontario Trust.

All told, in cash and shares, the two acquisitions cost Canada Trust $34.2 million, and as sometimes happens in takeovers, there were unforeseen expenses later. Lincoln Trust had been very successful gathering in deposits in the Niagara Peninsula but had been unable to invest all its funds locally. So it had made some big investments outside its own area which later became what are delicately called in the business "problem loans." A Canada Trust study, after the dust had settled, showed that in effect the losses increased the price paid for the company to approximately $25 per share.

Also, when Arthur Mingay first began to discuss the idea of purchasing Ontario Trust with Dr. Roberts, the company had earnings for the previous year of $937,000. Roberts told Mingay it would earn far more than that in 1976, but Mingay doubted it. However, Roberts introduced a rigorous cost-cutting campaign and by the time the sale went through the company had made more than $1 million in the first eight months of 1976 alone. Any satisfaction this improved performance might have had for Canada Trust was tempered when, under the anti-inflation controls then existing, the company was presented with a bill for several hundred thousand dollars in taxes on the increased earnings. Mingay journeyed to Ottawa to argue that the increase was not really a normal profit—that it had been achieved by extraordinary measures taken to facilitate the company's sale. As so often happens when someone contests a tax assessment, he was unsuccessful.

These unpleasant surprises notwithstanding, the acquisitions strengthened the company's coverage in key areas and brought its total number of branches across the country up to 123, which, in the words of the annual report at the end of the year, were "of great strategic value in an increasingly competitive environment."

The company's concern over that competitive environment had not been eased by a government White Paper published in August 1976, setting out proposed legislative changes to be adopted when the Bank Act came up for its ten-yearly revision the following year. In the eyes of Taylor, Mingay, and Lahn, and many others in the trust industry, the proposed changes threatened to follow on where the 1967 Bank Act revisions left off, by giving the banks even greater advantages, without doing anything at all for the trust companies and other financial institutions.

The practice of revising the Bank Act every ten years began in the year after Confederation. Its effect was to keep banking legislation in pace with the changing times and, as the legislation evolved, banks acquired what lawyers call "the powers of a natural person." In other words, the banks could do virtually anything they judged advisable with their assets. The trust companies, to their mounting indignation, were still hamstrung by legislation strictly prescribing what they could do with their assets—legislation substantially unchanged since 1914, long before the days of loans for cars and boats, credit cards, and a host of other modern practices.

As the financial industry awaited the new 1977 Bank Act it seemed that the government intended to accompany it with an overhaul of the legislation governing loan and trust companies. This was considered long overdue and particularly important because one of the changes proposed was to bring all institutions offering customers chequing facilities into a new Canadian Payments Association which would replace the system operated by the banks at that time to clear each other's cheques. All members of the association would have been required to maintain reserves bearing no interest with the Bank of Canada, as the banks were required to do. Canada Trust's annual report for 1976 pointed out that this would impose a double burden on trust companies because they were already required by legislation to make ample provision for their liquidity by holding a set percentage of short-term government bonds. If this was to be the future pattern of the industry, the report suggested, trust companies should be allowed to use the word bank in their corporate names. "The difference between chartered banks and trust banks," the report said, "would be clear and distinct, with chartered banks providing full banking services but not fiduciary services and trust banks providing fiduciary services with limited banking services."

As it turned out, the 1977 Bank Act revisions were delayed until 1980; and when they came they were unaccompanied by any updating of the legislation governing trust companies. One regulatory change Canada Trust had long been pleading for, of course, was the introduction of the ten-per-cent ownership restriction already applying to the banks. The federal superintendent of insurance, Richard Humphrys, was known to be in favour of this change, and when the government persisted in its refusal to introduce it, he suggested a method by which the company might try to protect its independence against any potential marauder. In 1975, at Humphrys's suggestion, Canada Trust applied for and obtained legislative approval for a corporate by-law preventing any shareholder or group of associated shareholders, no matter how large their holding, from voting more than fifteen per cent of the total number of shares outstanding. The fifteen-per-cent figure was set as a "grandfather" provision in deference to Max Meighen's holding; the ultimate aim of the by-law, which was achieved later, was to reduce any one shareholder's voting rights to ten per cent.

An arrangement such as this is open to the criticism that it might enable management to entrench itself in power by somehow bringing about the election to the board of only "captive" directors favourable to its own cause. By "packing" the board, the argument goes, management could abrogate the right of outside directors to dislodge a management with which they were dissatisfied. To counter this objection, a companion by-law was adopted preventing any active or retired employees of the company from sitting on the committee charged with the responsibility for recommending directors for nomination.

With the "ten-per-cent by-law" in place and thirty-five per cent of its shares still in the hands of the "friendly shareholder" group, the company seemed immune to attack. It would not be many years before the immunity was shown to be illusory.

19

The Struggle to Preserve the "Spread"

IN 1977, more than a year before any of the banks, Canada Trust became the first national financial institution to start paying daily interest on savings accounts. This innovation, which was soon extended to chequing accounts, was costly, but it put the company away ahead of the field until its competitors were able to gear up their systems to follow suit. The calculation and payment of daily interest would have been impossible, of course, without the computer. By now the company had gone through several generations of computers, each one more powerful and remarkable than the last, and its data-processing staff had grown to more than two hundred people.

About that time IBM announced that it would soon be introducing a revolutionary new computer, its 3033. This promised to be such an advance on all previous models that about thirty Canadian companies lined up to buy it, and IBM threw their names into a hat in a lottery to see who would get the first one available in this country. When Canada Trust won, a department-store chain offered it $100,000 for its right to be first in line. The offer was politely refused and the company replaced its four existing computers with the 3033 in 1978. By that time its annual expenditure on computer hardware had reached $4 million. Two years later its volume of business had grown so much and so many new uses were being found for the computer system that it had to install another 3033, and its hardware costs reached $5 million a year. By now data processing had become so vital that the company had built a high-security computer centre at Wilton Grove, in an industrial park in South London, with its own emergency electrical generators to guard against a power failure; and in 1987 it opened another back-up centre at Erin Mills, near Toronto. By then it had four even more powerful computers than the 3033 and its annual expenditure on hardware exceeded $35 million.

At the beginning of 1978 Allyn Taylor's long career with Canada Trust came to an official end when he retired from the chairmanship. In forty-two years he had seen—and been largely instrumental in—a growth in the company's assets from $45 million to $9.1 billion. As honorary chairman, he remained on the board of directors and the executive committee for a few more years, and in his early eighties he was still as busy as ever, organizing community fund drives, entertaining guests at testimonial dinners with his witty speeches, and playing golf. Arthur Mingay stepped into his shoes as chairman, and Merv Lahn became president.

Lahn once again took on his new responsibility at a challenging time. The double-digit inflation of 1974 and 1975 had eased somewhat, but not back to normal levels: in 1977, the consumer price index rose by 7.9 per cent. Interest rates, though, had dropped below the high levels of 1974 and 1976—for much of 1977 mortgage rates were below nine per cent—and the company's net earnings had risen to a record $30 million. Nevertheless, the country's economy was still sluggish, with high unemployment and an atmosphere of uncertainty that deterred investors.

Lahn sensed storm clouds still ahead and at a meeting of his top managers held at Foxfire, Georgia, he warned them that if they were to continue to make money for the company's shareholders they must redouble their efforts to increase efficiency and control costs, without impairing the level of service to their customers. Since he was asking them to make a supreme commitment to the company, he asked what they would like the company to do for them in return. Someone said, "Well, if we put in all this superhuman effort you're asking for we're probably going to be burned out by the time we're fifty-five. What about a stock-option plan so we can retire in peace?"

Arthur Mingay had introduced a management incentive plan related to the company's earnings when he took over the reins years before, but stock-option plans, a common incentive for executives in the rest of the business world, were unknown among financial institutions at that time; banks, in fact, were prevented by law from offering them. But when Lahn took the idea to his board of directors they approved it without hesitation. The superhuman efforts Lahn expected in return would certainly be called for in the troubled years ahead.

Even though the worrying inflation continued during 1978, the company still managed to report net earnings of $31.9 million, a slight increase on the year before. But there were disturbing developments. The prime lending rate increased six times during the year, rising from 8.25 per cent to 11.5 per cent. At the same time, because of intense competition and reduced demand, mortgage rates rose less than those paid on term deposits. The result was that the all-important spread had shrunk by the last quarter of the year to 1.71 per cent, compared to 2.24 per cent in the last quarter of 1977.

This was a trend that boded ill for the future, and in 1979, as inflation again edged up perilously close to the dreaded double-digit level, the effect on Canada Trust's balance sheet was dramatic. The interest paid on savings deposits rose five times during the year, from 9 per cent to 12 per cent. The spread shrank to 1.54 per cent, and the company's net earnings, at $24.4 million, were down 23 per cent from the year before.

If this shrinking of the spread could not be halted, it was clear that the company was on a course that could lead only to disaster, and Merv Lahn realized that something had to be done about it. The man he chose to do it had been trained not as a banker but as an engineer. Peter Maurice, son of a London locomotive engineer, enrolled in the University of Western Ontario with the idea of becoming a geologist. After a summer among the black flies in the northern bush he decided that that was not for him and switched to engineering. He graduated as a mechanical engineer and for three years worked on projects for Imperial Oil. Along the way he became interested in computers and the arcane technique known as mathematical model-building, and so he moved to a management-consulting firm, Stevenson & Kellogg.

After two years travelling the country building mathematical models for clients and advising them on corporate strategies, he decided he was not spending enough time with his family and took a more settled job as corporate planner for Maple Leaf Mills. When that company became embroiled in a takeover squabble, he left to join Canadian Wallpaper Manufacturers, a division of the large British Reed Paper group. By now his reputation was becoming established, and when Arthur Mingay went looking for a new corporate planning manager in 1972, Maurice received a call from a "head-hunter." When he was asked if he would like a job with a trust company he was not overly impressed; the trust business did not seem the most exciting area in which to build a career. But his wife was fond of London and he agreed to look into it, and when he examined Canada Trust's operation, particularly its progressive use of the computer, he became enthusiastic about the job.

As soon as he moved to London he had a computer terminal installed in his office. He was one of the first executives other than those immediately concerned with data processing to do so, and the others used to wonder what this young fellow—he was still in his mid-thirties—was doing, tinkering away at his little green-eyed monster. What he was doing can be summed up in retrospect as taking a fresh look at the company's business with an astute outsider's eye. And the contribution his mathematical model-building made to the company's financial planning, its implementation of the "cell" concept, and all the other exciting innovations going on in those days sufficiently impressed Merv Lahn that by the beginning of 1976 Peter Maurice, geologist-turned-engineer-turned-banker, was vice-president in charge of the southwestern Ontario region.

One day Maurice received a call from Merv Lahn. "I've got a new job for you," Lahn told him. "You're going to Toronto to run the finance area." Maurice protested that he didn't know anything about running a treasury. "Nonsense," said Lahn, "you'll have a lot of fun." So in the summer of 1979 Maurice moved to Toronto as group vice-president, finance. It was not a time that promised much fun. For the first half of that year interest rates had been relatively stable, though at a level that would have been unimaginable a decade earlier. In the fall they began to rise again, and it was clear that the company's earnings for the year would be down.

In a sense, the company was being victimized by its own success. Its imaginative promotions and innovations in the previous decade, particularly the introduction of "Eight to Eight" and daily-interest accounts, had brought in a flood of new money, and its deposits by now were growing at the rate of more than $1 billion a year. But most of that new money was short-term, subject to withdrawal on demand and to rapidly rising interest rates. And most of the company's investments were still long-term, at interest rates in some cases below what it was now having to pay for deposits.

It was the old problem of the mismatch, and it came to a head in 1980. In that year, double-digit inflation took hold again—the consumer price index rose by 10.2 per cent—and with it came the economic recession that had long been predicted. For a while in the spring and early summer the bank rate set by the Bank of Canada in its attempt to control the inflation exceeded 15 per cent, and other interest rates were correspondingly high. Canada Trust's spread for the year shrank again, to 1.48 per cent, and by the year-end its mismatch exceeded $1 billion, a dangerously large proportion of its whole balance sheet.

At the beginning of 1981 Merv Lahn handed Peter Maurice a challenging assignment: to eliminate the mismatch by the beginning of 1983. In essence, the problem was quite simple: if you lend money at a fixed rate for five years, even at the "usurious" rate of eight per cent, you are going to be hurt if two or three years later you are having to pay ten, eleven, or twelve per cent to raise new money. The question arises here: why would a company get itself into that fix? The answer is complex. First of all, that was the way companies had always done business, and before the dislocating gyrations in interest rates of the 1970s and 1980s, the peaks and valleys in their earnings had eventually balanced themselves out. Also, the concept that the company was in business to serve people was more than just a marketing device; it was deeply ingrained in the corporate ethos. If customers wanted a five-year mortgage, that is what the company would give them; and if customers wanted to lend the company money by investing in a six-month savings certificate rather than a five-year debenture, it would not turn them away. Finally, there was even a feeling in the industry that companies should not try to manage their way around the mismatch problem—that as financial intermediaries their historical role was to accommodate both borrowers and lenders and let the chips fall where they may; that was the normal risk of doing business.

Peter Maurice had first become interested in the complexities of the matching problem when he was still learning the business, in the bad year of 1974. At that time no one in the industry thought anything could be done about it, and as interest rates declined in the mid-1970s and the company's earnings recovered, the problem seemed less than urgent. But by 1979, when Maurice became the company's chief financial officer, the danger signals were flashing again. The company began to look for investments that would "float" with the interest rate and balance the "float-rate" liabilities represented by all the short-term money its branches were taking in over the counter, on which it had to pay the rapidly escalating interest rate.

In an attempt to generate float-rate funds the company had earlier tried to interest customers in short-term mortgages that moved upward or downward with the prime interest rate. They had proved unpopular. But in the uncertain economic atmosphere of 1980, when the company became the first financial institution to offer a six-month open mortgage, with an interest rate set one percentage point lower than the long-term rate, the response was more encouraging.

Another source of float-rate funds that the company had not previously tapped was unsecured loans to corporations, linked to, and fluctuating with, the prime lending rate set by the banks. The distinction between "corporate" loans and "commercial" loans secured by mortgages is somewhat blurred. The company had been making commercial mortgage loans ever since Allyn Taylor's day, though the board of directors had had grave reservations when Arthur Mingay asked it to approve the first $1 million loan it had ever contemplated. That was to build the Valhalla Inn on Highway 27 west of Toronto, and it was, of course, secured by a mortgage. By 1979 the directors had become accustomed to that sort of loan. But when Maurice presented them with the first proposed corporate loans—$2 million each to a couple of manufacturing companies in southwestern Ontario—they balked again. After much discussion, they agreed that the company could "do" half of each loan, whereupon the manufacturers took their business elsewhere.

Maurice persevered, however, and when the new department set up in 1980 to handle corporate loans started to bring in apparently rock-solid investments, the directors overcame their initial qualms. By the end of that year the company had made more than four hundred corporate loans totalling $270 million, all of them float-rate. It was only a small step along the way to curing the mismatch, but it was a promising start.

When Maurice was assigned the task of eliminating the mismatch, he enlisted the assistance of Tom Gunn, a Bay Street investment analyst who had joined the company in 1978 and two years later had become assistant vice-president, treasury systems. By its very nature the mismatch problem could not be solved overnight; most of the company's funds were lent out in mortgages on which the interest rate would change only when they matured. Also, the task was complicated by the fact that the inflationary storm reached its height in 1981. The consumer price index rose by 12.5 per cent during the year, and in the month of September the company had to pay 19 per cent on its demand savings deposits.

When Maurice had first tried to do something about matching, he was forced to work with information that was perhaps two months out of date, because of the time it took for reports to come in from the branches about the type of money they were taking in. So he and Gunn devised a computer program that monitored all the transactions in the branches as they were posted to the master files every night. This told them what sort of funds were coming in: long-term or short-term, fixed rate or float-rate. Then, working closely with the branches, they would try to shape lending policies to match the money going out with what was coming in. At one time, a quota might be put on mortgages; at another a loan sale might be held. Little stickers were attached to the rate cards distributed to branch managers saying, "Think float-rate."

There was also a drive to coordinate the company's various investments—the loans it made to banks and other financial institutions, its purchases of stocks and bonds, and so on—with an eye to generating float-rate assets. The biggest push came in the field of corporate loans. Bigger and bigger loans were made to Canadian corporations, including oil companies out west, steel and transportation companies in Ontario, and even IBM, which was provided with bridge financing for a huge new head office building at Markham, near Toronto. By the end of 1981 the company had lent more than $1 billion, mostly in float-rate funds, to Canadian corporations, and the mismatch had been reduced by more than half a billion dollars.

That was not enough, in that peak year of inflation, to prevent the spread from shrinking again, all the way down to 1.27 per cent. Mercifully, though, interest rates began to decline in the fall, and the company's fourth-quarter earnings rose dramatically, enabling it to finish the year with earnings of $28.7 million, slightly above those of the previous year. This translated to $2.53 for each common share, a dollar below the levels of the late 1970s.

The campaign to cure the mismatch achieved its objective in August the following year, several months ahead of schedule. Its success, and the continuing decline in interest rates during the year, restored the company's good health. The spread recovered to 1.81 per cent and earnings rose to a record $40.3 million, an increase of 41 per cent from the year before.

But no campaign is waged without casualties. The runaway inflation and soaring interest rates in those years damaged many Canadian companies and ruined some, particularly in the west, where the economy was devastated when the international price of oil failed to rise to the spectacular heights that had been predicted in the 1970s. One company hit particularly hard was Turbo Resources, an oil and gas company with a chain of retail gas stations, which had borrowed a couple of hundred million dollars from the Canadian Imperial Bank of Commerce to build an oil refinery in Alberta. The company had also borrowed $20 million from Canada Trust in an unsecured loan for general corporate purposes, and the loan went into default in April 1982. It was the first of the corporate loans to "go bad," and in the words of one executive, "It was large enough to get everybody stretched out."

In accordance with its traditionally conservative practice with bad loans—though in past years they had never been so huge—the company immediately wrote down $10 million of the apparent loss, and it wrote off a further $5 million the following year. At the time of writing, however, the books are not yet closed on the deal, since Turbo Resources was reorganized and Canada Trust in effect converted its loan into nine million Turbo shares.

Among those most "stretched out" over the Turbo loan was Alex Barron, an influential member of Canada Trust's executive committee. Son of a doctor in Paris, Ontario, Barron never finished high school because he wanted to make a million dollars and figured Bay Street, not school, was the place to do it. Little known outside the financial community, but a powerful figure within it, he was, as well as being Max Meighen's right-hand man, a director of many other companies, including Argus Corporation in its heyday.

A cautious, conservative man, Barron was known by other Canada Trust directors to have serious reservations about what he saw as the too feverish pace of the company's expansion. He worried that its marketing initiatives were bringing in so much money that it might not be able to develop the expertise to lend it all out safely, and he was concerned about the constant need the expansion created for injections of new capital—the company had begun to make a series of large issues of preference shares in the mid 1970s.[1] On the Turbo Resources loan, in particular, he perceived a potential conflict of interest, since as well as being a lender to Turbo the company was also a trustee for one of its bond issues.

Barron's concern triggered a great deal of what a former director called "uneasiness and conflict" between him and Merv Lahn. At one time Barron considered resigning from the board. But the potential conflict-of-interest problem was resolved when Canada Trust resigned as Turbo trustee and the account was taken over by Montreal Trust. Disturbed that the episode reflected on his management of the company, Merv Lahn asked the board for a vote of confidence. It was given, unanimously, and harmony was restored by the summer of 1982. But the suspicion lingers with at least one former member of the board that Barron's misgivings about the course the company was on may have contributed later that year to the disintegration of the friendly-shareholder group.

---

1. In 1987, shortly before his death, Barron told a former fellow director, "I never thought Canada Trust could go so far so fast."

20

"A Sad Comment on Government Lethargy"

THE beginning of the end of the friendly-shareholder group was, however improbably, intertwined with the fortunes of a company that originated just before the turn of the century with a Canadian investment in a street railway in Brazil, and the misfortunes of a London man who bought a church so that he could give organ lessons.

The company was Brascan, which had been the Brazilian Traction, Light and Power Company until various Brazilian authorities imbued with nationalistic fervour began, in the 1960s, to take over its huge empire based on its electrical utilities. As the compensation for its confiscated enterprises began to roll in, Brazilian Traction returned to its home turf, changed its name to Brascan, and became a powerful force on the Canadian business scene, beginning with its purchase of a twenty-five per cent interest in London's own Labatt's brewery.

The music teacher was a grandson of Joseph Jeffery—one-time inspector for the old Huron & Erie and founder of the London Life Insurance Company—and a member of the family that still controlled London Life. Gordon Jeffery's financial misfortunes began when his church burned down. (The family strongly suspected that someone who didn't like him set fire to it.) Undaunted, he bought another hall for his music lessons. Then, though he had so far demonstrated more interest in music than in business, he invested millions of dollars to build an apartment block in downtown London. His investment turned sour on him and his brothers loyally decided to sell some of the family's controlling shares in London Life to bail him out.

The buyer that came to the rescue was Brascan. A company called Lonvest was formed to take control of London Life in 1977, its three more-or-less equal partners being Brascan, the Jeffery family, and the Toronto-Dominion Bank. Canada Trust was invited to become a fourth partner, but Arthur Mingay decided that since the company held a large number of London Life shares in an estate account, its fiduciary duty prevented its participation.

Two years later, its treasury bulging with repatriated cash from Brazil, Brascan became a tempting target for a takeover attempt. Jake Moore, its president, sought to lay off the cash by trying to buy the huge Woolworth's department-store chain in the United States, a headline-making takeover attempt that failed. In the meantime, Edper Equities Ltd., controlled by the brothers Edgar and Peter Bronfman of Montreal, bought enough shares of Brascan on the open market to take control of it, and thereby inherited its holding in London Life.

As Brascan expanded under its new ownership—among other things it bought control of the mining giant Noranda—it acquired a substantial interest in Royal Trust. When Earl Orser, president of London Life, was invited to join the board of Brascan, he realized that because of the Royal Trust connection he could no longer sit on the board and executive committee of one of its competitors, Canada Trust. He told Arthur Mingay and Merv Lahn in May 1982 that he would have to resign, and that London Life would in due course dispose of its block of Canada Trust shares. "We are in no hurry about this," Orser wrote in a memo for the files after his meeting with Mingay and Lahn, "and in fact we feel we can get a better price after a market recovery, and we might add more stock to the position before disposing of it. Obviously we want to maximize the proceeds. It was agreed that Lahn and Mingay will keep me informed about any institution or any other prospective buyer who might have an interest in purchasing our position."

Orser, who had held senior financial positions at Air Canada and Eaton's, had joined London Life long after the gentleman's agreement was reached by the friendly-shareholder group in 1969. Had he been aware of the obligation to inform Mutual Life and Canadian General Investments about London Life's decision to sell its shares, some hurt feelings and misunderstandings might have been avoided in the months ahead.

By now London Life held almost 800,000 Canada Trust shares, close to ten per cent of the total outstanding. In the still unsettled economic climate of 1982 there seemed to be no buyer for such a large block, even though at one time during the year the stock-market price of the shares dipped to $18.25, its lowest level for two years. London Life was still waiting for the market recovery Orser hoped for and had not yet put its shares up for sale when, in August, it became known that the Manufacturers Life Insurance Company (ManuLife) had gradually acquired slightly more than ten per cent of Canada Trust's shares. ManuLife's management, like Mutual's years before, had decided that if the predicted deregulation of the financial industry came about, their company should have a foothold in a deposit-taking institution. It had originally bought a little over ten per cent of the Canada Permanent, but had sold that holding during a bitter takeover battle in 1981 and had begun to accumulate shares of Canada Trust on the open market.

In September, soon after the disclosure of ManuLife's purchase, Alex Barron telephoned John Panabaker, who had succeeded Ken MacGregor at the helm of Mutual Life and on the Canada Trust board of directors. Barron's nose for Bay Street news was as sharp as anyone's, and after his call Panabaker noted in his diary: "Someone is prepared to buy both the Canadian General and Mutual shares [of Canada Trust] at up to fifteen per cent above the market." By this time, with inflation on the wane and a business recovery beginning, the price of Canada Trust shares had recovered to $26. But Panabaker further noted in his diary: "I would not sell at these levels."

A few days later Barron called Panabaker again and told him he had been approached by a broker on behalf of a buyer who wanted 1.6 million Canada Trust shares and might be prepared to pay a premium of up to fourteen per cent above the market price. As the rumours and the bids from brokers continued, there was intense speculation among the Canada Trust directors about the identity of this mysterious buyer who seemed out to get control of the company. Was it Brascan? Earl Orser said not. Cadillac Fairview? Merv Lahn, who had recently joined the board of that company, said "No way." Perhaps it was ManuLife? Arthur Mingay doubted that. ManuLife's chairman, Syd Jackson, had given no indication that he intended to increase his position, and in any case Mingay thought he appreciated the company's stance that no single shareholder should vote more than ten per cent of its shares.

But in fact ManuLife, whose management considered Canada Trust the best-run trust company in the country, had commissioned three brokers—McLean Securities, Gordon Securities, and Capital Canada—to keep their eyes open for its shares. And when

London Life decided in October to put its shares up for sale the broker it chose to use was McLean Securities.

It was only when the sale of the shares came up at a meeting of the London Life investment committee that Earl Orser learned about the existence of the gentleman's agreement from Alec and Joseph Jeffery, London Life directors who had earlier also served on the board of Canada Trust. Orser immediately called Panabaker and Barron to tell them the shares had been put up for sale, thus formally, if belatedly, discharging the obligation entered into by his predecessor.

By that time Barron had already learned, or made a shrewd guess, that the London Life shares were going to be sold. He was hurt that he had not been informed in advance and began to wonder whether Canadian General, too, should sell its shares. By that time also, the Mutual Life lawyers, with all the rumours and bids flying around, had become concerned about the legal position of their chairman and chief executive, John Panabaker: the business world had changed considerably since the gentleman's agreement was reached in 1969 and everyone had become very sensitive about possible conflicts of interest.

The Mutual lawyers had two main concerns: first, that the company might be considered to be acting in concert with other shareholders and therefore be part of a control block; and second, that it might be considered as having traded with confidential information, because Panabaker and Mingay were on each other's boards, or because Mutual might be aware of the intention of other major shareholders to either buy or sell. The lawyers advised Panabaker that he and Mingay should refrain from participating in any discussion or decisions about the Canada Trust shares by Mutual's board or finance committee, and indeed that they should avoid any discussion about Canada Trust matters with other directors and officers of Mutual. As to the gentleman's agreement with Canadian General that each party keep the other informed about offers for the shares, the lawyers advised that any such discussions should be with Mutual officers other than Panabaker. They thought it was acceptable for either party to communicate to the other that it had received an offer, but not the name of the bidder or whether or not the company intended to accept it.

Panabaker accepted the lawyers' advice that he must insulate himself completely from whatever was going on with Canada Trust shares and wrote to Arthur Mingay on 2 November explaining his position. He sent a copy of the letter with a covering note to Barron. Unfortunately, it seems the letter did not reach Barron in time: he told the author shortly before his death that when he heard "on the street" about the impending deal for the London Life shares he called Mutual and was told they could not discuss it. That settled the matter for Barron; mistakenly, he assumed it meant that Mutual was going to sell and that Canadian General, instead of enjoying the prestige of being the largest shareholder in Canada Trust, would be left holding a large block of its shares with someone else in control. Perhaps he was also influenced by his misgivings about Canada Trust's expansion. At any rate, he immediately began to negotiate for the sale of the Canadian General shares, and at one stage told ManuLife chairman Syd Jackson, "We had this gentleman's agreement but now there doesn't seem to be one."

And so the die was cast. On 8 November ManuLife issued a press release saying it had agreed to buy 779,053 shares of Canada Trust from London Life at $33 per share—a total of $25.7 million. It had also agreed to buy 820,000 shares from Canadian General Investments at the same price, subject to a ruling from the Ontario Securities Commission that no follow-up offer to other Canada Trust shareholders would be required.[1]

The press release quoted Syd Jackson as saying: "We believe this is a good long-term investment for ManuLife's policy-owners. Canada Trust is a well-managed company with solid, long-term growth potential that adds balance to our Canadian investment portfolio. . . ." The announcement went on to say that the purchase of the London Life shares would increase ManuLife's holding of Canada Trust to just under twenty per cent; the Canadian General purchase, if it was permitted to go through, would raise its interest to just under thirty per cent.

Arthur Mingay and Merv Lahn were both surprised and angered by the news. After all, even though ManuLife was a repu-

---

1. The ruling was obtained, and the $27 million deal for Canadian General's shares was closed in January 1983. Even had it wished to achieve majority control of Canada Trust—and Syd Jackson assured Arthur Mingay he had no such intention—ManuLife could not have made a follow-up offer to the other shareholders. Under federal legislation, in making their investments, insurance companies cannot buy more than thirty per cent of the shares of any company's stock outside their normal business field.

table company that would presumably be a responsible shareholder, they could not overnight abandon their conviction that no single shareholder should be permitted to own more than ten per cent of a trust company. The directors shared this conviction, and after a hastily convened board meeting on the day after ManuLife's announcement, a press release was issued that made their position clear.

"Canada Trustco's letters patent," the release said, "prohibit the transfer [registration] of common shares if the total number of shares held by a purchaser and associates would exceed ten per cent of the issued common shares and those which may be issued under conversion rights. The letters patent also limit the number of votes which can be cast by any shareholder and associates at a shareholders' meeting to ten per cent of the issued common shares. . . ."

Having thus signified publicly that ManuLife's purchase of such a large block of shares was unwelcome, the directors soon afterward put a more serious roadblock in its path. Someone discovered a clause in the federal Loan Companies Act, under which Canada Trustco was chartered, which prohibited non-resident shareholders who owned more than ten per cent of a trust company's shares from voting any of them. The question then arose: was ManuLife a resident Canadian company? As a mutual life insurance company it is owned by its policy-holders, and it does much of its business outside this country. Just how many of its owners were Canadian residents, and how many foreigners? Bob Clarke, by now Canada Trust's general counsel and secretary, sought the advice of independent outside counsel, and ManuLife was informed that until its status was clarified, the legal advice was that Canada Trust could not permit it to vote its shares.

It was now ManuLife's turn to be angered. After all, the company had been founded in 1887; its first president was none other than Sir John A. Macdonald; its headquarters were in Toronto; its directors were Canadians. Also, the challenge to its Canadian status had wide ramifications, not only for ManuLife but for all other Canadian mutual insurance companies. Under the manifold restrictions on foreign ownership of Canadian companies, just what investments could Canadian mutual companies make if they were unable to demonstrate that they really were Canadian? Could they invest in oil companies under the National Energy Policy? What about investments in the broadcasting and cultural industries, where demonstrated Canadian ownership was required? The matter had arisen before, and in fact ManuLife thought it had been settled when it had been designated as Canadian for the purposes of the National Energy Policy. But that designation had been made under the Insurance Act. Did it also apply to the archaic legislation governing loan and trust companies? ManuLife joined with the other mutual companies to lobby the government for a clear statement of its position, and the issue was eventually resolved, but not until 1986, too late for ManuLife ever to cast any votes at Canada Trust shareholders' meetings.

ManuLife's acquisition of a thirty-per-cent interest in the company was particularly galling for Mingay and Lahn and the rest of Canada Trust's directors, for it came at a time when the government at last seemed likely to introduce legislation imposing the ten-per-cent ownership clause for loan and trust companies. On 30 July 1982 the federal government released a discussion paper examining the main issues to be considered in a proposed revision and consolidation of the out-dated Trust Companies Act and Loan Companies Act into one act which, it was suggested, might be called the Canadian Savings Banks and Trust Companies Act. This paper, prepared by the federal Department of Insurance, clearly favoured the general application of a ten-per-cent ownership constraint. "Interested parties" were invited to submit their views on it to the department, and after taking them into consideration the government proposed to introduce a draft bill in Parliament.

Canada Trust made a submission on its own and also took part in the preparation of a paper submitted by the Trust Companies Association.[2] But the draft bill, when it was drawn up, omitted the ten-per-cent ownership constraint, even though it had been publicly welcomed by the Canadian Bankers Association, William Kennett, inspector-general of banks, and numerous newspaper

2. A couple of years later Merv Lahn pulled the company out of the Trust Companies Association, a move interpreted in the press as a fit of pique brought on by its lack of support for his vigorous advocacy of the ownership restriction. In fact, Lahn had begun to wonder whether the company's continued membership met its own strict "cost-benefit" standards. As the largest member of the association, Canada Trust paid a substantial annual fee, and its executives devoted considerable time to its affairs, serving on committees, preparing briefs, and so on. Lahn polled all his vice-presidents in one of his celebrated memos, asking them if they considered the investment in time and money brought the company a worthwhile return. They were unanimous in their verdict that it did not.

editorials. The draft legislation also introduced a new provision that would have prohibited any company carrying on trust business from making loans to corporations whose stock was listed on recognized Canadian stock exchanges. This provision appalled the Canada Trust people, corporate loans by now being an important underpinning for its matching process.

In the annual report for 1982 Mingay and Lahn reaffirmed their conviction that the ten-per-cent constraint provision was essential to the public interest. Of the proposal to ban corporate loans, they said: "As the purpose of the legislation is broadening of powers rather than restriction, it is vitally important that this provision be significantly ameliorated." But on the whole, the report said, "the proposed legislation is viewed positively. For the first time in seventy years it will be a complete revision rather than patchwork amendments. It recognizes and incorporates modern business practices and is a major step toward bringing consistency to government legislation for different types of financial institutions. . . . Assuming legislation is passed in acceptable form, it is planned to seek shareholder approval to merge Canada Trustco and Canada Trust and to request approval of the name Canada Trust Savings Bank."

A year later that "major step" had still not been taken; the legislation had not yet even been introduced to Parliament. The 1983 annual report commented acidly: "Now the government's position, as recently enunciated by the minister of finance, is that the proposed act is not a priority item and a fourteen-member advisory committee is to examine the entire financial services industry. It is a safe bet there will be no concrete action until well after the next election. Thus, at least another few years of further erosion in competitive position vis-à-vis chartered banks are in prospect for federally incorporated loan and trust companies. All in all, this whole legislative picture is a sad commentary on government lethargy and political expediency at both federal and provincial levels."

Merv Lahn took up the cudgels in person in a speech to the Kitchener-Waterloo Kinsmen Club on 9 May 1983. The years since the British Mortgage debacle had seen a rash of scandals involving one-owner trust companies. Probably the biggest headlines had been made a few months earlier, when the Ontario government seized a group of companies—Crown Trust, Greymac Trust, Greymac Mortgage, Seaway Trust, and Seaway Mortgage—whose principals had pulled off a breath-taking triple "flip" of a large group of Toronto apartment buildings. By this manoeuvre, the supposed value of the buildings, which had originally been purchased from Cadillac Fairview Corporation for $270 million, was increased to $500 million. Lahn titled his talk, "Let's make sure we learn from the trust companies fiasco," and as usual he didn't pull any punches.

"What permitted the fiasco, disaster, heist, scam or whatever you care to call it?" he asked the Kinsmen. And he immediately answered his own question: "The single most important contributing factor was the ability, within current law and regulation, for one individual to control a trust or loan company. A deposit-taking trust or loan company is permitted to accept deposits of up to $25 for each $1 of owner's capital. What an attractive opportunity for white-collar crime. Not only can an owner keep his hands on his own money but he has access to $25 of someone else's money. A trust or loan company in unscrupulous hands is an open invitation to disaster."

The only opposition to the ownership restriction sought by Canada Trust, Lahn said, "has come, not surprisingly, from so-called 'Trust Company Investors,' an eclectic group of individuals and corporations having controlling interests in Canadian trust companies." The brief they had submitted to the federal authorities arguing against ownership restrictions "comes out long on self-interest but short in concern for the public good."

Lahn went on to name some of the owners included in the group: "Genstar, which owns Canada Permanent; Leonard Ellen and Reuben Cohen, who control Central Trust; Eaton's and The Bay, who own Eaton-Bay Trust; the Bronfmans of Brascan and the Reichmans of Olympia and York, who collectively control Royal Trust; and Hal Jackman, who through one pocket or another controls Victoria and Grey Trust."

He then detailed some of the Trust Company Investors' objections to the ownership constraint provision. In December 1982, he said, they had "largely staked their brief's case on the absence of serious abuse of existing ownership provisions and praised the positive effects of major shareholders in increasing the accountability of management and avoidance of conflicts of interest. January 1983 laid that delusion to rest for all time."

The group had classed widely-held institutions as "somnolent and comfortable." In rebuttal, Lahn reeled off a list of Canada

Trust's "firsts" and invited the Kinsmen to compare its record with single-owner companies. "The former chairman of the Trust Companies Association of Canada and president of a medium-sized company," he went on, "states that 'Honesty cannot be legislated and therefore the ten-per-cent rule is unnecessary.' I agree that honesty cannot be legislated but it is reverse logic to present that fact as supportive to individual ownership of trust companies. Widely-held ownership prevents a crook or a few crooks from looting deposit-taking institutions."

The group's brief had said that if trust-company holdings larger than ten per cent had suddenly to be liquidated, about $1.75 billion worth of stock would be thrown on the market, driving prices down to the detriment of all shareholders. That, said Lahn, could easily be avoided by a "grandfather" clause permitting divestment over a period of, say, ten years, or maybe even longer.

Hal Jackman had lately been quoted in a business magazine as saying that the banks supported the ownership restriction because it would finish off the trust companies. Lahn said Jackman had given "no sensible reason" why that should happen. "In fairness to Hal Jackman," he said, "he is a most responsible controlling shareholder of a trust company, as are several others in my view. However, in the public interest exceptions should not dictate the rule."

Lahn then turned to some other provisions he thought should be included in the new legislation. "Minimum capitalization required to start up a trust company should be raised to at least $10 million," he said. "The current figures of $1 million federally for a trust company and half a million for a loan company are much too low." The provinces, he thought, should abandon the field of trust and loan company regulation in favour of federal regulation, to ensure both consistency and efficiency. "Needless to say," he went on, "there is little hope of this happening."

Lahn added that he thought the largest single factor in permitting the establishment and continuance of unsound deposit-taking institutions had been the federal deposit insurance scheme. "While it might sound heretical and I must admit that I do not propose it," he said, "many potential problems would be resolved by elimination of Canada deposit insurance on a specified future date for demand obligations, but continuing coverage on outstanding time obligations until they mature. . . . Without CDIC coverage, how many people would have placed deposits with

Greymac Trust, owned by Leonard Rosenberg? Not very many in my opinion—or Seaway Trust, owned by Andrew Markle—or XY Trust owned by Mr. Who."

Lahn ended by saying that on behalf of Canada Trust's directors he had repeatedly asked the responsible federal ministers to state the government's position on the ownership question so that public debate on the legislation promised in 1982, and still not introduced, could continue.

"The lobbying power of the wealthy vested interests of the 'Trust Company Investors' is formidable," he said. "Notwithstanding, unless politicians act against the public good, which is possible but unlikely, a responsible and sensible long-overdue conclusion will be reached with introduction of restricted ownership provisions for all Canadian deposit-taking institutions."

It was not the most accurate prediction he had ever made. Before the government did anything at all about the problem, the horse would be out of the barn and galloping clean across the neighbouring county.

21

More Innovations – and the Business Booms

NEITHER the government's procrastination nor the ManuLife purchase of Canada Trust shares did anything to impede the company's day-to-day operations or its remarkable progress. By now the old Huron & Erie was a bank in all but name; at the end of 1984 the deposits lodged in its branches across the country exceeded nine per cent of the total held by all Canadian chartered banks.

The growing public awareness that Canada Trust offered its customers just as many services as they could get from any of the major banks was furthered in 1979, when it became the first trust company to issue a credit card. When he was still assistant general manager of Waterloo Trust, before the merger, Merv Lahn had recognized that its customers would appreciate the convenience of their own credit card. He approached the Bank of America, the lead bank in the Visa card operation, for a franchise. But as a small company operating in two counties of Ontario, Waterloo Trust did not stand much chance against the Toronto-Dominion Bank, which was seeking the franchise for the whole of Canada, and the Toronto-Dominion became the bank that introduced the Visa card to Canada. Other banks could, of course, negotiate with the Toronto-Dominion for a Visa franchise, which might cost them $20 million. Lahn did not have that kind of money to throw around, so Waterloo Trust never joined the Visa group.

Years later, when he was turning Canada Trust into a bank, Lahn received permission from the executive committee to seek a credit-card franchise and opened negotiations with the Toronto-Dominion and the Bank of Montreal; the latter had by that time introduced the MasterCard to Canada. Eventually he came to terms with the Bank of Montreal for the MasterCard, but there was one proviso: the bank retained for five years the right to what is called the "merchant deposit."

The way a credit-card system works is that whenever a purchase is made the merchant deposits the slip with a bank, and the price of the purchase, less a discount of approximately two per cent, is immediately credited to his account. In return for this discount the merchant gets instant payment for the sales he has made, and a guarantee of no bad debts; if a card-holder fails to pay up, it is the card-issuer's responsibility to collect the debt. The Bank of Montreal's proviso therefore meant that Canada Trust would be able to issue cards for the use of its customers, and if they did not pay their bills in full at the end of the month it would have the right to the interest charged on the outstanding balance. But it would not have the right to receive from merchants the deposit slips for sales made on its MasterCard.

Both Merv Lahn and Jack Speake (who was in overall charge of the credit-card introduction) knew that the operation would incur heavy start-up costs and that the company had a whole new "learning curve" to go through. A credit-card operation is known in the trade as a "high-volume, low-margin, high-risk-of-error kind of business." It is also labour-intensive. A "collections" staff had to be recruited and trained to recover bad debts. Other people had to be trained to field questions from irate customers who would find a charge on their monthly bill from "XYZ Company," of which they had never heard. The credit card department would then have to undertake a "tracer quest," by contacting the XYZ Company's bank, which would search its records and find a copy of the relevant sales draft, which would reveal that the customer's purchase was actually made at, say, the Britannia Boutique, owned by the XYZ Company, whereupon the customer would remember the purchase and pay up. Other people had to be trained to master the intricacies of authenticating, and calculating the foreign exchange on, a purchase which had been made, say, by a Canadian tourist in Egypt and had passed through the MasterCard International headquarters in the United States before turning up in London for payment.

The question arose at the beginning: how many people do you need to hire for this kind of operation? Too many, and your bottom line is going to suffer. Too few, and you're going to lose customers dissatisfied with the service. While Canada Trust was still learning the business in 1981, the credit-card operation lost $4 million. The following year, as the card department's expertise improved, and with what the annual report described as "stringent cost controls," the loss was reduced to $2.5 million. In 1983 the company was able to start taking merchant deposits, and thanks to an aggressive marketing campaign it had signed up more than 5,500 merchants by the end of the year. Even though the credit-card business amounted to about $140 million during the year, it still registered a loss of $1.3 million. But in 1984, with 12,000 merchants signed up and their sales for the year totalling more than $345 million, the MasterCard operation finally broke through into the black, though only to the tune of $676,000. After that breakthrough, the business grew rapidly, and in 1988, with almost a million card-holders and 64,000 merchants signed up, the MasterCard operation produced $6.3 million in pre-tax earnings.

From the introduction of the credit card it was a natural step to electronic banking machines from which customers armed with a card and a secret code number could withdraw cash from their accounts at any hour of the day or night. Canada Trust was by no means the first into this field; the banks had pioneered the machines and in 1979 the Canada Permanent had been the first trust company to install them, so the marketers knew they must come up with some catchy name to distinguish their machines from everyone else's. Frank Pratt gathered his troops around a conference table one day early in 1983 and they started to toss out ideas. Someone suggested "Casheteria"; someone else came up with "Harvey Wallbanker"; after the groans had subsided, someone threw out "Johnny Pay-Cheque." That sounded more like it, but then someone said half-jokingly, "We should call it Johnny Cash." There were a few chuckles, but then Pratt said, "Well, maybe we should explore Johnny Cash—what have we got to lose?"

As it happened, Johnny Cash had a concert date a few days later at the arena in Durham, north of London, and Don Park, who had joined the marketing department as a trainee with an honours degree in English, was deputed to go up and see what he could do about enlisting the popular country music singer's cooperation. Park had been active since his high-school days in what he describes as "pep rally-type things." He had been chairman of the booster club and president of the drama club at school and had done a little acting himself. But this would be his first experience in dealing with a real-life star.

When Park walked into a little office at the arena to talk to Cash's agent, Lou Robin, he found him counting the box-office takings and realized this was no time to open negotiations. Robin agreed to meet him at another concert in Hamilton the next night. When Park had explained his offer he agreed to talk to Cash about it. Cash's chief concern, Robin later reported, was that if he lent his name to the banking machine it had better be reliable; he had heard stories in the United States that the machines were always breaking down, and he had no intention of associating his name with a flop. But when the Canada Trust people were able to convince him that *their* computer system was totally reliable, top-of-the-line IBM equipment, he signed a contract to sponsor the introduction of the now-familiar Johnny Cash machines.

Part of the deal was that as the company installed the money machines in major centres—they were introduced gradually, one "cell" at a time—Cash and his wife, June Carter, would bring their show in for two or three days. On the first day they would do two concerts exclusively for the company's employees, after which they would perform two more concerts for the company's customers, who were offered reduced-rate tickets. The first machines were introduced in the London "cell," with attention being drawn to them by life-size cardboard cut-outs of Johnny. Then on the day chosen for the public launch the staff crowded into the ballroom of the Holiday Inn to cheer Johnny and have group photographs taken with him. Once again, there was some eyebrow-raising among the traditionalists, but the staff loved Johnny and June, and the "Johnny Cash" name certainly established Canada Trust's banking machines in the public consciousness.

One of Merv Lahn's characteristics that sometimes surprises other businessmen who have dealings with him for the first time is the extent to which, despite his reputation for toughness and "hands-on" management, he delegates genuine responsibility to his senior executives. He also seems to believe that executives, if they are worth their salt, should be presented with a challenge from time to time, to keep their creative juices flowing. As one of his lieutenants puts it: "He won't tell you what to do. He'll just say, 'I'd like to see us do something that will really knock the socks off the banks'."

One day in 1984 Lahn gave what has been called "a Merv nudge" to Stan Martin, who had recently been appointed vice-president in charge of savings services. Lahn said he had a feeling that the company was losing momentum in the savings area. The introduction of daily-interest accounts had been extraordinarily successful in increasing deposits, but everyone else had jumped on that band-wagon by now. It was time for something new, to attract attention and get the ball rolling again.

The best way Martin and his people could please their savings customers, obviously, was to pay more interest. But simply raising the rate on existing accounts by, say, half a percentage point could not be marketed as an exciting new departure. The customers would no doubt accept the new rate gladly enough, but it would do little in the campaign to increase the company's share of the total market and thus generate enough new business to compensate for the extra money that would have to be paid out in interest. After the usual brain-storming sessions the planners and marketers decided that the answer was a "tiered-rate" account, offering bonus interest on balances maintained at higher than a stipulated minimum amount. At first they considered setting the minimum balance at $5,000, but someone suggested that sounded like a rich man's account, and they were after the mass market. So it was agreed to make it $3,000. And since the convenience to the customer would outweigh any cost to the company, it was decided to make it a chequing account.

Company research had shown that even people with substantial balances in Canada Trust often dealt with one or two other banks. To encourage them to concentrate their funds in the new Canada Trust account, it was decided to accompany it with what is known in the business as a BOAT—a balance of account transfer: any customer switching $3,000 or more from another institution to the new account would receive a $25 bonus.

Now came the crucial question: what should the new account be called? Dozens of names were bandied about, and many of them involved the word "super"—Super Savings, Super Saver, and so on. None of them sounded quite right—until Stan Martin sent Frank Pratt a note suggesting "SuperRate," and Pratt knew his marketers had something to work with.

Much time was spent discussing how to "price" the new account. If the interest rate on balances above $3,000 was set at the same rate paid on deposit certificates, for instance, would that "cannibalize" the deposit certificate business? Eventually it was decided to offer ten per cent, which was two percentage points above the regular savings rate at that time and had an attractive ring to the marketers.

When Martin took the plan to Merv Lahn, it was a tough decision for Lahn to make. If SuperRate drew away too much money from the company's existing deposit certificate accounts, it was calculated, the cost in extra interest payments might go as high as $20 million in the first year, enough to have a devastating impact on the statement of earnings. But Martin and his planners believed the new account would attract $100 million in new money in its first year. So Lahn bit the bullet and gave it the go-ahead. SuperRate, introduced in 1984, proved so popular that the $100 million target was hit in only six weeks; and by the end of a year's operation it had raised more than $1 billion in new money.

SuperRate's success did not go unnoticed, and it was soon copied by the banks and other trust companies. After a while Merv Lahn decided that once again the savings area was losing momentum. In the fall of 1985 Martin received a call from Barbados, where Lahn and his senior management team were holding a meeting. His caller was Frank Pratt. The boss, said Pratt, was insisting that another new product be launched by the end of December at the latest. Martin got together with his people and came up with the idea for the "T-bill savings" account, another premium account with its bonus interest, paid on daily balances of more than $10,000, varying weekly with the rates paid at the government's regular auctions of treasury bills. Hitherto, investors had been able to take advantage of these attractive rates only through brokers and by investing large sums of money. The "T-bill" account, devised in record time and launched on Lahn's deadline, proved even more successful than SuperRate: it grew to $3 billion in its first year. And it, too, was soon copied, before Canada Trust could copyright the name.

The innovations continued in other areas of the company's business also. In 1984 Canada Trust became the first major lending institution in North America to offer customers the opportunity to make their mortgage payments weekly, which of course reduced the interest they would have to pay over the life of the loan. And one of the company's most successful promotions came out of a brain-storming session at which the product managers and the marketers were trying to come up with ideas for beefing up the mortgage business. Someone got the ball rolling by asking,

"What would you most like to do with *your* mortgage?" Someone else quipped, "Burn the damn thing."

So was born the monthly "Burn your mortgage" contest, in which the names of all customers taking out a new mortgage or renewing an old one during the month were entered in a draw. The winner, provided he or she could answer a skill-testing mathematical question, would receive a cheque equivalent to the balance owing on the mortgage. Bob Overholt, the product manager in charge of the promotion, announced the first winner early in April 1984: Mrs. Assunta Baretta, of Edmonton, whose outstanding balance amounted to $58,000.

Unhappily, by now the promotion had embroiled the company in two charges under the criminal code of Canada: the Alberta authorities had accused it of running an illegal lottery. The company was cleared on both counts in July, the judge ruling that the mathematical question, though not demanding the mental powers of an Einstein, was in fact a test of skill; and since the promotion and the prize were financed by Canada Trust's $8 million annual advertising budget, "the prize did not derive by reason of the fact that other persons had paid or given, or obligated themselves to pay or give, any sum of money or valuable security under the scheme."

To everyone's consternation the Alberta prosecutor appealed the acquittal to the provincial court of appeal. But in March 1985 the appeal was dismissed, and the "Burn your mortgage" draw became just one more popular and successful Canada Trust promotion.

Quite apart from the embarrassment caused by its prosecution of that case, Alberta in those years unwittingly constituted the largest single problem facing Canada Trust. The peak inflation at the beginning of the 1980s, and the extraordinarily interventionist policies of the Liberal government of the day, wrought chaos in the all-important oil industry and pitchforked the provincial economy into a disastrous slump. Turbo Resources, the cause of so much anguish at the upper levels of Canada Trust, was only one of the companies in trouble. As the provincial real estate market collapsed with the rest of the economy, the company was forced to write off millions of dollars in loans to such other companies as Daon Development Corporation and Carma Developers Ltd. Its investment losses in 1983 were $15.2 million, and in 1984, while somewhat lower, they still totalled $13.2 million. More than eighty per cent of those losses were incurred in Alberta. At the end of 1984, the company had more than $40 million in "non-performing" investments, three-quarters of them in Alberta.

The company was able to roll with the punches, thanks to its strong reserves and buoyant earnings. All the imaginative innovations and promotions had generated a tremendous expansion of its business and the "assets under administration" line in its annual report rocketed from $14.2 billion in 1980 to $25.1 billion in 1984. The rectification of the mismatch in the fall of 1982 had coincided with a dramatic drop in the rate of inflation. The consumer price index fell from 10.8 per cent in 1982 to 5.8 per cent in 1983 and to 4.4 per cent in 1984. This fortunate combination of circumstances prompted a recovery in the spread. From its dangerously low level of 1.27 per cent in 1981 it rose to 2.23 per cent in 1983, and the company recorded a phenomenal 59 per cent increase in its earnings, up to a record $64 million. The increase in 1984 was smaller, but nevertheless it was a satisfying 16 per cent, bringing earnings up to another record: $74.3 million.

By now the company had 7,500 full- and part-time employees in 208 branches across the country, two of which brought it some unwelcome press coverage in 1984. Local 304 of the Canadian Union of United Brewery, Flour, Cereal, Soft Drink and Distillery Workers, for convenience known as the Brewery Workers, had managed to organize the only two branches of the company ever to become unionized: Pen Centre, in St. Catharines, and Cambridge Preston, one of the old Waterloo Trust branches. After a round of tough negotiations the company and the union signed a one-year collective agreement covering the Pen Centre employees. When it came up for renewal, the union recommended, in February 1984, that the employees reject the company's final offer and go on strike. The employees, however, had come to feel that they were not as well off under the agreement as the staffs in other branches and voted to accept the company's offer.

During the negotiations for the first collective agreement at the Cambridge Preston branch, the company stuck firmly to its position that it would not give unionized employees better pay or benefits than those provided to other branch staffs. It had always paid on merit, based on regular performance evaluations, and it proposed to continue to do so. The union called the employees out on strike in March 1984 and filed a complaint with the Ontario Labour Relations Board alleging that the company was not bargaining in good faith. In a landmark decision in October the board upheld the company's position that it had no obligation to give unionized employees any more than it gave the rest of its staff and dismissed the complaint.

By that time all but four of the workers had returned to their jobs—the branch operations had continued without interruption throughout the strike—and no collective agreement was ever negotiated for the Cambridge Preston branch. Instead, the employees at both branches applied for decertification, their applications were granted, and the Brewery Workers' short-lived role at Canada Trust came to an end.

Having no desire for a repetition of these labour troubles, the company began to lay even more emphasis on its already extensive program to foster good morale among its employees. A separate unit of the human resources department now regularly canvasses the opinions of employees on a variety of what is termed "work-related concerns." Individual "feed-back" meetings are held with staff members who complete the survey, and they are told, "Okay, we'll do that right away," or "No, we can't do that, and this is why," or sometimes, "That sounds interesting, we'll look into it." The company also maintains a round-the-clock "hot-line" to the manager of the unit, who is in effect a corporate ombudsman, charged with investigating employees' complaints about everything from pay to a breakdown of the air-conditioning system. One innovation that came out of the employee-opinion canvass that might not have been popular with all the staff was the declaration of Canada Trust offices as a "smoke-free workplace."

As Merv Lahn told the shareholders at the annual meeting at the beginning of 1985: "We are committed to being a responsive and responsible employer, providing compensation, benefits, working conditions and opportunities for advancement comparable to other leading Canadian financial organizations."

In that address Lahn returned in his customary forthright way to the government's continuing failure to define its position on the ownership of loan and trust companies. Canada Trust's position that no one owner should have more than ten per cent of its control, he said, was well known. "The new federal government," he went on, "will surely announce its intentions some time this year. The issue has become almost a purely political one due to the sad fact that all major Canadian trust and loan companies, apart from Canada Trustco and bank subsidiary loan companies, are now controlled, directly or indirectly, by dominant shareholders—Canada Permanent, Royal Trust and National Trust having fallen over the last few years."

Though Lahn's own resumé lists him as a Conservative, he pressed on fearlessly: "With an election years away, a political decision might be swayed by the views of influential party backers and fund-raisers rather than by sheer logic, common sense and widespread informed opinion such as that of the Consumers' Association of Canada and other respected groups which favour ownership restrictions. Several of the 'trust company owners' fall into the category of influential Conservative party backers and fund-raisers. It would thus be naive to expect an ownership restriction to be forthcoming even with generous grand-fathering provisions. Should the status quo prove to be the case, Canada Trustco remains a 'sitting duck,' as it clearly is at the moment."

22

The "Sitting Duck" is Plucked

THE 1984 annual report contained a new section under the sub-heading "International," reporting the establishment of two wholly-owned subsidiaries on the Caribbean island of Barbados. This was not, in fact, the company's first venture overseas. In 1974 it had entered into a partnership with two United States banks—Northwest Bancorporation of Minneapolis and Southeast Banking Corporation of Miami—to form a company named Canadian American Finance S.A. Through its principal subsidiary, Canadian American Bank S.A., this was intended to carry on a broad range of international and merchant banking activities from offices in London, England, and Luxembourg.

Canada Trust's thirty-per-cent share of Canadian American cost it $1.6 million, but the company soon realized it was in over its head; competing on the sophisticated European financial markets was no cakewalk. As one senior executive recalled: "It's a jungle out there." With the outlook for worthwhile profitability at best uncertain, the company decided after a couple of years to back out, sold its interest in Canadian American to Northwest Bancorporation at cost, and put all hopes of international expansion aside for the time being.

Its re-entry into offshore operations in 1984 was motivated by domestic considerations rather than any ambition to be a large-scale international player. As its mortgage and personal loan portfolios mushroomed year by year, they generated a substantial amount of insurance business from customers taking out life or disability insurance on their loans. Historically, the company had been unable to take advantage of this business opportunity because of its archaic regulatory structure, and had had to farm out the policies on its loans to insurance companies. In 1984 the task of seeking some way of getting into the insurance business was assigned to John Richardson, a Toronto-born chartered accountant who had joined the company as its first tax consultant in 1972. In his twelve years with the company, Richardson had acquired a thorough acquaintance with all phases of its business. For a couple of years, until it was ruled unprofitable and sold, he had headed a department set up to help customers fill in their tax returns. Then he launched another product, income-averaging annuities, which proved highly successful. Later he served as comptroller for three years, and by 1984 he was executive vice-president for all regional operations.

When he began to cast about for some way of entering the insurance business, Richardson discovered that the minister of finance had the power to permit loan and trust companies to set up a subsidiary deemed to be an "ancillary business," that is, a logical extension of their main core business. He approached the superintendent of insurance, Bob Hammond, for permission to establish an insurance subsidiary to handle policies arising from the company's mortgage and personal loan business. Hammond did not like the idea and declined to recommend it to the minister.

Richardson then discovered that a foreign loan company was an ancillary business corporation permitted by statute, rather than by ministerial discretion. For several years the company had been offering U.S. dollar daily interest accounts, and in the matching process, as the deposits came in they were offset by the purchase of U.S. treasury bills. It would have been more profitable to make loans in U.S. currency, but under the regulations these would have had to be included in the seven-per-cent "basket clause," the upper limits of which were already being approached by the personal loans and credit-card operations. So it was decided to set up a foreign subsidiary to make loans to United States customers, and Richardson set out to find a suitable location for what became Canada Trustco International Ltd.

Barbados was chosen for several reasons: it had political stability, with one of the oldest parliamentary systems in the Commonwealth; its people were relatively well educated, with the highest literacy rate in the Caribbean; it had a good telephone system, and a pool of accounting and legal talent; and best of all, it had a taxation agreement with Canada, so that any profits the company made would be taxed in Barbados, and not subjected to double taxation when they were remitted to the parent company in Canada.

When Richardson and his legal advisers were examining the legislation governing offshore companies they also discovered that they were permitted by statute to have subsidiaries the company could not own in Canada without the minister's permission; so CT Insurance Co. Ltd. was formed as a subsidiary of Canada Trustco International. It is customary in the insurance business for the lead insurer to lay off part of its risk to other companies, and Mutual Life, which wrote the policies on Canada Trust's loan and mortgage business at that time, agreed to re-insure part of that business with CT Insurance.

Richardson became chairman of both companies, with a board consisting of four local directors and Bob Rudd, a former treasurer of Canada Permanent who was posted to Barbados as managing director of CT International. Since the company specializes in large corporate and real estate loans, it operates with only a small staff consisting of a local certified general accountant and a secretary, supplemented by help from the corporate loans department at head office when the work load demands.

Both the Barbados subsidiaries, though they do only a small fraction of the company's total business, quickly became successful. Four years later CT International had more than $110 million out in U.S. loans, and CT Insurance was contributing more than $6 million to the company's annual earnings.

Another new subsidiary formed in 1984 was CT Investment Counsel Inc. By now the assets administered by the company's personal and pension trust departments amounted to $13.4 billion, precisely double what they had been only four years earlier, in 1980. In an effort to ensure that these funds were invested in the most profitable way possible, CT Investment Counsel was established with an unusual incentive plan designed, in the words of the annual report, "to attract and retain highly qualified investment professionals." The essence of the plan was a "phantom equity" arrangement under which, though CT Investment is a wholly-owned subsidiary, its senior officers are paid as though they owned some of its stock, so that they share in both the profits and growth of the company.

As the company's operations were becoming more and more complex, so the competition it faced was becoming more and more intense. The 1980 Bank Act revisions, as part of the process of deregulating the financial industry, had permitted foreign banks to open branches in Canada. By the end of 1984 there were fifty-eight of these so-called "Schedule B" banks, all eagerly competing for loans with the existing Canadian banks—and with Canada Trust.

The distinct structure of the "four pillars" that had hitherto constituted the financial industry—the banks, insurance companies, loan and trust companies, and securities dealers—was clearly crumbling away piecemeal, like some ancient Assyrian ruin. As Allyn Taylor reflected in his retirement, "Everyone is getting into everyone else's business." But still the federal government seemed unable or unwilling to bring in the long-awaited legislation governing loan and trust companies that Merv Lahn and others had been pleading for to create "a level playing field." Instead, in April 1985, it released yet another paper for discussion, the "Green Paper on Regulation of Canadian Financial Institutions." Once again this expressed the view that the ten-per-cent ownership restriction was not necessary, and that any possibility of self-dealing by institutions with dominant owners could be prevented by strict regulatory controls. Lahn was both disappointed and disgusted. And, though he did not yet know it, the "sitting duck" was about to be plucked.

Later that month, on 29 April, a company named Genstar Acquisition Corporation bought 650,000 shares of Canada Trustco at $38.50 each, a deal amounting to more than $25 million. Next day it bought 15,900 shares at $37. Over the next couple of days it bought a further 1,156,400 shares, 1 million of them in one transaction but the rest in lots as small as 200. By 11 June Genstar Acquisition had accumulated a total of 2,147,300 Canada Trustco shares, just under ten per cent of the total outstanding.

Genstar Acquisition was a subsidiary of Genstar Corporation, an industrial and financial conglomerate with its head office in Vancouver but its executive offices in San Francisco, where its varied activities were presided over by two remarkably successful Canadian entrepreneurs, Angus A. MacNaughton and Ross J. Turner. From a comparatively modest beginning they had built Genstar into a multi-billion-dollar network of companies operating in both Canada and the United States.

MacNaughton and Turner had an unusual arrangement: they shared the duties of chief executive officer and every year switched their titles. One year MacNaughton would be chairman and Turner president, and the next year Turner would be chairman and MacNaughton president. For such a novel arrangement to work, the two men clearly had to be on the same wavelength. On business trips, they frequently travelled together in their luxurious Gulfstream II corporate jet. They were so close, it was said, that in negotiations one would often finish the other's sentence.

Genstar had begun life in Montreal as Sogemines, an offshoot of the huge Société Générale de Belgique, a company that was as much of an institution in Belgium as its royal family. The Société had been the prime mover in that country's industrialization in the nineteenth century and in the colonization of the Belgian Congo, where it developed some of the richest mines in the world. With the lowering of the Iron Curtain after World War II, Belgium lost the sources of many of the ores used in its Antwerp smelters. The Société Générale group sought to replace these supplies from countries with more settled political climates. One of these was judged to be Canada, where it formed an investment company in the early 1950s. In 1965 an experienced Belgian executive, August A. Franck, took over as president and chief executive officer and asked Angus MacNaughton, a young chartered accountant who had been employed by the company for ten years, to examine the investments made by the Belgian owners. MacNaughton concluded that they were not as profitable as they could be, recommended their reorganization into what became Genstar, and went on to become Genstar's chief financial officer.

MacNaughton's partnership with his fellow accountant Turner began when Genstar took over the Winnipeg-based BACM Industries Ltd., of which Turner had been executive vice-president and a director. Working together after Franck retired in 1976, they expanded Genstar's operations into a bewildering variety of new fields. By the time they started buying Canada Trust shares, Genstar was a leading manufacturer of cement in western Canada and a leading supplier of cement in California, Oregon, and Nevada; it was a major producer of lime products and building materials in both Canada and the United States, and one of the biggest American producers of gypsum wallboard and asphalt roofing tiles; it had become a large real-estate developer in both countries; it had companies operating tug-boats and building and repairing ships; and its subsidiary GSX Corporation was the third largest garbage collection and disposal company in the United States.

An associate who worked with him in the late 1960s recalled that from the start MacNaughton had wanted to get into the field of financial services. "His aim," he said, "was to diversify in such a way that the company would never be ruined by a depression, and the financial industry seemed more stable and less cyclical than some of their other companies. Besides, so much of what they did required capital." MacNaughton's opportunity to own a financial company came in 1981, when Genstar was invited to become a "white knight" by none other than the venerable Canada Permanent.

The Permanent had, of course, been the model for the formation of the old Huron & Erie, and both companies had developed along similar lines. The Permanent's first president, in 1855, was a hardware merchant, Joseph D. Ridout. Its vice-president, Peter Paterson, like Adam Hope, owned a dry-goods store. Another of its directors, J.D. Beard, had been mayor of Toronto in 1854. The Permanent expanded into the west long before the Huron & Erie, opening its first branch in Winnipeg in 1888. Ten years later it began, as the Huron & Erie had already done, to absorb other smaller companies. Its most important acquisitions came after World War II. In 1961 it merged with the Toronto General Trusts, the country's first trust company, which was founded in 1882 with the Hon. Edward Blake as its first president. And in 1967 it merged with the Eastern and Chartered Trust Company, which brought it twenty-nine additional branches.

While the Permanent did not enter the trust side of the business until 1913, twelve years after the Huron & Erie activated Canada Trust, as time went on it concentrated on its fiduciary business much more than the Huron & Erie's "Four Horsemen" had done. And until the advent on the scene of Allyn Taylor the Permanent had overshadowed the Huron & Erie as a repository for the fortunes of the "Toronto 400." So the Toronto establishment was shocked in April 1981, when Sam Belzberg, who with members of his family owned Vancouver's little-known First City Financial Corporation, launched a takeover bid for the Permanent. The close-knit Belzberg family, whose Polish immigrant father had begun his career in Canada by selling second-hand furniture in Calgary, seemed an unlikely suitor for the dowager empress of

Canadian trust companies; it was also an unwelcome one in the eyes of the Toronto elite, particularly since Belzberg proposed to pay for the Permanent largely with shares of First City rather than good hard cash.

The Permanent's management, headed by its chairman, Eric Brown, set out to find another suitor, a white knight to repel First City's advances. The resultant battle, which featured much legal and financial skirmishing, lasted for the rest of that summer. Brown despatched a courier to Ottawa with a letter to Allan MacEachen, the minister of finance, urging the government to declare that its policy was that no one person or company should control a deposit-taking institution. He received his reply, with no offer to intervene, only after the battle was over: it had been mailed during a long postal strike.

Among the others that Brown turned to for help was Merv Lahn. Several years earlier the Permanent had done a study of other companies, including Canada Trust, with which it might amalgamate over time. This had concluded that the two "corporate cultures"—the patrician conservatism of the Permanent and the gung-ho populism of Canada Trust—were too different to be successfully melded. Now Brown called Lahn and suggested that, to fight off First City, Canada Trust should top its bid for the Permanent and put the two companies together. It was a brief conversation. Lahn told Brown there was no way he was in business to create value for the Permanent's shareholders; if Brown wanted to foil First City he should make a premium bid for Canada Trust, thereby putting the Permanent out of reach of First City and creating value for Lahn's shareholders. "I knew they wouldn't do it," Lahn recalled to the author. "In other words, it was a polite way of saying, 'Thanks, but no thanks.'"

The Permanent had retained Dominion Securities as its adviser in the takeover battle, and as the deadline for Belzberg's offer approached with no rescuer in sight, Brown consulted Dominion Securities' vice-president, Jim Pitblado. Brown considered the First City bid "just a terrible junk bond offer," and he told Pitblado: "Jim, you've got to turn somebody up who's going to become live in this thing. Whoever buys us, he's got to pay my shareholders cash."

A couple of days later Pitblado called Brown and asked whether Genstar would be an acceptable white knight. "Hell," said Brown, "they're in the cement business. Where do they come in on this thing?" Pitblado replied that he had heard that MacNaughton and Turner had just done a refinancing in New York and had letters of credit for several hundred million dollars. And, he said, they had always wanted to have a financial company in their stable. "Okay," said Brown. "Let's do it. See if you can get them to swing through Toronto on their way home." Pitblado was successful, and when MacNaughton and Turner sat down with Brown, he did, in his own words, "the biggest selling job I've ever done in my life."

As a result, Genstar entered the fray and the battle ultimately became a stand-off, with Belzberg holding fifty-three per cent of the Permanent's shares and Genstar, which had offered $31 in cash for common shares and $36.90 for preferreds convertible into common shares, owning thirty-nine per cent. Control of the Permanent now became a matter for negotiation between Belzberg and MacNaughton and Turner. In due course Belzberg agreed to sell his shares to Genstar, at a reputed profit of $5.5 million, and Genstar, for an outlay of $288 million, became the owner of the Permanent.

MacNaughton and Turner had won the battle, but they soon became disenchanted with their victory; the Permanent was neither as adventurous nor as profitable as they thought it should be. Several years later, in a joint presentation to the parliamentary standing committee on finance, they said: "While the Permanent was a well-established national institution in Canada, it was operating well below its potential. . . . It became apparent to us almost immediately that the Permanent required quick changes in operating practices in order to repair a serious interest-sensitive mismatch of assets and liabilities. In fact, the Permanent lost money in each of 1981 and 1982 before taking into account gains on sales of securities and income tax recoveries."

The "quick changes" they mentioned were made in top management. Eric Brown was replaced as chairman and chief executive officer by John Hilliker, vice-chairman and a thirty-year veteran of the Canadian Imperial Bank of Commerce. Hilliker brought in a new crew and began to shake things up, but MacNaughton and Turner came to feel the Permanent was not large enough to compete successfully with the giants in the banking industry. Clearly, the fastest way to grow was by acquiring another trust company, a process likely to lead to economies of scale and possible synergistic effects, multiplying the strengths of both companies. So they initiated a round of studies and conversations with several companies. Eventually, they decided that Canada Trust, the only remaining widely-held trust company of any size, was the ideal merger partner for the Permanent, and they began to buy its shares on the market.

When their holding reached almost ten per cent, they invited Merv Lahn to meet them in their suite in Toronto's King Edward Hotel, scene of thousands of Bay Street deals since its opening in 1903. Lahn took along Peter Maurice, and MacNaughton and Turner disclosed the size of their holding and said they proposed to go on buying shares, with the eventual aim of merging Canada Trust with the Permanent. All that Taylor, Mingay, and Lahn had feared through the years seemed about to happen. To add insult to injury, the proud old Huron & Erie could end up being controlled by an industrial conglomerate. Lahn was appalled, but he could do no more than explain the company's long-standing position on the ownership constraint clause and promise to get back to them after he had reported their plans to his board of directors.

MacNaughton and Turner had also talked to Syd Jackson and Thomas Di Giacomo, ManuLife's senior vice-president in charge of investments, and suggested an arrangement by which Genstar might build up its holding to match ManuLife's thirty per cent, giving the two companies joint control of Canada Trust. This suggestion was no more palatable to Jackson and Di Giacomo than the advent on the scene of Genstar had been for the Canada Trust board, and it was not pursued. But grasping for an olive branch, the Canada Trust directors instructed Lahn to tell MacNaughton and Turner that they might find it acceptable if ManuLife cut back its holding to twenty per cent, Genstar built up to that level, and both parties signed standstill agreements undertaking never to increase their stakes above that percentage.

This arrangement would have enabled Genstar, for technical reasons having to do with accounting and taxation methods, to take its twenty-per-cent share of Canada Trust's earnings on to its own income statement, rather than merely including its dividends, as it would have to do if its holding remained at ten per cent. The resultant increase in earnings could have amounted to several million dollars a year. But when Lahn suggested this compromise agreement at another meeting with MacNaughton and Turner at the King Edward, they rejected it: it did not fit in with their long-term objectives. The Canada Trust directors instructed

Lahn to return to their previous tough stance that anything over a ten-per-cent Genstar interest would be unwelcome.

On the last day of July 1985, his talks with MacNaughton and Turner apparently stalemated, Merv Lahn took time off to drive to Niagara Falls with his wife Myra, his young daughter Peggy, and a boy who was visiting them from France. (Peggy had recently spent an enjoyable two weeks with the boy's family in Annecy, a historic town in the Haute-Savoie, and the Lahns were now returning the hospitality.) After the kids had seen the sights and enjoyed the customary roller-coaster ride, they were driving home when Lahn heard on the car radio that Canada Trust stock had suddenly jumped almost two dollars in that day's trading. "Well," he told Myra, "here it is."

Lahn's long-held suspicion that government inaction would lead to the end of Canada Trust's independence was confirmed next day, when MacNaughton and Turner called him soon after 9 a.m. to tell him trading in Canada Trust stock would not open on the Toronto Stock Exchange that morning, pending a Genstar takeover bid. The form of the bid had not yet been settled, but Genstar's directors were meeting the following day, a Friday, to consider it. There were several possibilities, MacNaughton and Turner said; they might even go for a hundred per cent of Canada Trust's shares; but they would let him know the decision after the board meeting. Lahn called Arthur Mingay to tell him battle had been joined, and the two men spent the rest of the day on the phone, Mingay trying to reach all the Canada Trust directors in Toronto and the west, and Lahn calling the rest.

Lahn and Mingay both knew that nothing could now prevent Canada Trust losing its independence, short of government intervention, and they had learned not to hold their breath waiting for that. But amid all the commotion of that day, Lahn found time to administer one of his celebrated "Merv nudges" to the government. He told a reporter for the Canadian Press that ownership restrictions on trust companies were the only way to protect the industry from conflicts of interest and self-dealing, and both the federal and Ontario governments were "wrong-headed" not to recognize it. "Owners will always be several steps ahead of the regulators," he said. "Hundreds of thousands of regulators would be required to monitor transactions on what would have to be a daily basis." As the next few weeks would show, the government proved less amenable to "Merv nudges" than his own executives.

In the absence of government intervention, all that Lahn and Mingay and the Canada Trust directors could do was to try to find a suitor they considered more acceptable and to obtain the best possible price for their shareholders.

Next day, while the Genstar board was meeting, Lahn and Mingay met ManuLife's Syd Jackson and Tom Di Giacomo, who could see their last chance to have a foothold in a deposit-taking institution disappearing. Jackson and Di Giacomo told them ManuLife might consider making a bid to counter whatever offer Genstar made, if Canada Trust's directors would agree to three conditions. These were that Canada Trust would accept a legal opinion obtained by ManuLife that it was indeed a resident Canadian company; that its shares should then be registered in its own name; and that it be permitted to vote them. Even though relations between ManuLife and Canada Trust so far had been decidedly cool, Lahn and Mingay preferred them as a suitor to a company whose chief interests were outside the financial field, and they agreed to support their case with the Canada Trust board.

That afternoon MacNaughton and Turner called Lahn and told him the Genstar directors had agreed to make a formal public offer for 12 million Canada Trust shares at a cash price of $44. With the shares they had already accumulated, these would give them slightly more than fifty per cent of the outstanding shares and thus control of the company, which they then proposed to merge with the Permanent. They felt that the two companies were a "good fit" and that the merger would be in the best interests of their customers, employees, and shareholders; and they hoped Lahn would go along with their plan and head the merged company. Lahn could only tell them that the Canada Trust board was meeting the following Wednesday, 7 August, to consider the situation and that a statement would be issued after the meeting.

Lahn spent the weekend at his cottage on Lake Huron, but it was not a relaxing interlude. He spent most of the time on the phone to Peter Maurice and Tom Di Giacomo, trying to devise a plan that would enable ManuLife to bring its holding in Canada Trust to just over fifty per cent, with the rest of the shares remaining widely held. ManuLife itself, of course, could not buy more shares because of the regulation preventing it from owning more than thirty per cent of the shares of another company outside its own field. But the ManuLife lawyers believed there was a precedent that would permit some of its subsidiaries to buy shares: Guardian Trustco of Montreal had recently been taken over by a Quebec-based mutual insurance company without any objection from the regulatory authorities.

Accordingly, on Tuesday, 6 August, Di Giacomo presented a plan to ManuLife's board of directors under which, using two subsidiaries, Dominion Life Assurance Company and Manuduke, a real estate company, ManuLife would make a public bid for 29.1 per cent of Canada Trust's stock, a little over 8 million shares, at $50 each. With the shares already held, this would give ManuLife firm control. ManuLife's directors apparently had some reservations about the plan, because the meeting broke up without a decision.

Next day the Canada Trust directors met in Toronto to consider the Genstar bid, which had been formally made the day before. Since the Genstar prospectus had not disclosed how the amalgamation with the Permanent could be brought about, they decided they did not yet have enough information to make any recommendation to their shareholders, as they were legally required to do. Before moving on to other business, Lahn reminded the board that the directors comprising the compensation/human resources committee had some time earlier discussed the possibility of accelerating the employee stock options, thus enabling members of the plan to exercise them in the event of a takeover bid, even if they were not yet due. Ted Donegan, of the legal firm Blake, Cassels & Graydon, who had been invited to the meeting to advise the directors of their legal responsibilities during a takeover bid, said there was no legal impediment to accelerating the options, and the board agreed to the move.

After the meeting a letter to shareholders was issued, reaffirming the directors' belief that Canada Trust should remain independent. "However," the letter went on, "in the present absence of statutory ownership restrictions for federal loan and trust companies, directors fully recognize that independence may no longer be possible. Canada Trustco is a unique property. It is the last major Canadian loan and trust company without a controlling shareholder and as such may well attract competing bids from parties interested in entering or expanding their presence in the financial services industries. . . . Accordingly, the board of directors strongly urges all shareholders not to take any action to accept the Genstar offer until your directors have met again and have so advised you."

The directors had voted at their meeting to retain Wood Gundy as their financial adviser during the takeover battle, and that afternoon Lahn and Maurice went over to discuss strategy with Wood Gundy head Ted Medland and some of his colleagues. Medland suggested a long list of potential suitors who might be invited to counter the Genstar bid, including some that Canada Trust's directors already had in mind: Bell Canada Enterprises, Canadian Pacific Enterprises, Power Corporation, Brascan, and the Thomson and Weston groups. Some other names were suggested, but a bidding war for a company as valuable as Canada Trust was something only a suitor with very deep pockets would be likely to enter. Medland agreed to join Lahn and Mingay in canvassing the most promising candidates.

By the end of the week the responses had begun to come in. Bell was not interested; nor was Canadian Pacific; nor were the Thomson and Weston interests. And Brascan, while it had not yet turned down the invitation to the dance, seemed lukewarm about accepting it. Arthur Mingay then recalled that a good friend of his in Toronto, a corporate lawyer named Purdy Crawford, had recently gone to Montreal to become president of Imasco Ltd., the giant holding company that had begun life as the Canadian subsidiary of the British-American Tobacco Co. Ltd. and had then diversified into drug-store and fast-food chains in both Canada and the United States. Perhaps, Mingay thought, Imasco might be interested in diversifying further—into the financial services industry. He called his friend Purdy and asked him whether he would like to buy a trust company. "God," Crawford replied, "I'd love to, but we just can't look at it right now." Imasco at that time had its hands full planning the possible acquisition of a major drug-store chain in the United States.

Only one potential saviour had shown interest from the beginning: Power Corporation, the aptly named empire created by Paul Desmarais from virtually a standing start with a small bus company in Sudbury. Desmarais himself was away that week on Anticosti Island, in the Gulf of St. Lawrence, but even before Lahn, Mingay, and Ted Medland began canvassing possible buyers a

Power emissary, Michael Pitfield, had called Lahn and said Desmarais might be interested if the Canada Trust board would consider his bid friendly.

Among the companies controlled by Desmarais was Montreal Trust, and the prospect of merging that company with the larger Canada Trust obviously had some appeal. Canada Trust at that time had only one branch in Quebec. Back in the early 1960s, when the company had begun to expand its branch system, its directors had given serious consideration to increasing its presence in that province. The expense of opening new branches there promised to be disproportionately high, because of the cost of operating and advertising in two languages, and so the company cast about for possible acquisitions, without success. Again, in 1970, after Desmarais had gained control of the then-troubled Montreal Trust, there were talks to explore the possibility of merging that company with Canada Trust, but the conservative Canada Trust directors eventually backed off; they were concerned that Montreal Trust had too many problem loans, and there had for some time been fears that Quebec might separate from Canada. They decided that whatever money the company could set aside for expansion would be better spent in English Canada.

Now, in 1985, the two companies looked like a "good fit," and after consulting his board, Merv Lahn called Power and said a Desmarais bid would indeed be considered friendly. Power then commissioned the investment dealer Burns Fry to prepare a report on the Canada Trust situation to bring Desmarais up to date on his return from Anticosti. Desmarais returned to Montreal on the afternoon of Friday, 9 August, and after being briefed called Wood Gundy. Ted Medland was away from his office, but his colleague Gord Homer fielded the call and reported to Lahn later that Desmarais had seemed interested and had asked many questions.

On Monday, 12 August, the directors of ManuLife met again to consider Di Giacomo's plan to make a public offer of $50 for enough shares to gain control of Canada Trust, and this time they approved it. The Canada Trust board met next day, formally voted to accept the three conditions ManuLife had stipulated, and issued a letter to shareholders explaining the rival bids. The last paragraph of the letter began with a couple of sentences that were certainly repetitive, and now sounded somewhat plaintive. "Your directors," they said, "continue to believe that it is in the public interest and in the best interests of the Company and its shareholders and clients that the Company remain independent of dominance by any one shareholder. However, given that there are now two offers for control of your Company, it appears clear that this objective will no longer be possible." In the circumstances, they said, the shareholders should consider the offers and choose the one they thought most attractive. As for the directors, they thought the ManuLife offer was better than Genstar's and they recommended that the shareholders should choose it.

By now the adrenaline was flowing on all sides, and next day Genstar escalated the war. It secured a temporary injunction in the Ontario Supreme Court preventing ManuLife from buying any more shares of Canada Trust on the grounds that by law it could not own more than thirty per cent of another company outside its traditional business field. The court set Friday, 16 August, as the date for a hearing on whether the injunction should be continued.

On that day, Merv Lahn, Peter Maurice, and David Jackson, of Blake, Cassels & Graydon, flew to Montreal for a pre-arranged meeting with Paul Desmarais. Desmarais had had Robert Gratton, president of Montreal Trust, and his aides working on possible strategies by which Power might secure control of Canada Trust. Lahn once again assured him that he would be a welcome bidder, explained Canada Trust's financial position, and expressed his confidence that the company would increase its net earnings in future years. Lahn and Maurice agreed when they left the meeting that a Power bid seemed unlikely.

But when Lahn flew back to Toronto and drove to his cottage for the weekend, arriving late in the evening, he found that Tom Di Giacomo had called him at around 6 p.m. on a matter he described as urgent. Lahn called Di Giacomo at his home and office but received no reply at either number. He finally reached him on the Saturday morning at his office. Di Giacomo told him that the previous afternoon, after Lahn and Maurice had left, Power Corporation had called to explore the possibility of buying all ManuLife's Canada Trust shares.

It was a busy weekend for Syd Jackson and Tom Di Giacomo. As well as pondering their response to the Power offer—at one stage they considered suggesting that Power acquire thirty per cent of Canada Trust's stock, to give it joint control with ManuLife—they also received, late on the Sunday night, a call from MacNaughton and Turner, who had decided, they said, to amend their public offer. Genstar now proposed to bid $45 for one hundred per cent of Canada Trust's shares.

This news put Jackson and Di Giacomo over a barrel. A bid for all Canada Trust's shares was beyond ManuLife's means; it could not be made without outside financing, which presented difficulties, since mutual life insurance companies cannot under the regulations raise capital by the sale of debentures. They had no wish to be left owning thirty per cent of a company in which someone else held seventy per cent, and therefore complete control. And if they accepted the Genstar offer, they would, of course, no longer be embroiled in any court action.

The hearing on the application for an extension of the Genstar injunction had been postponed by the court that Friday because of a backlog of other cases. Jackson and Di Giacomo had been assured by their lawyers that the arrangement for their public offer would stand up in court, and that if it didn't, they could use foreign subsidiaries to the same effect. But they had no appetite for continuing the case; they were apprehensive about the implications for the whole insurance industry of a provincial court ruling on something that was essentially a federal matter, since insurance companies operate under federal regulation. On the afternoon of Monday, 19 August, it was announced that ManuLife had sold all its shares of Canada Trust to Genstar at $45. When he called to tell Lahn about the sale, Di Giacomo said ManuLife had had no choice.

It looked as though the battle was over, but an hour after the sale of ManuLife's shares was announced Paul Desmarais called Lahn. He had been unable to make a deal with ManuLife—one of his aides told Peter Maurice later that the asking price quoted for the ManuLife shares had been "outrageous." But the Power people had not given up. Desmarais asked Lahn whether he thought a public offer of $50 a share would be enough to top the Genstar bid. Lahn said he thought it would. The advantage in takeover battles, however, always lies with the company that moves first: it has time to put alternative strategies into place in advance and knows how far it can go in the bidding. Companies trying to cobble together a competing bid keep running up against deadlines.

But Power persevered. Robert Gratton, president of Montreal Trust, called Lahn the next day, Tuesday, and said Power was still trying to devise a bid that could not be defeated. Twenty-four hours later he called Lahn again and said Gordon Securities, acting for Genstar, had bought 3.2 million Canada Trust shares that day, even though the official deadline for the Genstar offer was still a week away. Gratton said Power did not want to launch a bid unless it was sure it could win; and that prospect now seemed less and less likely.

The Canada Trust directors held a short and melancholy meeting on the morning of Thursday, 22 August, and bowed to the inevitable. They issued a letter to their shareholders afterward advising them to accept the new Genstar bid. In the absence of a better offer, the letter said, twenty-three of the directors intended to tender all, or virtually all, of the 219,500 shares they held. The members of the stock-option plan also decided to tender their shares. Merv Lahn made a pre-tax profit of more than $2 million on his own shares, and the other sixty-eight executives with options shared almost $14 million among them. Some of the old Huron & Erie loyalists looked a little askance at this when it was reported in the press, feeling that its management was profiting from the company's misfortune. But as Lahn remarked wryly to the author three years later: "There was no favour done to the senior personnel." Had they been able to predict the future and held on to their shares, they would have made perhaps $30 million more.

23

Under New Ownership Once More

ON 27 August 1985 Merv Lahn released a letter addressed to his staff which began: "The Genstar offer was completed this morning and, upon settlement of the transactions on September 4th, Genstar will own virtually all of Canada Trustco's outstanding common shares." The letter promised to keep the staff fully informed about the plan to merge Canada Trust and the Permanent, which had already received wide press publicity, and went on:

"Mergers are not new to Canada Trustco. In its 121-year history the company has entered into 18 mergers, the latest of which were undertaken in 1976. All have contributed to the growth and prosperity of our organization and there can be no doubt that the one now contemplated would do likewise. . . . Canada Trustco and the Permanent will be a 'good fit' if combined. While there would be some branch overlap it would affect less than six per cent of total branches. In those instances, the better located of the branches would be selected as the continuing operation. Staffs would be combined and there would be no jobs lost. Any overstaffing would be rectified by attrition through normal turnover.

"Regional offices would number eleven in a merged company, two greater than at present, and integration of staffs could be accomplished smoothly and without job loss. While integration and location of head office staffs would be more challenging and complex, it can be accomplished without significant relocation of people. Operations in London such as data processing, card services, etc. would undoubtedly be significantly expanded. . . . It is indeed business as usual. I thank each of you most sincerely for carrying out your duties in an exemplary fashion during a period when customer inquiries were undoubtedly at a peak."

The letter styled Genstar's directors and officers as "respected, capable and integrous people," and assured members of the staff, customers, and the general public that "Canada Trustco's integrity and financial strength will not be compromised in any way under the responsible ownership of Genstar."

The letter was clearly designed to restore the staff's confidence and morale. But, privately, Lahn had profound reservations about the new set-up, and the role he might be expected to play in it. He was in no way mollified when the directors of Canada Trust met its new owners for the first time at a board meeting in Toronto on 24 September. The meeting began at 9.30 a.m. and MacNaughton and Turner spent the first hour explaining Genstar's background and their plans for the merger with the Permanent. These included the establishment of an "Office of the President": there would be no single chief executive officer of the amalgamated company, but responsibility would be shared by MacNaughton, Turner, John Hilliker, chairman of the Permanent, and Lahn.

Convinced throughout his career that effective management demanded personal decisiveness, Lahn was astonished by this proposal. He considered it unworkable—and to him, certainly, unacceptable. But he held his peace while MacNaughton and Turner wound up their presentation and at 10.35 a.m. withdrew from the room while the board proceeded to other business. That other business included the appointment of MacNaughton and Turner as directors, to replace two board members whose resignations were accepted: Syd Jackson of ManuLife, and John Panabaker, of Mutual Life.[1]

Much of the rest of the meeting was devoted to the technicalities of preparing a formal application to the federal minister of consumer and corporate affairs for the removal of the voting-share constraint provisions in the company's by-laws, which were now clearly a dead issue, and application to the federal finance minis-

---

1. Mutual Life, sole survivor of the friendly-shareholder group, had not, despite Alex Barron's forebodings, sold its shares to ManuLife in 1982. But as Canada Trust prospered and its share price kept rising, Mutual's investment managers began to feel the Canada Trust block constituted too large a percentage of their total investment portfolio. So in August 1984 Mutual sold approximately a third of its holding, 237,500 shares, on the market. For the same reason, it sold a further 125,000 shares in May 1985. It sold the rest of its holding, 386,302 shares, to Genstar when it became clear that Canada Trust's fate was sealed.

ter for permission for the amalgamation of Canada Trust and the Permanent. But the directors also found time to review and approve the monthly reports from Merv Lahn's management team on various aspects of the company's operations, and to sanction a batch of corporate loans totalling almost $70 million and 2,762 mortgage applications totalling $170.9 million. One can imagine canny old Adam Hope's mind reeling.

Bill Grace, a director from Edmonton, where he was senior vice-president, finance, of Canadian Utilities Ltd., then proposed that "management look into the establishment of a special committee to consider all transactions or proposed transactions between Genstar and the companies." His resolution approved, the meeting broke up for lunch at 1.10 p.m.

Peter Maurice, who had attended the meeting as one of the executives presenting reports to the directors, was well aware of his boss's probable reaction to the idea of an "Office of the President." When the meeting ended, he caught up with Lahn on the way to lunch and urged him, "Don't do anything irretrievable." But after lunch Lahn sought out MacNaughton and Turner and, with as much amicability as he could muster in the circumstances, told them that since they owned the company they could organize it any way they wanted to, but he was gone. He advised them to replace him with Peter Maurice, stalked out of the building, and next morning drove home to London, where he told his wife, without noticeable concern, that for the first time in his life he was out of a job.

That afternoon Peter Maurice and Jack Speake, along with the third member of Lahn's top management triumvirate, John Richardson, executive vice-president in charge of all regional operations, were supposed to attend a meeting with a team from Bain and Company, a U.S. management-consultant firm which had studied the operations of the Permanent for Genstar. Instead, they constituted themselves an impromptu delegation to MacNaughton and Turner and assured them that Merv Lahn always meant what he said. Maurice reminded them that they had borrowed heavily to pay the $1.2 billion bill for Canada Trust, and warned them that if they wanted to repay that indebtedness they should not ruin its operation by breaking up its management team. "And you're in the process of destroying it," Maurice said.

There had already been speculation in the press that one reason for the purchase of Canada Trust had been to secure the services of

Merv Lahn, who was acknowledged to be one of the best chief executives in the financial industry. And certainly it was essential for MacNaughton and Turner to ensure the continued efficient operation of their new acquisition. So they reconsidered their plans, called Lahn that evening, and asked him to come back into the fold. Lahn set a number of stiff conditions, most notably that if he was going to be associated with the company in any way he would be *running* it, and a few days later Genstar announced that John Hilliker would be chairman of the merged company and Lahn would be its president and chief executive officer.

The extent of Lahn's victory became evident a few weeks later when it was announced that his management team would remain intact when the two companies merged on 31 December: Peter Maurice would become senior executive vice-president, with Speake and Richardson as executive vice-presidents. Furthermore, the merged company would be known as Canada Trust, and its headquarters would remain in London—fears had been expressed in the London press that widespread unemployment might result if it moved to Toronto, or perhaps even to Vancouver.

The new organizational chart, of necessity, left no room for Arthur Mingay, who retired as chairman at the end of 1985, after almost fifty years with the company. When Mingay became president, the company had assets under administration of $4.2 billion and net earnings of $12.9 million. When he retired, the amalgamated company had assets under administration of $49.2 billion and its net earnings in 1985 were $135.5 million. He remained a director and member of the executive committee as the merged company embarked on its enlarged operations.

Financial analysts and industry observers marvelled at the speed and smoothness with which the physical operations of the two companies were meshed into each other. From the start of the planning for the merger, in September, it was decided that they would operate as one entity from the time the doors opened for business on 2 January 1986. This posed enormous logistical problems, chief among them being to reconcile the two companies' computer systems. The Permanent was operating on a system installed by the Canadian high-tech company Geac. This was not only incompatible with Canada Trust's IBM system; it had reached its peak capacity and had the merger not taken place the Permanent would have faced huge expenditures to install a new system. So it was logical to stay with the Canada Trust system, and the cost of installing IBM terminals and other equipment in all the Permanent offices ultimately reached $18 million.

The fall of 1985 was a hectic time for all departments of both companies. With the decision to operate as one entity, all the employees—combined, they numbered almost 16,000—clearly had to be on the same personnel system. Here again, the Canada Trust system was chosen, and work was begun on the task of integrating the Permanent's employees into it and of training them in Canada Trust systems and procedures. The whole range of Permanent products—savings accounts, term deposits, and all the rest—had to be examined and compared with Canada Trust's products so that when the merged company opened for business the Permanent's customers could switch to the nearest Canada Trust equivalent. Plans had to be made for new signs for the converted Permanent branches, and they had to be supplied with Canada Trust forms and marketing materials.

The atmosphere of impending change, naturally enough, aroused some resentment among the Permanent's employees. Crudely lettered posters began to appear on notice boards. One of them—strangely, in view of the way he had fought against the takeover of financial institutions—portrayed Merv Lahn as a sort of home-grown Rambo intent on ravaging the peaceful preserve of the Permanent. Another urged employees worried about their jobs to "secure your future with the 'I love Merv Lahn' button"—the word "love" in the accompanying illustration being portrayed by a heart in the New York State tradition. "Buy now before attrition takes its toll!" the employees were advised.

In fact, as usually happens in such upheavals, most of the attrition took place at the top. Some of the Permanent's executives found other jobs before the merged company even began operations; most of the rest drifted away later, as the opportunity arose. Since the data-processing, personnel, and comptroller's departments were all based in London, about two hundred head-office jobs in Toronto became redundant. Some of the displaced employees were offered positions in London, but many of them left rather than move. All those who left were given generous severance settlements and offered relocation counselling to help them find other jobs.

When the merged company opened for business after New Year's Day 1986, it was billed as the country's sixth largest financial institution. The Permanent's staff and customers were soon given a dramatic introduction to the new corporate culture: in true Canada Trust marketing style, two-page advertisements in the press proclaimed, in bold letters two inches high, CANADA TRUST IS NOW AS BIG AS THE BIG BANKS. The advertisement went on to say: "The bigger and better Canada Trust is proud to have the confidence of millions of Canadians. In fact, we're larger than any bank, trust or insurance company in both the mortgage business and registered retirement savings deposits.[2] We're also a significant competitor in personal loans, credit cards, automobile dealer financing, commercial and corporate lending, personal, pension and corporate trust services, and real estate."

After explaining some of the services offered to customers, the advertisement went on to proclaim: "As part of the celebrations during this historic year for Canada Trust, we're going to make one of our customers a millionaire." This promotion, which was to run for the rest of the year, entitled customers with more than $3,000 in a savings or chequing account to one shot at the million-dollar prize for each $200 in the account every month.[3] If they had not realized it before, the former Permanent employees now knew they were playing in an entirely new ball game. It was one that most of them came to enjoy.

The new company had a total of 315 financial services branches across the country, about a hundred more than Canada Trust had before the merger. In the reorganization, 24 Permanent branches and 7 Canada Trust branches were either merged or closed. In addition, the new company had 23 offices devoted to trust business and 173 real estate sales offices, 44 of them in Quebec, where Canada Trust previously had none.

The merger greatly strengthened the company in the real estate sales field. The Permanent had always laid more stress on real estate sales than Canada Trust. The Huron & Erie had more or less drifted into the business in the early 1950s, as it began to beef up its trust operations and found it had more and more estate properties to sell. From there it was a logical move to begin listing properties for others, but at first it was a piecemeal operation. Some branches had real estate sales people but most did not. The com-

2. An accompanying chart showed that Canada Trust, with $17 billion in personal savings deposits, ranked ahead of the Toronto-Dominion Bank, the Bank of Nova Scotia, and the National Bank.

3. The prize was won by June Haydn, of Tottenham, Ontario.

pany had no separate real estate department until the late 1960s, when Arthur Mingay recruited a former registrar for real estate for Ontario, Walter Kucherepa, to set it up. The department grew under Kucherepa's supervision, until by 1972 there were thirty-six real estate sales offices across the country employing 245 salesmen; but as the company focussed its attention on its retail banking operations, the real estate department languished by comparison. At the time of the merger it had grown only to sixty-nine offices across the country.[4]

The merged company had been operating for less than three months when a new chapter in the long history of Canada Trust began. On Sunday evening, 23 March, Purdy Crawford called his friend and former neighbour Arthur Mingay at his home in Toronto and told him there would be an announcement next day that Imasco Ltd. was making a takeover bid for Genstar. This time, of course, as but one of Genstar's many subsidiaries, Canada Trust would be only a bystander in whatever boardroom battles might develop, but Mingay lost no time in relaying the news to Merv Lahn. Lahn received it calmly enough. Sure, if the takeover bid succeeded, he would have a new owner, but that was a prospect he welcomed; Imasco was a solid company with a reputation for permitting its subsidiary components to operate autonomously. And since he would not be involved in any of the negotiations anyway, he could only keep his powder dry and await developments.

Imasco had been considering expanding into the financial services field for some time. The deal it had been working on for the acquisition of an American drug-store chain had collapsed a few weeks after Mingay called Crawford inviting him to be a white knight. By that time it was too late to contest Genstar's bid for Canada Trust; but Imasco decided to commission its management consultants and investment dealers to do some studies to identify

---

4. The activities of the real estate department were always separate from those of Truscan Realty Ltd., a subsidiary established in 1972 as a holding and management company for all the company's real estate investments, comprising its own office premises and its interests in shopping malls and other commercial developments. Truscan's portfolio before the merger amounted to $222 million; two years later it had grown to $350 million, and the subsidiary's contribution to its parent's earnings exceeded $10 million before tax.

possible acquisitions in the financial services industry. The consultants came up with seven possible candidates, and eventually the choice fell on Genstar, because of its ownership of Canada Trust.

Wanting to ensure it had adequate financing before making its public offer, Imasco approached its traditional banker, the Royal. But the Royal was also one of Genstar's bankers and decided it had a conflict of interest. When other Canadian banks seemed lukewarm, Imasco went to Citicorp, in the United States, which put together a syndicate of fifteen U.S. banks to advance the $2.6 billion it was thought would be needed for a successful takeover bid. Imasco had also planned to use its investment dealer on Wall Street, Morgan Stanley and Company, as its adviser on the bid. But Morgan Stanley also did some work for Genstar and backed out because of the potential conflict of interest. So Imasco turned to another American firm, First Boston.

The Belgian group Société Générale still held almost twenty per cent of Genstar's shares, and in their initial planning the Imasco people did not think they would get the Belgians' support for their bid. But as luck would have it, First Boston had a representative in Europe who made frequent calls on the Belgian group and believed their shares might be available. So Rod Foster, one of Imasco's executive vice-presidents, flew to Brussels and after a couple of days of negotiations Société Générale agreed to tender their shares at the price Imasco planned to offer, $54, with the proviso that if Imasco had to raise its bid they would get the increased price.

With this substantial block of shares in his pocket, Purdy Crawford met MacNaughton and Turner in New York on Sunday, 23 March, and told them of Imasco's plans, and the public offer of $54 for all Genstar's shares was announced next day. By then the planned offering bid was lower than the price at which Genstar's shares were changing hands on the stock exchanges: in a flurry of trading just before the weekend they had jumped $11 to close at $55 on the Friday afternoon. This suggested that despite Imasco's best efforts the news of its impending bid had leaked out. There were suspicions that the buying had come from Europe, sparked by knowledge that Rod Foster was meeting with the Société Générale group. But with fifteen banks involved in the U.S. syndicate financing the bid, the leak could have come from anywhere.[5]

Purdy Crawford remains convinced that it did not come from within his own organization; and in fact the rise in price of the Genstar shares ultimately forced Imasco to sweeten its bid and pay four dollars a share more than its original offer for Genstar. Of more immediate concern to Crawford was that on the day the bid was announced Barbara McDougall, minister of state for finance, told the House of Commons she intended to use provisions of the proposed legislation governing loan and trust companies to "look at it very closely." The legislation had not yet been introduced, but the clear implication was that the government could derail the Imasco takeover if it chose to.

The minister's statement was a response to a demand from a back-bench Tory M.P. from Toronto, Paul McCrossan, that the government block the Imasco bid. McCrossan was a member of the parliamentary standing committee on finance, trade and economic affairs, and he had not been pleased six months earlier when the government had ignored the committee's view that large non-financial companies should be prevented from taking over large financial institutions, and had permitted the Genstar takeover of Canada Trust to go through without intervention. McCrossan and a group of his back-bench supporters now demanded that the government hold an emergency debate on the Imasco bid before the date on which it was due to expire, 25 April.

On 3 April Imasco raised its bid to $58 a share and the Genstar directors advised their shareholders to accept it. When Imasco had first made its bid, MacNaughton and Turner had tried to persuade Purdy Crawford to buy just Canada Trust and leave them with the rest of the Genstar assets. This proposal had some attraction for Crawford, since it was public knowledge that if the takeover succeeded Imasco intended to sell off the other Genstar assets, and at that stage no one knew how much they were worth. But having made a public offer to all Genstar shareholders, Crawford decided integrity demanded that he go through with it. MacNaughton and Turner then proposed an arrangement under which, if the takeover succeeded, they could buy back the rest of Genstar's non-financial companies.

---

5. Investigations into the last-minute flurry of trading were later launched by both the Ontario Securities Commission and the U.S. Securities and Exchange Commission, but at the time of writing the mystery remained unsolved.

This arrangement could have laid them open to allegations that they had a conflict of interest—that they did not want the price paid for the Genstar stock to be too high, so that they could buy back the other assets as cheaply as possible. Since they believed it was their responsibility to their shareholders to get the best price possible for their shares, they went to the Genstar board, explained their position, and said they wanted to dissociate themselves from any negotiations with Imasco on the price of the shares. The Genstar directors thereupon established a committee of independent directors, chaired by the head of Northern Telecom, Walter Light, which negotiated with Imasco and eventually settled on $58 as a fair price.

A few days after the new offer was made, Crawford and Imasco's chairman, Paul Paré, met Lahn in Toronto. Even before they knew anything about the impending Imasco bid, the Canada Trust directors had passed a resolution that the company would undertake no lending, investing, or trusteeship activities with any shareholder owning ten per cent or more of its shares. While this resolution did not have quite the legal force of a by-law, it was another attempt to preserve the company's independence and prevent any dealings with Genstar or, for that matter, any subsequent owner. Paré and Purdy now assured Lahn that they had no intention of interfering in the company's operations, and if the takeover bid succeeded they would ask for no more than a quarter of the seats on the Canada Trust board, thus ensuring that the resolution outlawing self-dealing would not be overturned under the new ownership.

Encouraged by this conversation, Lahn went public with his support for the Imasco bid. The parliamentary finance committee, still concerned that large financial institutions should not be controlled by large non-financial companies, had passed a unanimous resolution urging the government to ban the Imasco takeover. Lahn told reporters the committee's concern was misplaced. He was by no means the only observer surprised at the committee's apparent attempt to lock the barn door after the horses had fled: all the major trust companies in the country, including Canada Trust, were already controlled by large non-financial companies. And in the present case the committee seemed to be trying to make some distinction between a large Canadian non-financial company run from San Francisco, with a large Belgian shareholding, and a large Canadian non-financial company run from Montreal, with a large shareholding in Britain. Imasco's former parent company, BAT Industries PLC, still held forty-four per cent of its shares, though it had no directors on the board and Imasco operated autonomously in Canada. Lahn told the press he was "delighted" at the prospect of joining Imasco, because it was financially stronger than Genstar and its management was "highly capable, extremely well-respected and, I am quite confident, people with whom we can get along well."

Expanding on this theme in a CBC Radio interview a few days later, Lahn said he was confident Imasco would not try to sell assets into Canada Trust, as Genstar had done when it took over the Permanent. Among those who pricked up their ears at this apparently casual remark was M.P. Paul McCrossan, who promptly raised it at the next meeting of the finance committee. And on Monday, 14 April, the committee voted to summon Lahn, MacNaughton, and Turner to give evidence at a hearing a week later, on 21 April.

Lahn began his evidence before the committee by presenting the list he had been asked to provide of what he called "related party transactions" between Genstar and the Permanent. He assured the committee members that all the transactions had been approved by the Permanent's own internal audit committee, composed of independent directors; by its outside auditors; and by its board of directors. One of the transactions, in fact, had been approved by the Canada Trust directors: the $32 million purchase, early in 1986, of a package of mortgages generated by Genstar's land and development operations, which the Permanent had been negotiating before the merger. "They were mortgages," Lahn told the committee, "which, in the normal course of business, would be totally suitable investments for any trust or loan company."

Under questioning by committee members, Lahn left no doubt that even though it was too late to preserve Canada Trust's independence, he still believed that the government was abdicating its responsibility by not imposing the ten-per-cent ownership constraint on loan and trust companies, believing instead that strict regulation could control any potential self-dealing. New Democrat Nelson Riis reminded him of a speech he had made to the Kitchener Chamber of Commerce the previous summer, in which he had said: "In light of the failures of Seaway, Greymac, Crown, Fidelity and Pioneer, all deposit-taking institutions controlled by one or a few individuals and all involved in blatant and ruinous self-dealings with their sole shareholder or principal shareholders, the government's view is surely naive."

"Do you still stand by those comments?" Riis asked. "I have not changed my views one iota," Lahn replied. "With respect to my perhaps intemperate statement that the government is naive, I still believe that to be the case."

Riis thanked him for his frankness, and after some generalized questioning about trust company practices by other members the committee turned to MacNaughton and Turner, who had prepared a thirty-two-page brief to substantiate their contention that its dealings with Genstar had helped, rather than harmed, the Permanent. For instance, before they took over, the brief said, the Permanent had been unsuccessfully seeking ways of expanding into the United States. Genstar at the same time had been reorganizing its U.S. financial services. As part of that reorganization it offered to sell the Permanent its Genstar Securities Corporation, whose principal asset was Genstar Mortgage Corporation, one of the ten largest mortgage servicing companies in the United States. After independent valuations commissioned by the Permanent's directors, the price agreed upon was $43.3 million in cash and Permanent shares valued at $18.6 million. The deal took place in 1982 and was completed a year later, when the Permanent paid $54 million to a Genstar subsidiary for a ten-per-cent Genstar Mortgage note. And in the first year of its ownership, MacNaughton and Turner said, Genstar Securities accounted for more than forty per cent of the Permanent's net income of $23.4 million.

In another 1982 transaction, CanPerm Realty Ltd., the Permanent's real estate subsidiary, bought a Hamilton shopping centre owned by Genstar, Lime Ridge Mall, for $47 million in cash and Permanent shares valued at $25 million. These two transactions, MacNaughton and Turner pointed out, had increased the shareholders' equity in the Permanent by more than $43 million, a welcome increase in capital when it had previously been nudging close to the limits of its multiple.

After outlining several other transactions, MacNaughton and Turner stressed that they had all been made for sound business reasons, and all had been approved by the Permanent's board. At times the committee's questions seemed designed to elicit an admission that the various transactions—in all, the Permanent paid well over $200 million to acquire Genstar properties—meant that Genstar had, in effect, bought the Permanent with its own depositors' money. MacNaughton and Turner did not see things quite that way. They pointed out that since part of the purchase price for the Genstar properties had been paid in Permanent shares, Genstar had in fact injected equity into the company that they did not think the Permanent could have raised on its own.

"When we acquired the Permanent," Turner told the committee, "the amount of common shareholders' equity was $199 million, and when it was amalgamated in 1985 it was $325 to $330 million, which is a significant increase." MacNaughton and Turner both showed concern toward the end of the hearing, when Nelson Riis asked if they would consider the transactions self-dealing. MacNaughton did not like the use of that term, since it "implies that something might not be proper." He preferred to use the term "related party transactions." Turner seconded this view. "We kind of felt," he said, "flowing from your committee, that self-dealing was where transactions were thought to threaten the ongoing solvency and viability of a financial institution. And in our view, these related party transactions were to help the financial institution."

All in all, the committee's hearing was inconclusive, and it had certainly been overtaken by events. A few days earlier, Mrs. McDougall, the minister of state for finance, had announced that the government would permit the Imasco takeover of Genstar to proceed. The minister had forestalled the finance committee's call for an emergency debate on the issue by introducing amendments to the trust companies legislation in Parliament giving her the power to overturn any transfer of ownership of more than ten per cent of a trust or loan company's shares made without her written consent. "This bill," said McCrossan, "gives the minister all of the powers that the finance committee wanted her to have."

Amid the unwelcome rash of headlines that accompanied the Imasco bid, Purdy Crawford had sought a meeting with the minister and had shown her a copy of a press release Imasco was prepared to issue if she agreed. This contained a list of promises Imasco was ready to make if it would help the government to make up its mind on the takeover. First of all, there would be an absolute prohibition on self-dealing between Canada Trust and any other company in the Imasco stable. The board of Canada Trust would remain entirely independent. Imasco would undertake not to acquire any other financial institutions in Canada, at least until the government had secured the passage into law of its long-promised overhaul of the regulations governing loan and trust companies, whereupon Imasco expected to be accorded the same powers as any other corporation. Also, if the takeover succeeded, Imasco was prepared to sell a portion of its shares in Canada Trust to the public within a period of five years. (The government later ruled that Imasco should reduce its controlling interest to sixty-five per cent by the end of 1991.)

Given these assurances, Mrs. McDougall decreed that Imasco, which had already accumulated more than fifty-one per cent of the Genstar shares, could go ahead with its bid for the rest.[6] "These are very tough conditions we put on," she told the House. "They indicate that provided the public interest is served, we are prepared to allow the marketplace to operate."

Merv Lahn, still awaiting without much optimism the passage of whatever legislation might emerge from the tortuous political process, permitted himself a wry smile.

---

6. While the takeover was reported at the time to have cost $2.6 billion, the final price paid for Canada Trust has yet to be determined, since when it bought Genstar, Imasco inherited more than $2 billion in that company's contingent liabilities, or accumulated debt. Imasco and MacNaughton and Turner were unable to come to terms on the buy-back of Genstar's non-financial assets, so Imasco began to sell the other companies in the oddly assorted empire as separate packages to a variety of buyers. At the time of writing, the sales had brought in $2.8 billion, and it was estimated that when all the transactions were completed, the bill for Canada Trust would be about $2.2 billion.

Epilogue

ONCE again, the change in ownership was not permitted to impede the company's day-to-day operations: the marketing initiatives and product innovations, and the rapid growth in business volume, continued without interruption.

One of the first fruits of the predicted synergistic effect of the merger came in 1986, with the introduction of a trust account called the Financial Commander. The personal trust business had been the backbone of the Permanent, and its experienced trust officers were well suited to handle this new account, made possible only by Canada Trust's sophisticated computer system. Intended for customers with portfolio assets of more than $100,000, the Financial Commander was billed as "the ultimate in hassle-free financial control." In addition to the usual savings, chequing, and credit-card facilities, it provided customers with professional management of their investments, the sale and purchase of securities at reduced commissions, the payment of bills—even household staff, if any—accounting services and tax advice, all detailed in monthly statements. As its advertising proclaimed: "A financial partnership with Canada Trust brings all your financial matters under one roof." The new service proved so popular that by mid-1988 there were more than 9,000 Commander accounts, and the book value of their assets exceeded $4 billion.

The drive to win customers with new and more convenient services continued to dominate all aspects of the company's business. In 1986, for instance, the Johnny Cash machines were linked with the Interac network, enabling Canada Trust card-holders to obtain cash around the clock at more than 4,000 automated banking machines at other financial institutions in Canada. A year later, the company joined the Plus network, giving its customers ever-expanding access to more than 19,000 machines in the United States and Europe and ultimately around the world. Also, in the fall of that year, 1987, a new credit card—SuperCharge—was launched with a splash as carrying the lowest interest rate of any card in the country: 13.5 per cent at the time of writing.

And so it went, as the country's largest trust company continued to challenge the banks on their own turf and to keep all its competitors on their toes with its car give-aways and mortgage burnings and a stream of new products such as SuperLoan—"larger loans for less"—and PowerLine, a line of credit with interest approximating the prime rate charged by banks to their best customers.

Internally, too, the drive for efficiency continued, with the launching in 1987 of another of Jack Speake's brain-children, the Canada Trust Management Institute. The company's personnel department had for many years conducted courses for junior managers and those aspiring to join their ranks. But gradually Speake and some other senior managers came to feel that the logical people to train managers were those who were already successful managers.

From his early days as a Scoutmaster, Speake had been dedicated to what he calls "personal development." Explaining the philosophy behind the institute, he told the author: "The world is changing so fast that something different is needed to compete in the nineties. We will not compete on technology as much in the future as we have in the past; we will not compete in marketing as much as we have in the past, because competitors eventually catch up. I believe we will compete more in the future on people's ability—the *human* part of the service equation—and that means we have to put a great deal more support into the development of our people, and their leadership."

Though it has no bricks and mortar or ivy-covered walls, Speake likes to think of the management institute as a university, and indeed he carries the official title of Dean. "In the past," he says, "our people support in the company was largely skill training. But the whole concept of the institute is to *educate*." The educational process began with the selection of a group of senior executives who were temporarily relieved of their normal duties to attend five-day "training the trainer" sessions. Having learned some pertinent class-room techniques, these managers—assistant vice-presidents and up—held training sessions for the next level of managers below them. They in turn took on the task of educating—and, it was hoped, inspiring—the supervisors and newly promoted junior managers lower down the ladder. "It's seventy-five per cent self-learning," says Speake. "What you do is create an environment where people learn from each other, within a very disciplined structure. Nobody graduates—there's no finish to it. You keep going back, with five-day courses every year."

In 1987, with the merged company now in full stride, all the conscientious striving to give customers more and better services and to improve the company's operating efficiency paid off where it was intended to: on the bottom line. At the annual meeting early in 1988 Merv Lahn[1] was able to report 1987 net earnings of $201 million, a huge increase of sixty-one per cent over the previous year and the highest earnings of all Canadian financial institutions for that year. By now the company had almost $26 billion in customers' savings deposits, more than fourteen per cent of the country's total. But it was still shackled by archaic regulations framed more than seventy years ago, when our legislative forebears could not possibly have envisaged today's rapidly changing business climate. In mid-1988 the federal government had still not introduced its long-promised loan and trust company legislation to the House. And with election talk heavy in the air, and high-priority items such as free trade on the legislative agenda, Merv Lahn had little hope that it would be introduced, let alone passed, before the approaching election. And each year's delay created new problems for Lahn and his team.

The federal foot-dragging left a vacuum that the provincial governments of Ontario and Quebec moved to fill with their own legislation, which conflicted in several important ways with the proposed federal legislation. In earlier years, when any federal legislation affecting Canada Trust was passed, the company invariably consulted the Ontario government, which would usually amend its own legislation so that harmony prevailed and the

---

1. At the annual meeting a year earlier, Lahn had stepped up to the post of chairman, replacing John Hilliker, who had resigned to become president and chief executive officer of Bimcor Inc., Bell Canada Enterprises' pension fund management unit. In accordance with company tradition, Lahn remained chief executive officer for a transitional period. Peter Maurice became president and chief operating officer of Canada Trustco, Jack Speake became president of the subsidiary Canada Trust, and both joined the Canada Trustco board.

company was able to conduct its business in compliance with both sets of regulations. But under its new legislation, proclaimed early in 1988, Ontario decreed that all financial institutions licensed for operation in the province must play by Ontario's rules. Since these permitted certain practices not permitted under the federal legislation, by which Canada Trust is bound, and proscribed certain other practices permitted under the federal legislation, the company was left at the time of writing in an untenable position.

"When we finally get through the current stage of financial institutions reform," Merv Lahn told the Society of Management Accountants of Saskatchewan in a speech in June 1988, "governments must give top priority to the harmonization question."

In the fall of 1987, in an attempt to navigate around the legislative shoals, the company was restructured, with Canada Trustco and its subsidiaries becoming in turn subsidiaries of a new parent holding company, CT Financial Services, which is not regulated by either federal or provincial loan and trust company legislation. Imasco exchanged its 98.6 per cent holding of Canada Trustco shares[2] for shares of CT Financial, on a three-for-one basis. Shortly afterward the 1.4 per cent of Canada Trustco shares remaining in public hands were also exchanged for shares of CT Financial, again on a three-for-one basis. So Imasco ended up owning 98.6 per cent of CT Financial, which in turn owns 100 per cent of Canada Trustco.

The legislative uncertainty, Lahn told the annual meeting early in 1988, had left the company no choice but to reorganize its structure. "Our operational activities," he said, "were at the point of being stifled due to various arbitrary, quantitative, regulatory limitations, particularly in the loans area. Without the reorganization, the company would not be able to continue to compete effectively and vigorously in the financial services industry."

The restructuring, of course, did not relieve Canada Trust of its obligation to observe whatever regulations were eventually put in place. But it enabled CT Financial to form new subsidiaries, per-

---

2. About that same time, in accordance with its commitment to the government to reduce its holding of Canada Trustco to sixty-five per cent, Imasco was preparing its first sale of shares to the public. But that summer shares of financial institutions had fallen sharply and it was decided to postpone the issue—just a few days before 19 October, the day of the stock-market crash now known as Black Monday.

haps in entirely new businesses, that Canada Trust could not own. The first two of these, CT Credit Corporation and CT Retail Finance Inc., were formed to escape the tyranny of the company's old nemesis, the basket clause, by holding some assets, mostly in the form of personal loans, which, had they been left on Canada Trust's balance sheet, would have pushed the company above the seven-per-cent ceiling.

That the failure of successive governments to amend seventy-year-old regulations forced them to adopt this stratagem (though it is perfectly legal) does not sit well with Canada Trust's management. "Everyone agrees the legislation is anachronistic and unworkable," says Peter Maurice, "and it gets to the point of being silly. But as long as you obey the form, the substance doesn't matter. If any teacher started teaching my child this, I'd be in there hammering him on the head. But the fact is that if you obey the form you can get some relief on the substance. Watching the whole process does not give you a lot of comfort."

As this book goes to press, the steel is rising in the heart of Toronto's financial district for a new, fifty-one-storey Canada Trust Tower, centrepiece of the billion-dollar BCE Place, right across from the gleaming office tower occupied by the country's largest bank, the Royal. Occupying a whole city block, from Bay to Yonge between Front and Wellington, BCE Place is designed to have a six-level "galleria" linking Canada Trust Tower with another office building of forty-two storeys. With a twenty-per-cent equity interest in its new tower, at a cost of $120 million, Canada Trust plans to occupy roughly twenty per cent of its 1.2 million square feet of rentable space.

But pending a resolution of the legislative uncertainty it is impossible, at the time of writing, to predict what kind of activities the company will be conducting in its new quarters, planned for occupation some time in the middle of 1990. Under existing rules, Imasco's majority ownership precludes the attainment of the company's long-held ambition to be a bank. But the formation of CT Financial opened the way for a whole new range of activities. And as Canada Trust heads into the 1990s, no one can foresee its future shape, any more than Adam Hope, Verschoyle Cronyn, and the other founding fathers assembled above Daniel Macfie's dry-goods emporium back in 1864 could have imagined the present scale and scope of the organization they created as the Huron & Erie Savings and Loan Society.

Appendix

Appendix

Chairmen, Presidents, and Directors of the Huron & Erie Mortgage Corporation, the Canada Trustco Mortgage Company, and the Canada Trust Company

The Huron & Erie Mortgage Corporation/Canada Trustco Mortgage Company

Chairmen[1]

T.G. Meredith	1925 to 1943
I. Leonard	1943 to 1958
V.P. Cronyn	1958 to 1968
J.A. Taylor	1968 to 1978
A.H. Mingay	1978 to 1985
J.A.C. Hilliker	1986
M.L. Lahn	1987 to present

Presidents

A. Hope	1864 to 1867
E.W. Hyman	1867 to 1871
J. Birrell	1871 to 1874
C. Stead	1874 to 1879
W.P. Saunders	1879 to 1887
P.R. Street	1887 to 1888
J.W. Little	1888 to 1909
T.G. Meredith	1909 to 1926
H. Cronyn	1926 to 1933
T.G. Meredith	1933 to 1943
M. Aylsworth	1943 to 1958
J.A. Taylor	1958 to 1973
A.H. Mingay	1973 to 1978
M.L. Lahn	1978 to 1987
P.C. Maurice	1987 to present

1. The position of chairman of the board was created in 1925.

The Canada Trust Company

Chairmen

J.A. Lougheed	1899 to 1900
T.G. Meredith	1926 to 1943
I. Leonard	1943 to 1958
V.P. Cronyn	1958 to 1968
J.A. Taylor	1968 to 1978
A.H. Mingay	1978 to 1985
J.A.C. Hilliker	1986
M.L. Lahn	1987 to present

Presidents

J.A. Lougheed	1899 to 1900
V. Cronyn	1900 to 1907
T.G. Meredith	1907 to 1926
H. Cronyn	1926 to 1933
T.G. Meredith	1933 to 1943
M. Aylsworth	1943 to 1958
J.A. Taylor	1958 to 1973
A.H. Mingay	1973 to 1978
M.L. Lahn	1978 to 1987
J.H. Speake	1987 to present

Directors

Director	*Huron & Erie*	*Canada Trust*
J. Birrell	1864 to 1875	
E. Leonard	1864 to 1891	
A. Hope	1864 to 1867	
C.W. Kent	1864 to 1877	
J.I. McKenzie	1864 to 1886	
J.G. McIntosh	1864 to 1888	
S. Barker	1864 to 1875	
E.W. Hyman	1864 to 1875	
C. Stead	1864 to 1879	
C.C. Coombs	1864 to 1879	
P. McKenzie	1864 to 1904	1899 to 1905

Director	*Huron & Erie*	*Canada Trust*
F. Smith	1864 to 1868	
W. Boyer	1866 to 1868	
H.S. Strathy	1867 to 1869	
	1879	
F.W. Thomas	1870	
J. Jeffery	1870	
W. Saunders	1875 to 1905	1899 to 1914
	1907 to 1909	
	1911 to 1914	
B. Cronyn	1875	
G.M. Gunn	1875 to 1879	
W.P.R. Street	1876 to 1888	
J. Beattie	1876 to 1893	
J. Lyman	1879	
H.E. Blake	1879	
J.W. Little	1888 to 1909	1899 to 1909
A.W. Porte	1888 to 1897	
F.E. Leonard	1891 to 1923	1899 to 1923
V. Cronyn	1893 to 1907	1899 to 1919
J.A. Lougheed		1899 to 1900
G.A. Somerville		1899 to 1914
C.S. Moore		1900 to 1903
T.H. Purdom		1900 to 1909
W. Bell		1900 to 1912
T. Macbeth	1904 to 1905	
W.M. Gartshore		1904 to 1910
J.B. McKillop		1905 to 1922
T.G. Meredith	1905 to 1943	1907 to 1943
F.R. Eccles	1906 to 1924	1907 to 1924
J. Christie	1906 to 1907	
A.T. McMahen	1906 to 1910	1907 to 1910
H.S. Blackburn		1907 to 1930
H. Cronyn	1908 to 1933	1907 to 1933
H.E. Gates	1909 to 1938	1910 to 1938
R. Fox	1906 to 1921	1911 to 1919
G.T. Brown	1910 to 1926	1911 to 1926
W.J. Christie		1911 to 1916
P. Pocock	1915 to 1929	1911 to 1929
J. Cowan		1911 to 1926
E.P. Clement		1911 to 1919

Director	*Huron & Erie*	*Canada Trust*
R.O. McCulloch		1913 to 1921
J. Labatt	1897 to 1915	1915
A.H.M. Graydon	1915 to 1928	1915 to 1928
F.E. Macdiarmid		1916 to 1921
I. Campbell		1916 to 1929
M. Aylsworth	1929 to 1958	1916
		1926 to 1958
N.R. Howden	1921 to 1936	1919 to 1936
G.H. Belton	1923 to 1937	1920 to 1937
H. Blake		1920 to 1930
J.B. Davidson		1922 to 1954
J.G. Kerr		1922 to 1928
I. Leonard	1926 to 1968	1923 to 1968
S.C. Mewburn	1925 to 1937	
A.R. Bartlet		1925 to 1946
S.F. Washington		1926 to 1933
C.J. Clarke	1939 to 1942	1926
	1943 to 1949	1928 to 1934
		1938 to 1939
		1941 to 1945
E.E. Reid		1927 to 1929
C.H. Houson	1934 to 1936	1928 to 1936
D. McEachern		1929 to 1933
		1943
V.P. Cronyn	1929 to 1941	1930 to 1941
	1949 to 1972	1948 to 1972
R.M. Winslow		1930 to 1931
C. Brown	1936 to 1941	1931 to 1941
A.R. Cairncross		1931 to 1935
W.H. Gardner		1931 to 1951
T.W. McFarland		1933 to 1943
A.C. Spencer	1949 to 1967	1933 to 1967
J.E. McConnell	1941 to 1957	1934 to 1952
J.W. Hobbs	1938 to 1951	1934 to 1951
J.W. Spears	1936 to 1940	1936 to 1940
S.J. Smith		1936 to 1967
E.A. Wilson	1938 to 1963	1936 to 1963
J.W. Riddell		1939 to 1968
F.P. Dawson	1942 to 1962	1939 to 1962
G.F. Laing		1940 to 1955

Director	*Huron & Erie*	*Canada Trust*
R.H. Cronyn	1941 to 1948	1941 to 1948
J.J. McHale	1942 to 1964	1942 to 1964
H.E. Cochran	1951 to 1966	1942 to 1966
W.H. Cooper		1944 to 1952
W.L. Mara		1945 to 1956
A.S. Gordon		1946 to 1953
W.H. Carter		1947 to 1962
G. Farrell		1947 to 1972
A. Meighen		1947 to 1960
J.S. Moore		1947 to 1954
H.R. MacMillan		1947 to 1959
A.E. Silverwood		1947 to 1961
J.E. Smallman		1947 to 1965
J.G. Thompson		1947 to 1971
R.F. Lawson	1950 to 1956	1947 to 1956
J. Hart		1948 to 1956
G.J. Ingram		1949 to 1958
G.A. Forbes		1949 to 1960
R. Fennell		1951 to 1955
R.P. Baker	1951	1951
	1957 to 1969	1956 to 1969
E.L. Harvie		1952 to 1967
L.O. Breithaupt	1959 to 1960	1952 to 1960
J.A. Taylor	1957 to 1981	1954 to 1981
R.A. Robertson		1955 to 1960
G.W. Robinson		1955 to 1971
C. Wallace		1957 to 1972
W.J. Blackburn	1980 to 1984	1957 to 1984
T. Lawson	1956 to 1985	1957 to 1985
J. Jeffery	1961 to 1969	1957 to 1969
J.P. Collyer	1958 to 1960	1956
		1959
F.M. Ross		1958 to 1968
H.H. Leather	1959 to 1972	1951 to 1972
J.B. Morgan		1960 to 1962
C.D. Shepard		1960 to 1961
M.C.G. Meighen	1959 to 1982	1961 to 1982
R.H. Reid	1961 to 1972	1961 to 1972
M.A. Dhavernas		1961 to 1964
A.E. Barron	1963 to 1987	1961 to 1987

Director	*Huron & Erie*	*Canada Trust*
N. Torno	1981 to 1982	1962 to 1982
R.A. Knighton	1968	1962 to 1964
		1971 to 1974
A.E. Walford		1962 to 1972
R.B. Wilson		1963 to 1980
F.P. Galbraith		1963 to 1970
G.E. Creber	1974 to 1978	1963 to 1969
		1974 to 1978
J.V. Clyne		1964 to 1970
		1972 to 1977
R. Chagnon		1965 to 1969
G.E. Sharpe		1966 to 1982
J.J. Stuart		1966 to 1982
H. Borden	1966 to 1977	
J.D. Wilson	1964 to 1980	1967 to 1980
A.H. Mingay	1964 to present	1967 to present
W.J. Sprague		1967 to 1980
G.E. Whitaker	1968 to 1973	1967 to 1969
		1970 to 1975
M. Wills		1968 to 1969
C.W. Brazier		1968 to 1982
W.A. Bean	1968 to 1982	1968 to 1982
A.H. Jeffery	1969 to 1980	1969 to 1982
R.D. Wolfe		1969 to 1974
I.E. Houser	1982 to 1983	1970 to 1983
C.O. Nickle	1982 to 1984	1970 to 1984
R.W. Stevens	1982 to present	1970 to present
T. Edmondson		1971 to 1980
O.E. Manning	1969 to 1975	1972 to 1975
K.R. MacGregor	1970 to 1979	1972 to 1980
W.J. Beatty		1972 to 1978
G.M. Bray		1972 to 1974
D.W. Brown		1972 to 1976
H. Campbell		1972 to 1982
G.H. Dobbie	1982 to 1989	1972 to 1989
W.W. Foot		1972 to 1976
C.S. Glassco		1972 to 1975
W.H. Hemphill	1982 to 1985	1972 to 1985
C.A. Martin		1972 to 1976

Director	*Canada Trustco*[2]	*Canada Trust*
H.S. Matthews		1972 to 1978
E.D.L. Miller		1972 to 1974
J.E. Motz		1972 to 1975
H.L. McCulloch		1972 to 1973
W.J. McGibbon		1972 to 1978
D. McIntosh		1972 to 1982
G.E. Robertson		1972 to 1975
E.G. Schafer		1972 to 1980
J.E.F. Seagram		1972 to 1979
J.D. Stevenson	1982 to present	1972 to present
A.S. Upton		1972 to 1974
C.N. Weber		1972 to 1974
C.R. Clarke	1973 1975 to 1977 1979 to 1980	1972 to 1980
W.J. Stenason	1980 to 1985	1972 to 1985
J.D. Harrison	1972 to 1980	1972 to 1980
E.C. Phillips		1973 to 1975
L. Rasminsky	1973 to 1981	1974 to 1981
G.B. Currie		1974 to 1975
F.W. Dakin	1977 to present	1975 to present
P.N.T. Widdrington	1982 to 1984	1975 to 1984
K.G. Murray	1982 to present	1976 to present
R.P. Bratty	1982 to present	1977 to present
E.F. Findlay	1982 to present	1977 to present
J. Anderson		1977 to 1978
K.A. Fowler		1977
C.C. Knudsen		1977 to 1979
K.A. Roberts		1977 to 1980
R.A. Wheeler		1977 to 1980
M.L. Lahn	1978 to present	1978 to present
R. Gardhouse	1982 to 1986	1978 to 1987
J.B. Cronyn	1972 to present	1978 to present
J.H. Panabaker	1979 to 1985	1979 to 1985
F.T. Metcalf	1982 to present	1980 to present
D.H. Parkinson	1982 to present	1980 to present
E.K. Roberts	1980	1980
J.W. Adams	1982 to present	1981 to present
E.H. Orser	1981 to 1982	1981 to 1982

2. Effective January 1976.

Director	*Canada Trustco*	*Canada Trust*
B.M. Ivey	1982 to 1989	1981 to 1989
H.R. Stephen	1982 to 1983	1982 to 1983
W.D. Grace	1982 to 1985	1982 to 1985
J.T. Hill	1982 to 1987	1982 to 1987
E.S. Jackson	1983 to 1985	1983 to 1985
S.I. Bata	1983 to present	1983 to present
D.M.M. Goldie	1984 to present	1984 to present
P.G. White	1984 to present	1984 to present
A.A. MacNaughton	1985 to 1986	1985 to 1986
R.J. Turner	1985 to 1986	1985 to 1986
H.G. Emerson	1985 to 1986	1985 to 1986
J.W. Pitts	1985 to present	1985 to present
P.J. Hill	1985 to present	1985 to present
B.I. Ghert	1985 to present	1985 to present
J.A.C. Hilliker	1986	1986
R.D. Wilson	1986	1986 to present
D.F. Miller	1986 to 1988	1986 to 1988
D.E. Somers	1986 to 1989	1986 to 1989
R. Stollery	1986	1986
R.L. Beaulieu	1986 to 1987	1986 to 1987
D.R. Bloom	1986 to present	1986 to present
A.L. Campbell	1986 to present	1986 to present
J.H.C. Clarry	1986 to present	1986 to present
R.C. Dowsett	1986 to present	1986 to present
D.L. Johnston	1986 to present	1986 to present
B.M. Levitt	1986 to present	1986 to present
P.D. Lewis	1986 to present	1986 to present
J.W. Lindsay	1986 to present	1986 to present
T.J. Wylie	1986 to present	1986 to present
J.H. Speake	1987 to present	1987 to present
P.C. Maurice	1987 to present	1987 to present
H.P. Crawford	1987 to present	1987 to present
L.D. Hyndman	1988 to present	1988 to present
F.I. MacDonald	1989 to present	1989 to present
C.E. Medland	1989 to present	1989 to present
W.J. Bennett	1989 to present	1989 to present

Index

Index

A.E. Ames & Co., 56-7
Aikins, Mrs. Augusta W., 54
Air Canada, 197
Alison and Dickson, Messrs., 31-2
American Association for the Advancement of Science, 36
American Civil War, 6-7, 129
American Management Association, 166-7
American Pharmaceutical Association, 36
Ames, Alfred Ernest, 56-7
"ancillary business," 218
Anglican diocese of Huron, 15, 18
Argus Corporation, 194
Ash, William H., 23
Atlantic Acceptance Corporation Ltd., 143-6
Atlas Loan Company, 57
AVCO loan company, 137
Aylsworth, Morley, 79n, 80, 81, 94, 100, 102, 103, 108, 117, 118, 174; appointed president, 96-8; Depression years, 86-7; early years with company, 71-5; London & Western purchase, 105-7; post World War II expansion, 109-13; pre-retirement years, 121-3
Aylsworth, Sir Allen, 72

BACM Industries Ltd., 221
B.C. Telephone, 106
Bain and Company, 236
Baker, Robert P., 73-5, 102, 104, 106-7, 111, 122; and Depression era, 91-4; retirement, 117
Ballard, Harold, 172
Bank Act (1967), 113n, 149, 154, 162, 163; proposed revisions, 184
Bank Act (1980), 220
Bank of America, 207
Bank of Canada, 154, 185, 191
Bank of Commerce, 33, 56
Bank of London, 43, 63
Bank of Montreal, 44, 62, 81n, 92, 113, 142, 207-8
Bank of Nova Scotia, 239n
Bank of Toronto, 97n, 108
Baretta, Mrs. Assunta, 213
Barron, Alex, 153, 194-5, 195n, 198, 199-200, 235n
"basket clause," 163, 163n, 164, 218
BAT Industries PLC, 244
Baxter, Bill, 108, 112
BCE Place, 252
Bean, Brigadier Walter A., C.B.E., 145-6, 156-60, 161n, 173, 176
Beard, J.D., 222
Beattie, John, 48
Beatty, John S., 161
Bell Canada Enterprises, 229, 250n
Belzberg, Sam, 222-3, 224
Benallick, H.L., 110
Betts, Frederick Pimlott, 44, 52
Biggs, Jack, 181
Bimcor Inc., 250
Birrell, John, 30, 32
Black Monday, 251n
Blackwell, Bert, 104
Blake, Cassels & Graydon, 228, 231
Blake, Reverend Dominick, 20n
Blake, Honourable Edward, 20n, 25, 50, 222
Blake, Samuel, 20n
Blake, Sophy, 20
Blake, Honourable William Hume, 20n
Boards of Review, 92
BOAT, 211
Borden, Sir Robert, 71

Boyer, William, 16, 20
Brascan, 196, 204, 229
Brazilian Traction, Light and Power Company, *see* Brascan
Brewery Workers, Local 304, 214
British Canadian Trust Company, 124-6, 126n
British Mortgage and Trust Company, 144-6, 156, 203
British Reed Paper group, 189
British Treasury, 68
British-American Assurance Company, 43
British-American Tobacco Co. Ltd., 229
Bronfman, Edgar, 197
Bronfman, Peter, 197
Bronfman family, 204
Brown, Eric, 161n, 223, 224
Brown, Jim, 90
Bruce County, 27
Building Society Act of 1846, 12, 13
Building Society Act of 1859, 13
Burley, Cornelius, 2
"Burn your mortgage" contest, 213
Burnett, Jack, 182
Burns Fry, 230
Burrard Dry Dock Company Ltd., 106

Cadillac Fairview Corporation, 204
Cambridge Preston, 214
Cameron, D.M., 79
Cameron, H.D., 26-9
Campbell, A., 22
Canada Act (1871), 18
Canada deposit insurance, 205
Canada Deposit Insurance Corporation, 146
Canada Life Assurance Company, 56
Canada Permanent, 29, 65, 113, 158, 161-2, 198, 204, 209, 216; merger with Canada Trust, 234-7; takeover bid, 222-33
Canada Permanent Building and Savings Society, 13
Canada Permanent society, 21
Canada Trust Company, 52-5, 66, 67n, 95, 100, 169, 235n, 239n; and computers, 131; and marketing, 131; and Huron & Erie, name change, 122; merger with Canada Permanent, 234-7; name change, 122; pension plans, 114-16; purchase of British Canadian Trust Company, 126; purchase of Community Trusts Corporation, 105; purchase of Consolidated Trusts Corporation, 105; takeover bid, 225-33
Canada Trust Investment Fund, 130
Canada Trust Management Institute, 249
Canada Trust Savings Bank, 203
Canada Trust Tower, 178n, 252
Canada Trustco, 183, 251n; and London Life, 197-8; and ManuLife, 198-202
Canada Trustco International, 218-9
Canada Trustco Mortgage Company, 182n
Canadian American Bank S.A., 217
Canadian American Finance S.A., 217
Canadian Bank of Commerce, 23
Canadian Bankers Association, 202
Canadian Broadcasting Corporation, 171
Canadian General Investments, 149, 197-200, 200n
Canadian Guaranty Company, 39-40
Canadian Imperial Bank of Commerce, 194, 224

Canadian Pacific Enterprises, 229
Canadian Pacific Railway, 33, 63, 102, 150-2
Canadian Payments Association, 185
Canadian Political Science Association, 91
Canadian Savings and Loan Society, 58, 63
Canadian Union of United Brewery, Flour, Cereal, Soft Drink and Distillery Workers, Local 304, 214
Canadian Utilities Ltd., 236
Canadian Wallpaper Manufacturers, 189
CanPerm Realty Ltd., 245
Capital Canada, 198
Carling Brewing and Malting Company, 43
Carma Developers Ltd., 213
Carmichael, Florence, 165
Carter, June, 210
Cash, Johnny, 209-10
CBC Radio, 244
"cell concept," 181, 182, 190
Central Trust, 204
Christie, W.J., 63
Citicorp, 241
City of London Building Society, 20, 21
Clark, Harold, 121
Clarke, Charles J., 73-5, 100, 102, 106-7, 110, 111, 122
Clarke, Robert, 103, 139-40, 201
Coate, Fraser, 115-16
Cohen, Reuben, 204
Coleman, D.C., 102
Collyer, Percy, 111-12, 115
Colonial Church and School Society, 15
Commerce Bank, 113
Community Trusts Corporation, 105
Consolidated Trusts Corporation, 105
Consumers' Association of Canada, 216
Cooke, William, 28-9
Cornish, Francis Evans, 7-8, 129
County of Middlesex Building Society, 25
Cowan, Farmer, 28
Cox, George Albertus, 56
Crawford, Purdy, 229, 240, 241-2, 243, 246
Crimean War, 4
Cronyn, Reverend Benjamin, 16, 18-20, 20n, 38-9, 44
Cronyn, Major Hume Blake, 52, 59n, 63, 66, 73, 79n, 109-10; death, 86; manager, Huron & Erie, 59-61; personal kindnesses, 71n; vice-president, 76-7
Cronyn, Hume (actor), 59n
Cronyn, John B., 17
Cronyn, Katherine, 59n
Cronyn, Margaret, 20n
Cronyn, Mary Goodhue, 44
Cronyn, Rebecca, 20n
Cronyn, Richard, 59n, 94, 101, 103
Cronyn, Verschoyle Philip, 17, 18, 48, 59n, 117n; early years at Huron & Erie, 20; elected president of Canada Trust, 52-3; investigates misappropriation of funds, 39-40; memoirs, 88; retirement, 61; and scandal over Benjamin, 44
Cronyn and Betts, 59
Crown Trust, 203, 244
Crump, Norris "Buck," 150-1
Crystal Block, 20, 21
CT Credit Corporation, 252
CT Financial Services, 251-2
CT Insurance Co. Ltd., 219
CT Investment Counsel Inc., 219

CT Retail Finance Inc., 251

D.B. Weldon library, 105n
Daon Development Corporation, 213
Das Kapital, 23
Davidson, Roy, 124-6
Davis, The Very Reverend Dean, 61
de la Hooke, Edward, 23
Debtors' Act, 5
deGroote, Michael, 182-3
DeLatre, 32
Department of Insurance, 202
Desmarais, Paul, 229-31, 232
Di Giacomo, Thomas, 225, 227-8, 230, 231-2
Dominion Bank, 15, 158
Dominion Cerealist, 37
Dominion experimental farm system, 42
Dominion Life Assurance Company, 228
Dominion Savings and Investment Society, 78
Dominion Securities, 223
Dominion Steel, 56
Donegan, Ted, 228

Eastern and Chartered Trust Company, 222
Eaton-Bay Trust, 204
Eaton's, 197, 204
Ebert, John, 27
Eccles, Dr. F.R., 54
Eccles, Martha L. Wood, 54
Edper Equities Ltd., 197
"Eight to eight," 180, 181, 190
Elgin Loan & Savings Company, 57
Ellen, Leonard, 204
Enniskillen Township, 6
Entomological Society of Canada, 36
Expo 67, 155

Farmers and Mechanics Society, 12
Farmers' Creditors Arrangement Act, 92
Farrell, Gordon, 106, 108
Federal Bank, 43
Fidelity Trust, 244
Financial Commander, 248
First Boston, 241
First City Financial Corporation, 222-3
Flavelle, Sir Joseph, 82
Fletcher, Miss Nellie, 70n
Forbes, George D., 109-10
Ford Foundation, 143-4
Ford Motor Company, 170
Foster, Janet, 171
Foster, John, 171
Foster, Rod, 241
"Four Horsemen," 74-75, 86-95
Franck, August A., 221
Fruit Growers' Association of Ontario, 36

Geac, 237
General Act (1899), 50
General Electric, 114
General Motors, 114
Genstar Corporation, 204, 220-1; Imasco takeover bid, 240-7; merger of Canada Permanent and Canada Trust, 234-6, 235n; and takeover bids, 222-33
Genstar Acquisition Corporation, 220
Genstar Mortgage Corporation, 245
Genstar Securities Corporation, 245
Getliffe, Ray, 94
Gibson, George (Mooney), 64
Gibson, Lawrence, 32, 33
Gibson, Manager, 39
Gillean, Mr., 39
Girdlestone, Mr., 62

Givins, Harold W., 63-4, 77, 84-5
Givins family, 64
Glidden Paint Company, 141
Goodhue, George, 44
Goodhue, Mrs. George Jervis, 3n
Gordon Securities, 198, 233
Gore Bank, 23
Grace, Bill, 236
Grand Theatre, 129
Gratton, Robert, 231, 232-3
Great Western Railway, 4, 23, 43
Green Paper on Regulation of Canadian Financial Institutions, 220
Greene, Lorne, 171
Gregory, W.H., 144
Gregory, Wilfred P., 144-5
Grey & Bruce Trust and Savings Company, 158
Greymac Mortgage, 203
Greymac Trust, 203, 206, 244
Group of Seven, 171
GSX Corporation, 222
Guardian Trustco, 228
Guelph and Ontario Investment and Savings Society, 47, 109
Guelph Mercury, 47
Guelph Trust Company, 109
Gunn, Mr., 20
Gunn, Tom, 192

Haig, Betty, 101
Hall, Bill, 119
Halton & Peel Trust and Savings Company, 158-62, 173n
Hamilton Provident & Loan Corporation, 14n, 78, 89, 110
Hamilton Provident society, 29
Hamilton Trust, 182, 183
Hammond, Bob, 218
Hammond, Mr., 45
Harding, John P., 21
Harley, John, 59n
Harris, Walter, 115
Harrison, John, 150
Hart, Arnold, 142
Hart, James, 21
Harvie, Dorothy, 122
Harvie, Eric, 122, 124-5
Haydn, June, 239n
Hellmuth, Reverend Isaac, 14-15, 36
Highland Light Infantry, 157
Hilliker, John, 224, 235, 237, 250n
Hobbs, John W., 102
Holmes, 45
Home Bank, 76-7, 143
Homer, Gord, 230
Hope, Adam, 14n, 16, 20, 23-5, 29, 78, 179, 222
Hope, Charles, 14n
Hope, George, 14n
Hotel London, 128, 129
Hughes, Don, 167
Hull, William, 52
Hume, Anne Margaret, 20n
Humphrys, Richard, 185
Hunt, Mr., 27-8
Huron & Erie: acquisition of General Trust Corporation of Canada, 52; and the adding machine, 131n; assets (1882), 35; assumption of People's Loan & Savings Corporation, 81-2; and debentures, 31-2; Depression years, 86-95; disclosure policy, 34; early loan policies, 21-3; early working conditions, 38; expansion to west, 63; London headquarters, 30; merger with Canadian Savings & Loan Company, 58; merger with London Permanent, 25; merger with Southern Loan and Savings Company, 57n; merger with Western Counties Permanent Building and Savings Society, 25; name change (1976), 182; open hours, 30; purchase of

Hamilton Provident & Loan Corporation, 78; purchase of London Loan & Savings Company, 83; purchase of Southern Loan & Savings Company, 79; purchase of Waterloo Trust and Savings Company, 15662; real estate sales, 239-40; takeover of Dominion Savings and Investment Society, 78
Huron & Erie Mortgage Corporation, name change (1915), 67n
Huron & Erie Savings and Loan Society, 9, 13
Huron College, 15
Hutton, Hugh, 121, 133n
Hyman, Ellis W., 14, 16, 29, 30
Hyndman, Margaret P., 173

IBM, 193; 402 accounting machine, 132; 1401 computer, 133; 360/30 computer, 168; 3033 computer, 187; data centre, 168, 169; equipment, 210; system, 237
Imasco Ltd., 229, 241-3, 251-2; takeover bid for Genstar, 240, 246-7, 247n
Imlach, Punch, 171
Imperial Oil Ltd., 6, 43, 111, 189
Insurance Act, 202
Interac, 248
Investors Overseas Services, 172
Ivey, Livermore & Dowler, 135-6

Jackman, Hal, 204, 205
Jackson, David, 231
Jackson, Syd, 198, 200, 200n, 225, 227, 231, 235
Jacot, Georges, 128
Jeffery, Alec, 199
Jeffery, Gordon, 196
Jeffery, Joseph, 26, 196, 199
Jeffery family, 197
Jewell, George F., 33, 33n, 43
John Labatt Limited, 2
Johnny Cash machines, 209-10, 248
Jones, Harry, 106n

Karloff, Boris, 64
Kennett, William, 202
Kent, Charles W., 39
Kent, Malcolm, 38, 39
Keppel Township, 26
Kerr, Archie, 181
Kitchener Chamber of Commerce, 244
Kitchener-Waterloo Kinsmen Club, 203
Knighton, Bob, 44, 161
Kucherepa, Walter, 240
Kuhn, Loeb and Company, 143

Labatt, John, 16, 43, 105
Labatt, John, 2nd, 52
Labatt's Brewery, 196
Lahn, Mervyn Lloyd, 174, 181, 189, 190, 192, 197, 200, 210, 250n, 251; ability to delegate, 210; annual meeting held in 1985, 215-16; appointed president, 188; becomes chairman, 250; and Canada Permanent, 223, 225-33; and the credit card, 207-8; early background, 175-80; joins Canada Trust, 161, 161n, 162n; merger of Canada Permanent and Canada Trust, 234-40; ten-per-cent ownership legislation, 202-6, 220; and Trust Companies Association, 202n; and University of Waterloo, 176n
Lahn, Myra, 180, 226
Laidlaw Transportation Ltd., 182
LaMarsh, Judy, 182
Lambton Loan and Investment Society, 12

Lawrason, Mr., 20
Lawson, Honourable Ray, 106, 106n, 107, 148n
Lawson, Lt. Col. Tom, 106n, 148n
Lawson & Jones Ltd., 106n
Lawson Mardon Group Ltd., 107n
Ledat, Mr., 88
Leonard Boilers, 84
Leonard, Honourable Elijah, 15-16, 49n
Leonard, Frank E., 52
Leonard, Colonel Ibbotson, D.S.O., 15, 84, 97, 117n
Light, Walter, 243
Lime Ridge Mall, 245
Lincoln Trust and Savings Company, 183; takeover bid, 182-3
Little, Colonel John W., 42n, 44-5, 47-9, 60, 61, 105
Livermore, lawyer, 135-6
Loan Companies Act, 201, 202
Loblaw's, 165
London & Western Trusts Ltd., 52, 105, 106-8, 148n, 173
London Advertiser, 78, 106n
London Free Press, 4, 5n, 32, 43, 64, 78, 83
London Horticultural Society, 69
London Hunt and Country Club, 8
London Life Insurance Company, 14, 26, 133, 151, 152, 153, 196-7
London Loan & Savings Company, 83
London Permanent, 20, 25
London Permanent Building Society, 24
London Street Railway, 59
London Transportation Commission, 135
Lonvest, 196-7
Lougheed, James A., 52
Luther Township, 28

McCabe, Mr., 21
McCrossan, Paul, 242, 244, 246
McDonald, Hugh Forbes, 26
Macdonald, Sir John A., 33, 201
McDougall, Barbara, 242, 246, 247
MacEachen, Allan, 223
McEachern, Danbert, 73-5, 102-3, 104, 106-7, 109-11, 122
Macfie, Daniel, 9, 14, 20, 129, 179
MacGregor, Ken, 151-3, 173n, 198
McGregor, Peter, 1-2
McKenzie, John, 14n
McKenzie, Philip, 49n, 52
McKinley, Jean, 128
McLean, Don, 141, 167-71, 180
McLean Securities, 198, 199
McMahen, Adam, 60-1, 66
McMichael, Robert, 171
McMichael, Signe, 171
McMichael Canadian collection, 171
MacMillan, H.R., 106, 108, 112
MacNaughton, Angus A., 220-1, 224, 225, 226, 227, 231, 235-7, 241-3, 244-6, 247n
McNiece, Burd, 87
Manning, Oswald Earl (Oz), 158-60
Manuduke, 228
Manufacturers Life Insurance Company, 58-9, 198
ManuLife, 198-202, 200n, 225, 228, 231-2
Maple Leaf Gardens, 172
Maple Leaf Mills, 189
Mardon Son & Hall, 106n
Markle, Andrew, 206
Martin, Stan, 210-12
Marx, Karl, 23
Mason, J. Herbert, 12, 13
Massachusetts Mutual Life, 144
MasterCard, 207-9
Maurice, Peter, 225, 227, 229, 231-2, 250n, 252; and "cell" concept, 190; early years with company, 189-93; and Merv Lahn's resignation, 236-7

Medland, Ted, 229-30
Meighen, Arthur, 106-7, 148
Meighen, Colonel Maxwell G.C., O.B.E., 148-50, 185-6, 194
"merchant deposit," 207
Merchants' Bank of New York, 32, 42, 62
Meredith, Charles, 62n
Meredith, Edmund, 9, 62n
Meredith, Henry Vincent, 62n
Meredith, John, 62
Meredith, John Stanley, 62n
Meredith, Llewellyn, 62n
Meredith, Richard Martin, 62n
Meredith, Thomas Graves, K.C., 65, 68, 72, 85, 98, 105, 151, 174; and Allyn Taylor, 100; annual meeting, 1912, 67; assumes title of chairman and president, 86; background, 61-2; chairman of the board, 79n; forced to resign, 97; and stock-market crash, 1929, 80
Meredith, William Ralph, 43, 62n
Metcalfe, George E., 70
Methodist New Connexion Church, 35
Mewburn, Maj. Gen. the Honourable Sydney Chilton, K.C., C.M.G., 81n
Midland Doherty Ltd., 105n
Midland Securities Corporation Ltd., 105n
Miller, Don, 155
Miller, Reverend Orlo, 71n, 129
Mills, Walter, 97
Mingay, Arthur Hammond, 121, 160-1, 161n, 164, 170, 174, 176, 177, 178, 183-4, 189, 192, 197, 199, 200, 200n, 202, 226-7, 229, 240; appointed chairman, 188; early background, 103, 165-7; elected president, Trust Companies Association, 182; hires marketing manager, 140-1; move to pension fund division, 114-16; retirement, 237
Minns, Eric, 132, 133, 133n, 135, 179-81
Molson's Bank, 43
Monetary Times, 43, 63
Montreal Canadiens, 94
Montreal Trust, 113, 114, 115, 150, 195, 230, 231
Moore, Jake, 197
Moore, John S., 45
Morgan, Campbell Powell, 143
Morgan Stanley and Company, 241
Morrill, Simeon, 14
Mortgage Regulation Act, 34
Murray, Charles, 43
Mutual Life, 173, 197, 198, 199-200, 219, 235, 235n
Mutual Life of Canada, 151-3
Mutual Life company, 58-9
Mutual Life insurance company, 50

National Bank, 239n
National Energy Policy, 202
National Policy (1879), 33
National Trust Company, 82, 113, 158, 159, 216
Nelson, William, 28
Noble and Lewis, Messrs., 21
Noranda, 197
North-West Rebellion, 59
Northern Telecom, 243
Northwest Bancorporation, 217

O'Hara, Charles, 94-5, 104, 110, 136
O'Keefe Breweries, 141
Olympia and York, 204
Ontario Catholic League, 15
Ontario College of Pharmacy, 36
Ontario Heart Foundation, 166
Ontario Investment Association, 43-4, 63

Ontario Labour Relations Board, 214-15
Ontario Securites Commission, 200, 242n
Ontario Supreme Court, 231
Ontario Trust Company, 182-4
Operation Mayflower, 134, 136
Organization of Petroleum Exporting Countries, 177
Orser, Earl, 197-9
Orton Act *see* Mortgage Regulation Act
Orton, Dr., 34
Overholt, Bob, 163, 213

Paddell, Doug, 139
Panabaker, John, 198, 199, 235,
Paré, Paul, 243
Park, Don, 209-10
Paterson, Peter, 222
Pearson, Prime Minister Lester, 155
Pearson Formula, 155
Pegler, Sarah, 62
Pen Centre, 214
People's Loan & Savings Corporation, 81-2
Petrolia, 6
Philips, Mr., 27-8
Pigott & Sons, 83
Pioneer Trust, 244
Pitblado, Jim, 223-4
Pitfield, Michael, 230
Pittsburg Pirates, 64
Plus network, 248-9
Port Sarnia Building Society, 12
Port Sarnia Syndicate, 12
Porteous, Robert, 22
Porter Royal Commission on Banking and Finance, 154
Power Corporation, 229-33
PowerLine, 249
Pratt, Frank, 180, 209, 211-12
Private Act (1896), 50
Prudential Insurance Company, 146
Purdom, T.H., 78

Queen's Own Rifles, 59

Rebellion of 1837, 2
Redgwell, Bob, 126n
Registered Retirement Savings Plans, 115-16
Reichmann brothers, 204
Reid, Bob, 151, 152, 153
Reid, Ed, 151
"review of performance," 167
Ricci, Ulysses, 84
Richardson, John, 218-19, 236, 237
Ridout, Joseph D., 222
Riis, Nelson, 244-6
Robarts, John, 145
Robert Simpson Company, 132
Roberts, Dr. Kenneth, 183-4
Robin, Lou, 210
Robinson, Reverend Joseph Hiram, 35
Robinson, Sarah, 35-6, 37n
Robinson, William, 14
Rosenberg, Leonard, 206
Rowley, George, 57
Royal Bank, 113, 241
Royal Society of Canada, 36
Royal Trust, 99, 113, 158, 159, 197, 204, 216
Roynat Ltd., 130
Rudd, Bob, 219

Salter, Dr., 35
Saskatchewan Farm Loan Board, 91
Saunders, Charles, 37
Saunders, Fred, 37n
Saunders, Henry, 37n
Saunders, Percy, 37n
Saunders, Sarah Robinson, 35-6, 37n
Saunders, Will, 37n
Saunders, William, 35-42, 37n, 52, 61
Sauvé, Leo P., 182, 183

Scatcherd, John, 21, 24
"Schedule B" banks, 220
Scratchley, Arthur, 11
Seaway Mortgage, 203
Seaway Trust, 203, 206, 244
Security Capital Corporation, 158
Shack, Eddie, 171-2
Sherlock, John, 133n
Silverwood, A.E., 107
Simcoe, John Graves, 1
Sinclair, Gordon, 171
Sinclair, Ian, 150-1
Skilbeck, Robert, 12
Slack, Samuel, 27
Smallman, Col. J.E., 108
Smith, Frank, 15-16
"smoke-free workplace," 215
Smylie, Robert W. 33-4, 38, 39-40, 44-5
Société Générale de Belgique, 221, 241
Society of Management Accountants, 251
Sogemines, 221
Somerville, George Anderson, 46-53, 50n, 58
Somerville, Walter H., 50n
Southeast Banking Corporation, 217
Southern Loan and Savings Company, 57n, 79
Speake, Jack, 135, 136, 137, 166, 167, 236, 237, 249-50, 250n
Special Act (1898), 57
Special Act (1922), 53n
Stead, Charles, 32, 32n, 33, 35
Stead, W.T., 32n
Steele, Arthur, 133n
Stelco, 114
Stevenson & Kellogg, 189
Stewart, J.W., 79
Street, William P.R., Q.C., 42
SuperCharge, 249
SuperLoan, 249
SuperRate, 211-12
Supertest, 107

T-bill savings, 212
Talbott, Edward, 22
Taylor, E.A., 14
Taylor, Henry, 42-3, 63
Taylor, John Allyn, 117, 129, 139, 141, 142, 145-7, 154-5, 161n, 164, 165-6, 170, 176, 177, 184, 192, 220, 222; and computerization, 133-4, 168; disbands advisory boards, 173, 173n; early background, 98-104; and Max Meighen and Huron & Erie shares, 149-53; and Waterloo Trust, 156-61; policy initiatives, 118-27; retires as chairman, 188; retires as president, 174; vision of future of Canada Trust, 105-15
Tecumseh Hotel, 45
Teperman and Sons, 83
The Bay, 204
Third Canadian General Investment Trust, 149
Thompson, Col. J. Gordon, 107
Thomson, Tom, 171
Thomson and Weston groups, 229
"tiered-rate" account, 211
Toronto Board of Trade, 56
Toronto Building Society, 12
Toronto General Hospital, 56
Toronto General Trusts Company, 50, 222
Toronto Printing Pressmen's Fund, 114
Toronto Star, 78
Toronto Stock Exchange, 56
Toronto Street Railway, 15
Toronto-Dominion Bank, 113, 144, 197, 207
Tory, J.S.D., 150
Tovey, Hamilton, 3n
Tovey, Admiral John Cronyn, 3n
Treasury Board, 160, 162

Truscan Realty Ltd., 240n
Trust Companies Act, 202
Trust Companies Association, 115, 145, 156, 176, 202n, 205
Trust Companies Association of Canada, 117
Trust Companies Association of Ontario, 117
Trust Company of the Bahamas, 158
Trust Company Investors, 204, 206
Trust and Loan Acts, amendments, 162
Trustee Guaranty Company, 78
Turbo Resources, 194, 195, 213
Turner, John, 172
Turner, Ross J., 220-1, 224, 225, 226, 227, 232, 235-7, 241-3, 244-6, 247n
Turner, William E., 39-40

U.S. Securities and Exchange Commission, 242n
U.S. Steel and Carnegie Pension Fund, 143
Union Party, 71
University of Toronto, 56
University of Western Ontario, 15, 36, 42n, 54, 105n, 121, 135, 176
Usury Law, 11

Valhalla Inn, 192
van den Berg, Gijsbertus, 152
Victoria and Grey Trust Company, 12n, 146, 158, 204
Victory Bonds, 69, 97
Visa, 207

Wallace, A.E., 57
Wallace, Honourable Clarence, 106, 108
Waterloo College, 176, 176n
Waterloo Lutheran University, 176n
Waterloo Trust and Savings Company, 145, 152, 156-62, 161n, 168, 173n, 176, 207
Weldon, Lt. Col. Douglas Black, 105, 105n
Westby, Colonel E.B., 108, 112
Western Canada Tennis Tournament, 101
Western Counties Permanent Building and Savings Society, 25
Whitaker, George, 166
White, Norman, 132, 133n, 136, 137, 169
Whitely, James, 22
Why a Corporate Executor? pamphlet, 53
Whyte, Sir William, 66
Whyte, William, Jr., 66, 100-1
Wilfred Laurier University, 176n
Wilson, Jack, 92, 103-4, 111, 112-13, 121, 172-3
Windsor Business School, 165
Winnipeg Grain Exchange, 87
Winslow, Mrs., 45
Wood Gundy, 229, 230
Woods, Cyril, 114
Woods Gordon, 133, 134
Woolworth's, 132, 197
World War I, 65, 68
World War II, 96
World's Fair, Paris (1886), 37

Yaneff, Chris, 170
Young, Venerable Archdeacon, 60